Survivals in Belief Among the Celts

By

George Henderson

First published in 1911

Published by Left of Brain Books

Copyright © 2023 Left of Brain Books

ISBN 978-1-396-32624-0

First Edition

All rights reserved. No part of this publication may be reproduced, distributed, or transmitted in any form or by any means, including photocopying, recording, or other electronic or mechanical methods, without the prior written permission of the publisher, except in the case of brief quotations permitted by copyright law. Left of Brain Books is a division of Left Of Brain Onboarding Pty Ltd.

PUBLISHER'S PREFACE

About the Book

"This long out-of-print book [...] reviews the extensive literature on survivals of pre-Christian beliefs in the Celtic area. It covers customs from Ireland, Scotland, the Isle of Man, Cornwall and Brittany, and relates them to other traditional cultures world-wide. This is a work of scholarship, and cites from authoritative literature, including many now hard to obtain sources, and several short texts in the original Gaelic. Among the fascinating topics covered are the evil eye, geis (taboos), doppelgangers, beliefs relating to animals and shape-shifting, lustration, second-sight, and healing rituals. Of particular interest is the discussion of pagan elements in the Carmina Gadelica."

(Quote from sacred-texts.com)

CONTENTS

PUBLISHER'S PREFACE
PREFACE 1
    THE FINDING OF THE SOUL 2
    THE FINDING OF THE SOUL (PART 2) 24
    THE WANDERINGS OF PSYCHE 47
    THE WANDERINGS OF PSYCHE (PART 2) 74
    THE WANDERINGS OF PSYCHE (PART 3) 100
    THE EARTHLY JOURNEY 127
    THE EARTHLY JOURNEY (PART 2) 154
    THE EARTHLY JOURNEY (PART 3) 181
INDEX 208
ENDNOTES 222

PREFACE

THIS volume gives the substance of my first series of public lectures in Folk-Psychology delivered in the University of Glasgow.

THE treatment is objective in the sense that there is throughout a unifying thought. Though I cite widely it is not a mere collection of folk-belief: it is a history of soul-belief, over a given area, treated in a comparative light. That the contents are taken from our own land does not lessen its interest. I use the term Celtic as a linguistic convenience, not as racial: the bulk of the material is from among the Gadhelic-speaking area, where I was naturally able to draw upon my own knowledge of facts which awoke in me an early curiosity.

I am again beholden to the Carnegie Trust for their help by a grant in aid of publication, for which I offer my grateful thanks.

   THE UNIVERSITY,
GLASGOW, May, 1911.

THE FINDING OF THE SOUL

SURVIVALS may be defined as primitive rites believed and practised, rites which once were 'faith' but which from a later and higher conception simply 'remain over' or survive. A survival may remain over both as 'belief' and as 'rite'; in either case it is the equivalent of the Latin 'superstitio.' But the English 'superstition' is too bare a term for it. For a belief or ritual custom once existed as a living force ere it sank into the position of a survival. A survival is what has been left stranded while all around it there has been more or less of change, of development, due to the growth of thoughtfulness and to the action of environment and of historical forces. What has once become a survival, if it have a future, has only a future of decay: its life now is in decay, it has no development as a whole. But manifestly in a social organism there are different rates of progress. Not all parts of the life of a social system develop at the same time, at the same rate, or in the same way. Nor is there the same continuous development over the same period of time. Accordingly there are strata of belief and ritual in any and every social system, in the most recent as in the most archaic.

It is well to examine those archaic survivals one knows best; to endeavour to reduce them in an unpretentious way to some system from the point of view of a comparative study of man. Presupposed is the unity of mankind, i.e. of man as a thinking and moral being. Consequently, while this study is, on the whole, confined to customs among the Celts, I feel at liberty to read these in the light of analogous customs where possible. I do not know that in origin they are all Celtic. Ere the Celtic migrations these islands were inhabited by other tribes whose beliefs were most probably preserved among the Celts. It is not likely that Celtic and non-Celtic tribes would have at the same period the same beliefs and practices, which might be accounted for by both having been on a different plane of development.

It would be most instructive and interesting to assign to each tribe its own special belief and rite: in part that is attempted by the folk-lorist. Here it is no mere collection of beliefs or of rites that is aimed at, but the interpretation of these in the light of the 'soul.' At first, I believe that the non-Celtic tribes preserved their own belief and ritual for the reason that they were not admitted to full legal status among the Celts. Yet the Celtic tuath or tribe and the Celtic fine or clan were incorporating organisms, and through inter-marriages new and alien customs were introduced and preserved, especially among the mothers. The Pictish matriarchal system is of special importance. In the light of 'mother-right' and all that inheres therein one may perhaps read such traces as may be found of the couvade and of the aire chlaidh, 'kirkyard watch' or 'grave guardian,' of which anon. A psychical anthropology of the Celts is much wanted; but that of any single branch is best read in the light of the rest, indeed of comparative religion. What Edmund Spenser said of the 'wild Irish,' of whom he wrote in 1595 in his View of the State of Ireland, is equally true of the Highlands: "All the customs of the Irish, which I have often noted and compared with what I have read, would minister occasion of a most ample discourse of the original of them, and the antiquity of that people, which in truth I think to be more ancient than most that I know in this end of the world: so as if it were taken in the handling of some man of sound judgement and plentiful reading, it would be most pleasant and profitable." In this search, which is of great intricacy and excessive delicacy, as treating of belief-complexes which really reflect soul-movements, it is only by some understanding of the whole that one may interpret the part. Some curious rites, which in undertones I learned of long ago in the Highlands, came down through the native midwives, a breed that is now extinct in so far as the old rites are concerned: it was the thought of understanding these in the light of the whole that first led me to make this attempt. I make no doubt but the distinction of rites between the Celtic and non-Celtic tribes was once as firm as the distinction between tribesman and non-tribesman, which Mr. Seebohm has shown to be an important feature of Celtic law. [1]

A help in the solution of the problems of Celtic psychical anthropology would be to classify all customs, beliefs and rites which have the same conceptions of life. The mythic influence of the conquered tribes ought not to be forgotten. But it needs consideration likewise that tribes now united into a nation may formerly have held customs quite different from what they do now. The common Gadhelic sayings: 'it is mother-affinity (friendship) that is nearest'; [2] 'I will not say brother save to the son that my mother bore,' [3] point back to the Pictish social system, according to which descent was reckoned in the female line. This, it has been argued, is a feature which the Picts owed to non-Aryan predecessors. But may not a race in the course of its long history be led to change its customs from within? Wherever we meet with descent reckoned in the female line, are we in presence of the non-Aryan? Mr. Frazer shows how in royal families in Latium and in Greece the daughters were kept at home, and the sons went forth to marry princesses and reign among their wives' peoples;[4] he says that "among the Saxons and their near kinsmen the Varini it appears to have been a regular custom for the new king to marry his stepmother."[5]

And further: "Attic usage always allowed a man to marry his half-sister by the same father, but not his half-sister by the same mother. Such a rule seems clearly to be a relic of a tune when kingship was counted only through women."[6] He instances also the great house of Aeacus in Greece, the grandfather of Achilles and Ajax, and the family of the Pelopidae. The relation of mother to child is of the first importance, and cults and customs ought not to be read without keeping it in view. After all, as Professor Gilbert Murray[7] has pointed out fitly, the Matriarchate is one of the great civilising influences of mankind.

What is now but a mere 'survival' was once the sole substitute for our philosophy and religion; the mere superstition of to-day is in unbroken continuity with the dateless ages of earliest faiths. Progress and change there have been throughout, but hardly such breaks as efface the possibility of our recognising the religiosity of man as part of his psychical being. Survivals,—making all allowance for diversities of customs springing from different races within different eras of time, and sometimes possibly temporarily resumed within a race which has discarded them within its own past,—are but disguises which point to the inherent unity of human thought in thinking itself out; to lift these disguises into their unconscious system is to come upon the soul at work, speaking to us half-aloud, and revealing what St. Augustine perceived long ago,—the inherent unity of all religious feeling. In his Retractions, the Bishop of Hippo declares that what is now called the Christian Religion existed among the ancients, and in fact was with the human race from the beginning.[8] It is his way of expressing the idea of religious persistencies. These have various origins, although the composite elements are ultimately brought under one dominant thought which was latent in the rites from the beginning. Religion is the body of sacred rites or scruples embodied in observances which a man finds binding on himself with regard to the wills or Will, which to his consciousness are in connection with and have regard to his life. As given or revealed it is the Deity that covenants. Man is bound thereby to his fellows and has regard for social ties. In course of man's development in a social order, ancestral souls, the souls of the dead, enter into his life for good or ill, as also Nature-Spirits conceived as active in air, earth, water and fire, culminating at length in the One Nature-Spirit.

It is in the rite that concrete religion is posited. The rite is the correct inherited ancestral custom, having at bottom the idea of what has been measured or numbered, and thus fixed by the convenience of the ancestral community. It foreshadows the idea of Harmony. 'Follow, thou, closely the fame of thine ancestors' (lean-sa dlùth ri cliù do shìnnsear) is a Highland maxim favourable to survivals. What served the past is good for us also. A particular religious obedience every man is free to impose upon himself. But man does not often reach his fundamental self: "the moments at which we thus grasp ourselves are rare, and that is just why we are rarely free. The greater part of the time we live outside ourselves, hardly perceiving anything of ourselves but our own ghost, a colourless shadow which pure duration projects into homogeneous space. Hence our life unfolds itself in space rather than in time; we live for the external world rather than for ourselves; we speak rather than think; we 'are acted' rather than act ourselves." [9] As living in space man becomes involved in a system of ritual prohibitions: do not. They are solemn declarations framed for his well-being, and need to be tested in practice. The taboos of other races are present with the Gael as gessa or sacred restrictions. It is their religious quality which imparts them persistency. Religion now reveals its life in the way whereby one approaches God; there are various avenues of approach to the Power regarded as divine, and in approaching by these ways it is felt that one should have regard to approaching aright and with due care. There is no religion without its ritual. In the rite is expressed devotion to the object for which one feels a care. Outwardly worship must necessarily manifest the worshipper as one who is giving in order to get; he may give goods or self, but in either case his actions imply a Power that can give what may be gotten. Religion is ultimately a progress in Life, and this implies the exercise of reflection which ultimately eliminates idols. Acts of devotion may be manifested (a) with relation to souls and with relationship of souls to the Highest Soul or God; (6) and may be conditioned by sympathetic association with objects regarded as having souls, or as being alive (Animism). Devotion thus embraces all phases of Manism (of which what is known as Totemism is but a moment). In Gadhelic, devotion is expressed by cràbhadh, piety (in rite); old Irish crabud, 'faith'; cognate with Cymric crefydd. In the Highlands the adjective cràbhach is applied to one who is devout and observant of pious rites. The root of the word is met with in Sanskrit vi-çrambh, 'trust.' The rites of religion [10] (cràbhadh) are the various avenues of approaching the Being in whom one has trust, expressed or implied. But heart-giving has a side which implies belief inclusive of heart-consent. In Gadhelic this is expressed by the word creideamh; Old Irish cretim; Cymric credu; all cognate with Latin 'credo,' I believe'; Sanskrit çrad-dadhâmi, 'I give heart to.' The attitude of mind thus attained to is expressed by the Old Irish iress, 'faith' (literally 'on-standing'), which only survives in the negative in the modern Gadhelic amharus, 'doubt'; Old Irish amairess, 'unbelief, infidelitas.' Religion therefore, so far as an examination of the Celtic languages leads, is seen to embrace:

1. the rite (cràbhadh, trust expressed in rite),

2. the heart-consent (creideamh),

3. faith (in the object or end of the rite): iress.

This inclusive attitude of mind, so far as the objects of attention are concerned, may have reference to

1. The Word:

(a) the word of prohibition or restriction (geas): the negative word;

(b) the word of magic or the positive power of the Word spoken (òb, òrtha, guidhe): the positive word;

(c) the lustral rites. Ordeals.

2. The Soul or Souls, which embrace

(a) soul-parts, or soul in association with parts of the body;

(b) the internal soul or soul proper;

(c) the external soul or the soul in sympathy with, but imagined as outside the body (sympathetic association).

3. Nature-spirits and Ancestral Spirits (Animism).

4. Communion of Life:

(a) the Word by the blood-soul, the god-in-the-blood; by the swearing relics of a saint (minn, mionn, i.e. oath); by the virtue of the elements, by the sun and moon; by the tribal god (tong a toing mo thuath).

(b) the Word to the God (Prayer: urnuigh, guidh);

(c) the Word to the Soul:

(a) in the omen (manadh);

(b) in the portent (tuar);

(c) in the vision (fīs);

(α) in dreams (aisling);

(β) in second-sight (taibhsearachd, an dà-shealladh);

(γ) in prophetic knowledge (dailgneachd; tairrngearacht); taisbein or revelation.

5. Sacrifice:

(a) partaking in thankfulness with the god (uibhir aig Dia de chuid);

(b) giving to get (do ut des);

(c) giving to appease (do ut abeas).

6. The God-land:

(a) the land of the young (Tír na n-Ōg); the island paradise;

(b) the conquest of the Sīdh and its joys (oibinnius in t-sída);

(c) the land of promise (tír tairrngire), the shadows of the immortals; and the twilight of the gods.

The Word has freedom. It has also the danger that accompanies freedom: it may be made an idol. Words are the manufacturers of idols. As 'spell, taboo, charm' the word is geas, E. Irish geis, derived from the root in the verb guidh, 'entreat' (Old Irish guidiu, gude, guide), cognate with Gothic bidjan 'ask,' and English bidding, surviving in 'the bidding prayer.'

The potency of strong entreaty is witnessed to in the Highland saying: 'a witch will get her wish though her soul should not receive mercy.' [11] Even the dead can take fuller vengeance than the living, and the death-bed entreaty [12] binds the survivor.

The religious sentiment includes belief in the potency of the word. Hence the easy and too common delusion that religion derives from magic. To start with, religion embraces more than the magic word: hence a study of all 'survivals' reveals more than 'magic'; it shows acts and objects of faith in which the heart either rests or works its way out of towards a more abiding content. The rhythmic formula or carmen (whence charm), older can-men, in root cognate with Gadhelic, can, 'to say,' had such occult power that, according to Virgil, it could draw the moon from the sky. [13] And so close is the connection between the prayer and the spell that the word that once signified the former may be degraded to signify the latter. One example is the following.

When a witch has bespelled a man, the modern Gadhelic phrase is: 'she has put the ōrth (spell) in him.' [14] This word, however, is but a loan from the Latin orationem; the accusative in Early Irish is orthain, 'prayer,' in which sense the word is met with on an Iona tombstone. As in everything else, there is such a thing as deterioration in religion, as the above transition of meaning manifests. One must guard against deriving religion from magic or identifying it therewith. For 'charm, incantation,' the native word is obaidh. [15] When a witch is credited with having bespelled a man the Highlander says: 'she gave him a word.' [16] Connected of old with the power of the word was that of the satirist, who could raise blotches on the face or rhyme an enemy to death.

Further, the word could make the absent one visible by apparition: the spell for this purpose is known in Uist as Fāth-Fīth. [17] Irish has fāth, 'a kind of poem,' which I suggest is cognate with Cymric gwawd, panegyric; O. English wóet; O. Norse ōðr, song, poetry, metre. Near allied are Irish fáith, prophet, Latin vates, Gothic vōds, man. With the side form fīth is to be compared the Welsh gwiddon, 'a witch,' a word used in D. ab Gwilym's poems; the plural occurs in 'Llys y Gwiddonod,' the Witches' Court, where the witches are associated with prophecy and prediction in a way that allows them being regarded as the authors. Rhŷs asks why the Gadhelic women warriors in Gloucestershire were described in Welsh as witches (gwiddonod), and adds: "It is unfortunate that the etymology of the word eludes my search." [18] I believe it is from the magic power of the word. Fīth has no connection with the term fī still met with in the asseveration: Gu'n gabh am Fī thu = may the Evil One take thee! Here Fī is cognate with Ir. fī, bad (Cormac, O'Clery); (there is also fī, 'poison,' cognate with L. vīrus, Gr. ἰός, Skr. visha). The power of the word is so great that a witch's wish when expressed in words may produce gonadh, a wounding or wasting away, which may take various forms; it is reputed by some to produce even childlessness. Thus, on Eilean Aigais, an island on the Beauly River (Uisge Farrar in the upper reaches, but now Abhuinn na Manchuinne in the lower), it is said that a woman was hung wrongously on a tree and eaten to death by the flies; ere dying she pronounced a curse imprecating childlessness on those who should hereafter live there, a curse that was held to have been literally fulfilled. A deathbed entreaty (corrachd, [19] Ir. coruigheacht) had special force because of the revenant (tathaich) spirit which was credited with power to injure the living. I've heard a person declare to another as to coming back after death: 'when I rise up it is thou who wilt get the first slap or blow' ('nuair dh'ēireas mi's tu gheobh a chiad sgailc).

The positive side of the magic word leads to sorcery (buitseachd, draoidheachd), the negative aspect includes the rites that are taboo (geas); the positive precepts that are to be used are spells or charms (ōrtha, ōrthachan; ubagan); the negative precepts are taboos (gessa). The positive word of magic says 'do'; the negative word of magic says 'don't.' It is assumed that all things are in sympathy, and act on one another: things which have once been in contact continue to act on each other even after the contact has been removed. Thus, a man I knew of would never start from his home before sunrise to go on any business without first putting his left knee sunwise thrice round the horse's head. This sained the animal and prevented it from seeing supernatural spirits, for it had been in contact with a man who blessed it in name of the Trinity. Again, like things produce like things; and thus, if you wish to injure a man, injure something like him. This rests on a fallacy in elementary reasoning; but much experience has been necessary to convince mankind of errors which, however apparently simple, have issued in gross deeds. An instance of this magic is that of 'turning-the-heart in lead' (cridhe luadhainn, tionndadh cridhe), which I have seen done in the Highlands several times. A rite somewhat similar existed in the Austrian Tyrol, and in parts of Germany, and J. Grimm traced it to Greece. [20] In the Highlands, when a friend has something the matter with the heart, a wise man who knows this rite,—living at a distance makes no difference,—melts some lead which he pours through a key taken from the outer door over a basin of cold water, making mention of the heart of the person whom he names, and invoking the Trinity: if the shapes as they form in the water can be got to resemble a heart, much virtue ensues to the healing and strengthening of the friend who is far off. The friend often knows that such a rite is practised on his behalf, and that prayers of faith are offered for his recovery.

Another rite which I have often heard of is that of the clay-body (corp criadh), the magic of which rests on the principle of similarity. It is fairly common in Celto-Latin lands. [21] A figure is made of clay, and either the whole or the parts which it is desired to injure are covered with pins and nails to the accompaniment of maledictions; the image is then buried in the ground or placed in a stream in a somewhat inaccessible locality, on the principle that the sooner the clay-body dissolves, the sooner will the body of the person thus represented be wrecked. For the Isle of Man there is a good instance given where an image was turned before a large fire, and pins stuck into it while a rhyme was being muttered, coincident with which the minister was found suffering with wracking pains. On a search having been made, the supposed effigy of the minister was found, as also an old bladder, with pins, rusty nails and skewers. This female practitioner was sentenced to be executed, "and just before she was bound to the stake, confessed the crime for which she was about to suffer." [22] In the Highlands there are instances of quite recent occurrence. I quote from a reliable writer of recent date, simply changing the spelling Creagh into Criadh, as being more correct philologically:

"A rather gruesome relic of a barbarous age which I have heard of as happening within the last few years, is that ugly one known as the Corp Criadh. As its name indicates, this is a body of clay rudely shaped into the image of the person whose hurt is desired. After a tolerably correct representation is obtained, it is stuck all over with pins and thorns, and placed in a running stream. As the image is worn away by the action of the water, the victim also wastes away with some mortal disease. The more pins are stuck in from time to time, the more excruciating agony the unfortunate victim suffers. Should, however, any wayfarer by accident discover the Corp in the stream the spell is broken, and the victim duly recovers. A case of Corp Criadh has been known to occur in Uist within the last five years; and in a parish adjoining ours, it was whispered that the death of a certain young man was due to a spell of this nature.

"Another case that was told to me was concerning a young woman who set her affections upon a certain young man. But on this occasion Barkis was not willing, and he would have none of her. To revenge herself for his shocking want of taste, she resolved that if she was not fated to get him, then neither would any possible rival. In this dog-in-the-manger frame of mind, she made a Corp Criadh for the luckless youth. But it so happened that one day a neighbour (who is the mother of my informant) went into the girl's father's barn to look for some eggs, and hidden among some hay she found, not eggs, but the Corp. There is reason to believe that during the land agitation and strife which have of recent years occupied the Highlands, the rite was practised in connection with some of the land-leaguers who had made themselves obnoxious to their fellows." [23]

The power of the 'word' is seen in magic charms to stop blood and bleeding. Moore [24] gives instances for the Isle of Man. And I know of instances where persons yet alive believe in the Blood-spell, and have a charm for stanching blood (Eolas, Casga Fola). In Sutherland, Ross and Inverness its efficacy depends on its being transmitted from male to female, and from female to male.

In former times there was another term, not now used in the Highlands, viz., Ir. bricht, 'magic, magical spell,' apparently the ceremonially conceived word on which J. Grimm lays stress as the essential requisite of the magic if it is to be effective. Osthoff would equate bricht with Icel. bragr, 'poetry, art of poetry,' and with the Sanskrit brahman, on the assumption that it means 'magic, witchcraft.' [25]

The power of the word even as acting at a distance is still tacitly believed in: e.g. the phrase, Cearr nam ban is deas nam fear, is repeated when there is a sudden reddening of one of the ears: if it be the left ear, the inference is that it is women who are speaking about you; if the right ear, that it is men.

The Greek for a word as something spoken was, μῦθος, 'anything delivered by word of mouth, word, speech,' whence our 'myth.' The spoken word is essential for religion. A South Pacific myth tells that when the Creator of all things had ordered the solid land to rise from the primeval waters, he walked abroad to survey his work. "It is good," said he aloud to himself. "Good," answered an echo from a neighbouring hill. "What!" exclaimed the Creator, "Is some one here already? Am not I first?" "I first," answered the echo. Therefore, the Mangaians assert, the earliest of all existences is the bodiless voice. It is their way of saying, "In the beginning was the Word." [26]

Unless one named the day, a witch could hear one speaking of her on a Friday even if far off. Hence one said: an diu Di-h-aoine, cha chluinn iad mi air muir no tir = to-day is Friday; they will not hear me on sea or land.

A parallel to this belief in the power within the word may be found in the phrase: Tha facal aice = 'She has a word,' said of a witch who is credited with power to cause one in virtue of her word to do her bidding. One is reminded of the phrase used by the people when the demoniac was cured at Capharnahum: τίσ ἐστι οὗτος λόγος, 'What sort of word (or language) is this? for with authority and real power He gives orders to the foul spirits and they come out' (Lc. 4:36). By λόγος, or word, here the people may have meant some formula of exorcism, some cabalistic 'word' which forced the demons to obey.

If such be the power of the magic word, how much more important is the word which is or contains the name (ainm) itself! All the spells and charms for averting the evil eye that are in use end by inserting the name of the person to be cured, adding thereto the sanctifying clause: in the Name of the Father, the Son and the Holy Ghost. To counteract evils the name is even changed. [27] For the soul is regarded as in the name. It is forbidden to awaken one who is suffering from night-mare (trom-laighe) [28] unless one has first summoned him by name. The inference is that his soul is away and is to be called back by the ritual use of the person's name; the old folks therefore enjoined one: na dūisg e gun ghairm air ainm = do not waken him without calling him by name. To do otherwise is gessa, or taboo now; at an earlier day, the fear was that a man might die, for his soul was but a tenant of the body, not in any way in relation to or a result of its functions.

I find with many that it is a matter of extreme importance to call a child by the name of a deceased ancestor; death is but a minor affair so long as the name is kept up. This is known as: togail an ainm = lifting or raising the name (of the deceased relative). Perhaps it is owing to some association of belief with the old idea of the name-soul that so many saints had double names, e.g. Crimthann, 'wolf,' the first name of St. Columcille, the 'church dove.' And many heroes of the Fionn-Saga have double names. I have seen the custom of naming a child after a deceased relative explained by the intention of securing rest in his grave for the latter; the child when grown up was bound to brave the influence which caused its relative's death. But on Celtic ground I have not heard of such an explanation. The practice of "giving a new-born babe the name of a deceased person is to be traced back in the old Icelandic sagas, where a dying person often appeals to another to name a future child after him, because he expected advantage from it." Mr. Hartland infers that he thereby expected to secure a new birth. [29] In the case of a child's death, if he has borne the name of a deceased relative, it is often held unlucky in the Highlands to give the same name to another child; but that is aside from the main desire of 'raising the name.'

The Gadhelic ainm, 'name,' is cognate with Welsh anu, enw; Gr. ὄνομα, Prussian emmens, Old Bulgarian imę, the root ono allied to no in L. nomen, E. name.

In Wales English names were regarded as very unlucky for fishermen (Trevelyan, 329).

Of great import of old was an asseveration by the name of the tribal god. No doubt many Celtic god-names would have been kept secret, and it is probable that often only epithets have survived. However that may be, we find the phrase tong a toing mo thuath = 'I swear what my tribe swears' (with an occasional variant, 'I swear by the god of my tribe') of frequent occurrence in Irish literature: and if tong be cognate with L. tango, 'I touch,' as it seems to be, the idea underlying is that of 'touching ' some sacred thing, be it stone or something else,—a habit continued in Christian days by taking the mionn or oath, E. Ir. mind, 'oath, diadem,' by touching the swearing relics or insignia of a saint. Cognate is O. Welsh minn, 'sertum'; MacBain compares O.H.G. menni, 'neck ornament,' Ag. S. mene, 'neck chain,' L. monile. [30] How far the idea of the soul is expressed under the sense of touch we will consider later under the custom of 'touching the corpse.'

It is of interest to notice that a prickly sensation in the nose is known as menmain, a word which is but a variant of O. Ir. menme, g. menman, 'mind, mens,' cognate with Skr. mánman, 'mind, thought,' L. mens; also memini, 'remember,' E. mean, mind. The menmain is a sensation which prognosticates the coming of a stranger or visitor. On the other hand a secretion such as the saliva (seile) is of special virtue in ratifying bargains or in curing warts: this is because originally the spittle was conceived as possessing soul-force. At markets I have noticed that bargains are still sealed by spitting on the hand ere two parties clasp hands on coming to an agreement. I have heard also of a belief that some of the Clan Campbell, through a certain feeling in the eye-brow, foreknew of a Campbell's death. A sneeze (sreot) is also a sort of omen: a 'spirit ' is thought to take possession of one; when one sneezes involuntarily it was etiquette with some to say, 'God be with thee' (Dia leat). The kidney (adha, ae; O. Ir. óa, ae; W. afu) is specially an organ of the soul, and there are certain prescriptions regarding it: children must not partake of it until they can pronounce the word or name for it (Inverness-shire); if you eat a whole kidney it will come out on the body (Sutherland). From its connection with the soul the skull or brain-pan (copan cinn) has curative virtues: to drink water from the skull of a dead man is believed in as a cure for epilepsy, and has been to my knowledge faithfully carried out lately (1909). A draught of the spirit of human skull was a part of the medical treatment in vogue in former times in higher circles.[31] Even the human hair as associated with the idea of soul is beloved as a keepsake, and is treasured as a remembrance in far-away lands. A stanza from a Highland poem runs:

Tha t'fhalt-sa, 'ghaoil, na mo spliūcan rōin
Is bithidh, a ghaoil, fhad s a bhios mi beō;
'S 'nuair dh'fhalbhas triūir leam 'ga m' ghiūlan chon an fhōd
Bidh t'fhalt-sa cuide rium an ciste chaoil nam bōrd.

'Thy hair, oh darling, is in my pouch of seal-skin, and will be so long as I live; and when three bear me away carrying me to the sod, thy hair, my dear one, will be with me in the narrow chest of boards.'

The soul-life is thus held to be associated with parts of the full-grown body. But even at birth the body has its ritual. One could say, before birth, inasmuch as it is held to be unlucky for two women who are great with child to come into the same room if either be near confinement. To contravene this rule was gessa or taboo in the code of old Highland midwives, who held that the infant of one of the parties must die or be stillborn (Inverness-shire). The after-birth had its special ritual. To my knowledge the following was the belief held not so long ago: "The old women were very careful of the after-birth; if it were burnt in the wrong manner the wife would have no more children. The midwives had great fear of this in case of taking away the lives of others. But if the wife would eat the after-birth of another woman, the children would come back. It was the custom of the late Mrs. G. (a certain midwife) to cause women who for the first time became mothers bite the placenta thrice. The mother thereafter would not suffer the pains of childbirth." [32]

On no account was the after-birth to be carelessly thrown outside, lest dogs should get it; it was to be decently buried under a tree or carefully burnt. The old midwives sometimes were wont to keep a portion, and this when roasted they ordered to be drunk with water in cases of sterility. In Ireland I find that "an after-birth must be burned to preserve the child from the fairies." [33] The omphalos [34] was in the Highlands ground to powder after it fell off on the ninth day or so, and was mixed with water and given to the child to drink. The cord was sacred, as it united the unborn infant to the life of the mother; it was held to retain life in some mysterious manner. In Greece the navel or omphalos is the symbol of the Earth-Mother; [35] for Brazil, Southey [36] says: "Immediately upon a woman's delivery the father takes to his hammock, covers himself up, and is nurst there till the navel string of the infant has dried away; the union between him and his progeny is regarded as so intimate that care must be taken of him lest the child should suffer." The omphalos was a favourite amulet among the Crees, according to Mackenzie's History of the Fur Trade (p. 86). Among American Indians it was a frequent custom to carry it to a distance and bury it; in later life it was the individual's duty to go alone to that spot and perform certain ceremonies. From other parallels, therefore, I conclude that the Celtic ritual of the navel-string was due to some connection with the life of the soul, as it was imagined. "The navel-string and the placenta are often regarded as external souls." [37] Blood drunk from the child's navel and eating the dried remains of the navel-string are approved folk-cures for sterility elsewhere. [38]

Further, among body-parts mythic thought interprets the soul as in the eye (the Evil Eye).

The singular malific influence of a glance has been felt by most persons in life; an influence that seems to paralyse intellect and speech, simply by the mere presence in the room of some one who is mystically anti-pathetic to our nature. For the soul is like a fine-toned harp that vibrates to the slightest external force or movement, and the presence and glance of some persons can radiate around us a divine joy, while others may kill the soul with a sneer or frown. We call these subtle influences mysteries, but the early races believed them to be produced by spirits good or evil, as they acted on the nerves of the intellect. [39]

All races have a belief in the power of the eye which but expresses the soul. The soul is not thought of as confined to any one single organ of the body. The Romans spoke of the fascination of an evil tongue: mala fascinare lingua (Catullus, vii. 12); ne vati noceat mala lingua futuro (Virgil, Bucol. Ecl. vii. 28).

But the Romans [40] were pre-eminently familiar with the evil eye and its cure; in Spain [41] the evil eye is known as causing illness (querelar nasula); Italy abounds with the belief; Sébillot [42] gives several instances of talismans used for preserving one from the effects of the evil eye (à la préserver du mauvais oeil). The evil eye is due to soul-magic. In Scotland it is well known; suffice it to refer to the collections on this topic by the late Rev. J. G. Campbell [43] and by Dr. R. C. Maclagan. [44] Young infants are frequently believed to be overlooked; likewise cattle; a man may lay the evil eye even on what is his own property, as when a husband must on no account see the churning operations, as his glance would prevent the butter coming. The great remedy is būrn airgid, 'water into which silver coins have been put,' as also gold and copper if you like, but silver by all means. The water has to be raised with a wooden ladle from a stream over which pass the living and the dead, in the name of the Trinity; the sign of the cross is made over the contents of the ladle, and a rhyme is repeated wherein the opening word of the Lord's Prayer, Pater, in G. Paidir, is repeated seven times, but alternately in name of the Virgin and of the King (or Lord). Then the ritual says: "In the door of the city (of heaven, i.e.) Christ gave three calls full just: seven 'paters' in name of the Virgin will avert the evil eye, whether it be on human creature or on brute: whoso hath laid on thee the eye, may it return on themselves or on their children, and, if children fail, on their substance: [the person's name here], may'st thou be in thy full health, in name of the Father, of the Son and of the Holy Spirit." [45] The water is then partly given as a drink to the child, partly sprinkled over it, and the rest is poured out over a large stone or boulder that is never moved by human hands. When rents make their appearance in such stones, these are ascribed to the penetrating and disintegrating force of envy, and the saying goes: 'Envy breaks up the stone' (brisidh farmad a chlach). From the kind of coins that may adhere to the wooden ladle on being emptied, and from their position, some of the wise ones would divine whether the evil eye in the special case was that of a male or female. Such is the ritual of averting the evil eye in Strathglass neighbourhood. I now give an example or two from S. Uist, which I owe the late Rev. Allan MacDonald.

"If a person came and saw a cow or other creature belonging to you, and he began to praise it, e.g. if he were to say, tha ùth mór aig a' bhoin, 'the cow has a big udder,' or anything similar of a complimentary nature, this act of praising was called aibhseachadh; and as it might lead accidentally to gonadh, or evil eye, or wounding of the cattle, as a preventative it was customary to say to the person making the complimentary remarks: Fliuch do shūil = 'wet your eye.' This wetting of the eye was generally performed by moistening the tip of the finger with saliva, and moistening the eye with it thereafter.

"If a person were much afflicted by the toradh, or 'milk produce,' being taken from him, he was advised to adopt the following remedy: Whenever one of his cows calves, to take away the calf immediately before he draws milk from his dam, then to take a bottle and draw milk from the four teats into the bottle, the person so doing being on one knee, and saying:

Gum beannaicheadh Dia na cŭilean [46] so
Tha mise 'g iarraidh so 'n ainm Dhia
S cha n eil mi 'g iarraidh ach mo chuid fhéin.

The bottle is then tightly corked and hidden in a safe place. Here is a magic way of retaining the whole by keeping the part. If the cork were to be put in loosely, it is feared that the toradh would be at the mercy of any one who had the faculty of filching it. Another Uist informant, Duncan M'Innes, said that he heard the effective way of recovering the toradh was to snatch a bundle of thatch from the threshold of a suspected person and to burn it beneath a churn (Tubhadh an fhardoruis a thoirt leat s a losgadh fo thōin a chrannachain); and John Mackinnon, Dalibrog, said: Na'n cailleadh to 'n dul air ceann na buaraich chailleadh to 'n toradh = 'If you were to lose the loop on the end of the cow-tie, you would lose the milk-produce."'

A further stage of the concept of the Body-Soul is that of Blood Magic or the Soul in the Blood. The connection of the soul-life with the blood would naturally have been perceived from of old. Once the body was drained of the blood death ensued. The Irish collection of Church Canons quotes Lactantius [47] as to the nature of the soul, where he states that some held the soul to be fire, others said it was spirit, others that it was blood: fire, for it vivifies the body; spirit, for it breathes through the members; blood, for with the blood the soul passes away. Such speculations might have become known among some of the people, but their appeal to the folk-mind, in so far as blood is concerned, would have been easy. For, as Faust, who covenants in blood with Mephistopheles, says: "Blood is a juice of very special kind,"—so much so that in Vedic ritual sprinkling by blood is practised to lay evil spirits, while in the Highlands the blood of a black cock is spilled at the spot where the demon of epilepsy first made its presence manifest. A blood-mark connected with a foul deed was held in the Highlands to be impossible to be wiped out. To drink blood was an earnest token of true love. A lady who entertained Prince Charlie in Harris became full of sorrow on hearing of her lover having been drowned on his way to marry her, and she sang in lines which I may render thus:

Would, my God, I were near thee, my love,
  on what bank soe'er or creek thou art cast;
My liking, oh love! were thy body's blood,
  and the red wine of Spain were nothing to me,
Will they, nill they, my drink were thy blood,
  the blood that is flowing from out of thy breast,
The blood of thy body, dear love, I love best.

Again, in literature there is the case of Gregor MacGregor of Glenstrae, put to death at Kenmore by Sir Colin Campbell, who became laird of Glenorchy in 1550 and proved himself a bitter foe to Clan Gregor. Sir Colin caused his daughter's husband, Gregor of Glenstrae, with whom she eloped, and whom she married against her father's will, to be executed at Kenmore in 1570. A brother of hers also took the father's side. To escape vengeance Gregor and herself and child had to wander about, but were at last captured, and she was forced to witness her husband's execution at

Taymouth Castle. In her cry for vengeance on the head of the perpetrator, she says:

Would that Taymouth and Finlarig
  were a-flame,—razed to the ground;
And Gregor's white palms, O Gregor the fair,
  clasped in mine arms around.

No apples have I to-day, to-day,
  though apples for others there be;
My apple so sweet, my apple, my meat,
  lying in cold earth is he.

To her bairn, fearing lest he may not attain manhood to execute vengeance for the deed, she croons sadly:

On Lammas morn and early
  my love and I were merry;
But ere the sun came to mid of day
  mine heart was heavy, heavy.

On high-born kith and kindred
  my curse for my sorrow's plight;
By stealth my love was taken
  and unawares by might.

Were twelve there of his kindred
  with Gregor at their head,
Mine eyes were not a-shedding tears
  my bairnie friendless made.

On a block of oak they set his head,
  they shed his blood with a will;
On the ground they spilt it, and had I a cup
  I would of it have quaffed my fill. [48]

Martin, in his Western Isles, says of the islanders: "Their ancient leagues of friendship were ratified by drinking a drop of each other's blood, which was commonly drawn out of the little finger. This bond was religiously observed as a sacred bond; and if any person after such an alliance happened to violate the same, he was from that time reputed unworthy of all honest men's conversation." [49]

The cro-codaig or blood-covenant was known among the Gael of old. Thus Branduff, king of Leinster, in 598 A.D., as he was preparing to fight the king of Ireland, met a party of Ulidians, whom he induced to abandon the king of Ireland and fight under Branduff's own standard in the battle of Dunbolg. The king of Ulidia replied: "A blood-covenant (cro-codaig) and an agreement shall be made between us." "They seated themselves on the mountain and made a cotach or bond of fellowship that should never be broken." The name of the mountain, formerly Sliabh Nechtain, was afterwards changed to Sliabh Codaig, 'the mountain-slope of the covenant'—the present Slieve Gadae (the old name slightly corrupted) on the road from Hollywood to Donard, Wicklow.

The Ulaid, hereditary enemies to the race of Conn-of-the-Hundred-Battles, were glad to desert, and Conchobar, their king, is said to have had a vision regarding this blood-covenant, as is told in the story of the Boromean tribute:

I beheld a vat of crystal, with splendour of gold.
By me, on the midst of my house, in Bregia, at the Boyne,
A third of the vat (was filled) with the bloods of men, strange assembly!
There was but one third of new milk, in its midst,
Another third was noble (?) wine, strange to me!
Men with bowed heads surrounded it (men who had come over a clear sea). [50]

Conchobar beheld the Leinster men and the Ulaid around the vat, drinking its contents. "And I know," said the king of the Ulaid, "that this is the covenant that was foretold therein. For this is the blood that was seen in the vat,—the blood of the two provinces in meeting. This is the new milk—the canon of the Lord, which the clerics of the two provinces recite. This is the wine, Christ's Body and His Blood, which the clerics offer up." And he was explaining it in that wise, and he uttered a lay:

Make for us a covenant, let it be for ever!
With the 'trees of wine,' with the kings from Liffey. [51]

The poet Spenser relates that during his stay in Ireland he saw a woman at Limerick drink the blood of her foster-son on his having been executed. He saw her "take up his head whilst he was being quartered, and suck up the blood that ran from it, saying that the earth was not worthy to drink it, and steep her face and breast with it, at the same time tearing her hair, and crying out and shrieking most terribly." And we have Highland evidence. In a song composed to a Macdonald warrior after the battle of Cairinish in 1601, his foster-mother sings:

Thy body's blood flagrantly
  a-soaking thy linen
And I myself sucking it
  till hoarse were my breath.

Another singer says:

Thy wounds I did staunch
  and many were they;
Thine heart's blood I drank,—
  sweeter than wine, I will say.

And in a well-known Hebridean song to Ailean Donn there is a direct mention of blood-drinking:

"I could drink, though to the aversion of others, not of the red wine of Spain, but of the blood of thy body after being drowned." [52]

Irish references pointing to the idea of the soul in the blood may be met with, as we read of bursts of blood from the tips and nostrils of the man who knew that King Eochaid had the ears of a horse; [53] of a swelling which grew from the head of the lad who knew the secret of King Labraid's ears; [54] of washing in the blood of a king for leprosy. [55] And the late Dr. Wilde, in his account of Irish folk-remedies, mentions the blood of the Welshes as well as that of the Keoghs and Cahills as a cure. [56] In Lewis blood taken from above the patient's ankles was given as recently as in 1909 with a view to curing epilepsy,—an instance I formerly only tentatively included in the Appendix to my treatment of the Norse Influence on Celtic Scotland, but I am aware that it need not be due to any outside influence although blood-brotherhood is likewise met with in Scandinavia. Du Chaillu, in his Viking Age (ii. 64), quotes from Egil and Asmund's Saga (ch. 6), and says: "They took oaths that whoever lived the longest should have a mound thrown up over the other, and place therein as much property as seemed to him fitting, and the survivor had to sit with the dead one for three nights, and then depart if he liked. Then both drew their blood and let it flow together; this was then regarded as an oath." Blood-brotherhood in the Highlands was not extinct at least until after Iain Lom's time; for tradition has it that by origin he was not of Lochaber lineage, but that owing to a peculiar circumstance his father fled to Lochaber from Argyll and made blood-brotherhood (fuil-bhrāithreachais) with the Campbells' deadly enemies, the Macdonalds. Iain Lom Macdonald was Gadhelic poet laureate to Charles II. I am now only concerned with the tradition that blood-brotherhood was practised in his age, even if the story in detail may, at least at a first consideration, be at variance with the poet's received pedigree.

It is said that the poet had no hair at his birth, nor afterwards, and that accordingly he was given the epithet lom, or 'bare, without hair.' Such cases are rare, but I know personally of one. Briefly, the story is that Iain Lom's mother was a MacCalmain from Muckairn, who married one Campbell, who resided near to or in Kilmartin, Argyll. This Campbell in a quarrel stabbed another Campbell who, on his round as deachadoir or tithe-collector, insulted Mrs. MacCalmain Campbell. The upshot was that she and her husband fled and took refuge with the Campbells' enemies, and specially under the banner of Macdonell of Keppoch, who initiated them into his own clan by the rite of blood-brotherhood (rinn iad fuil-bhrāithreachais riutha). The child born to them soon thereafter was the future Iain Lom Macdonald the poet, and named after the Macdonalds. Said Keppoch to his father: "The more Campbells you kill the better." The poet became more Macdonald than the Macdonalds themselves.

This tradition I heard recited by Dr. Alex. Carmichael at a meeting of Lorne men in Glasgow, when the lecturer was Mr. Malcolm Campbell Macphail, the Glenorchy Bard, and a native of Muckairn. It was accepted. And I take the tradition as pointing to the belief in the soul-in-the-blood, which is the basis of the solemn covenant blood-rites of many peoples. Stanley tells how he often had to take part in the rite of blood-brotherhood in Africa, and Trumbull's Blood Covenant gives many instances. Its force among the Irish of old is apparent from The Wooing of Emer: when Cūchulainn wounded his love, Dervorgil, in the form of a sea-bird, with a stone from his sling, he contracted blood-brotherhood by sucking from the wound the stone with a clot of blood round it. "I cannot wed thee now," he said, "for I have drunk thy blood. But I will give thee to my companion here, Lug-aid of the Red Stripes." [57]

The artificial tie of blood-brotherhood being reckoned a barrier to marriage pertains to a matriarchal stage of society, wherein descent is reckoned on the mother's side, and where the father is not reckoned as belonging to the kin of his children. [58] The father is not akin to his child. It is the ethic of this stage that is reflected in such a tale as Conlaoch killing his own father Cūchulainn: the son avenges his mother's kin upon his own father. It is a stage which has its own strata of explanations of such things as conception, generation and the origin of the soul. The custom of foster-brotherhood conceivably may have had its origin herein: the child is put out to be fostered among its mother's kin, and out of the father's house. Until capable of bearing arms it is taboo for the child to appear in his father's presence: it is prohibited for the warrior to have any sympathetic association with the weakness of youth. Even the marriage-ring might be held to be a remnant of some old custom of binding the blood-covenant upon the hand.

THE FINDING OF THE SOUL (PART 2)

AMONG certain savages the strip cut off at circumcision is bound on the arm; and in the Jewish ritual some of the blood mingled with wine is quaffed by the operating priest. What is tasted by man is a covenant-sign for deity. Clay Trumbull [59] says: "Even down to modern times, the rite of circumcision has included a recognition, however unconscious, of the primitive blood-friendship rite, by the custom of the ecclesiastical operator, as God's representative, receiving into his mouth, and thereby being made a partaker of, the blood mingled with wine, according to the method described among the Orientals, in the rite of blood-friendship, from the earliest days of history."

In Ireland of long ago, I have read somewhere that a usual gift from a woman to her betrothed husband was a pair of bracelets made of her own hair, as if a portion of her very self entered into the covenant rite. The blood especially was the very self. It is this belief that explains the idea that the corpse of a murdered man bleeds in the presence of, especially at the touch of the slayer. There are references throughout the literature of the Middle Ages to the bleeding-corpse or cruentatio. It occurs in the Nibelungenlied. And in the Ivain of Chretien de Troies, there occurs a scene where the corpse is brought into the hall where Ivain is, and then begins to bleed, whereupon the men feel confident that the murderer must be hidden there, and they renew their search. The soul is regarded as speaking through or by the blood. In the Highlands [60] I feel confident that there are remnants of such a belief, pointing back to a belief similar to the thought of the Hebrews when they held that "the blood is the life" (Deuteronomy xii. 23). To be remembered, too, are Homer's expressions: "The blood ran down the wound" (Iliad, xvii. 86); "the life (ψυχή) ran down the wound" (Iliad, xiv. 518). A Greek, quoted by Aristotle (De Anima, i. 2, 19), declared that the soul was the blood. The Arabs say "the soul flows" (from the wound), i.e. he dies.

When associated with crime the stains of blood are regarded in folklore as indelible. Let me give a piece of Inverness-shire folklore from my notes of 2nd May, 1887. It illustrates other points as well:

"There lived an hotelkeeper at B------ with his wife and three children. Having made him drunk with brandy and taken his head off with the axe, she buried him among the brackens, and put his clothes on the banks of Loch X------. A search was instituted, but the body could not be found. There lived a godly minister not far away, and he dreamed a dream, in which he saw the body among the brackens. When the report was spreading among the people, the wife had the body removed. The people, however, were suspicious of her, and their suspicions were confirmed by marks of blood at the top of the stair; however often the boards were cleaned, or even renewed, the stains of blood would appear. A letter-carrier was passing by one evening at the inn. He put up there at her request, as she wanted him to kill a goat in the morning. She sent him to bed along with her two boys. He slept; but the boys awoke, and their scream startled him out of sleep. They said that they saw something. But he slept off again. This was repeated, and on the second occasion he went down to the kitchen, where he found the woman sitting by the firelight. She told him that she had never gone to bed since her husband was lost. He then twigged that the tathaich, or revenant of the dead, was in the house, and he went off.

"Now, the godly minister referred to owned a white or grey horse; its saddle was always kept beside the entrance door, to which the horse would come of its own accord, and as often as he did so the minister accepted it as a beckoning from God to go and make known His ways to men.

"The minister mounted on this occasion, and followed to where the horse led, and he arrived at the church of B-------. This church was a barn, which had a gable of matted willow twigs in which there was a breach. The woman referred to sat outside this breach, with a shawl on her head and with her back to the man of God. In course of his sermon the minister stopped: 'I cannot proceed any further,' he said, 'I have something else to say; there is a murderess in the congregation; and she is troubling me.' He repeated himself, and threatened to name her,—but the woman, being outside, quietly left, as was afterwards found out. On her deathbed she confessed the whole, and related that one day as she was out herding she saw a number of small men playing around her, the husband among the number; he came up to her and gave her a blow, which left on her a blue mark, of which she died. The mark was visible after death."

On the occasion of witnessing an execution there was a special rite to prevent dreams of the dead: to dream of the dead was the next step to their coming back as revenants. When Alex. Mackintosh of Borlum was executed at Muirfield (for an assault on one M'Rory, a Beauly cattle-dealer who was suspected of having wrongly identified his assailant, and who afterwards was an outcast in Beauly, where he took his own life), we learn how "with mingled feelings of sorrow and horror the multitude slowly and silently dispersed, many, if not most of the company, placing a small piece of bread under a stone, which, according to a superstitious tradition, would prevent after-dreams of the unfortunate Alexander Mackintosh." [61]

Blood innocently shed might readily call out for vengeance; for the soul was in the blood.

In the etiquette of paying one's parting respects to the dead, before the corpse is buried, no custom is more tenacious in the Highlands than that of touching the body with the finger. To neglect doing so is thought to expose a person to dreaming of the deceased, and by consequence to the danger of being visited by the dead, and of being open to the dread haunting of the ghost. This is the relic of the old ordeal upon the corpse of the murdered—a custom not confined to present Gaeldom, but current in a wider area. For instance, the minister of Pitsligo testifies: "The opinion prevailed till not very long ago, and even yet lingers, that in case of murder, if the murderer touches the corpse, blood flows from the wounds." [62] To touch the body is therefore a sort of folk-ritual to signify that one is at peace with the deceased. In a case of murder, there is a noted instance on record in the Highlands. Let me quote:

"A singular providence, under presidency of the minister, Mr. James Fraser, for the discovery of the murderer of Donald Mackwilliam Chui (i.e. Dhuibh): [63]

"The signal providence that appeared in this matter was, that though the dead body had layn upon the sod within the flood mark, and the sea ebbed and flowed six times during its being there, yet not taken away. Upon the 3rd day the herdsmen bringing up their cattle discovered the dead man, hasted in to the place, found it was their neighbour, Donald Mackwilliam Chui, murthered. . . . All the people presently flockt to the place, and perceiving that he had been three days missed, and his corps lying upon a flat piece of the bank within the flood, wondered that the sea ebbing did not drive him away, the wind being southerly all the time. But the hand of God was in it to discover the murther of the innocent. The corps is carried to the churchyard, and laid in the common reer with the chapel, and a despatch sent express to the Shirref Deput, Alexander Chisholm, living in Bunchrive, who peremptorly convenes the whole parish, causes strip naked the corps, and lay it exposed upon a broad plank at the entry of the chappel, and chairs set round; and all the gentlemen of the 3 parishes present, concluding that this murder was an act of malice and revenge, and not of gain or lucre, the poor young man being but a servant and had no great trust. The list of the parishioners being read, every one as he was called touched the bare body, laying his hand on it, non of quhat degree soever excepted, men and women to the number of 6 or 700. At length, the murtherer, John Mackeanvore, laid his hand most confidently upon the bare breast, and I narrowly observed (sitting at the head of the coffin) that the greatest wound opened and a drop of blood gushed out. I desired he should lay on his hand again, which he did, and men observed a drop of blood issue from the nose. He is suddenly seized and fettered, brought in to the church, and after serious prayer for the discovery of this horrid work of darkness, he is examined and a torture threatened; but no confession. His mittimus signed, and sent in to the vault of Inverness, and secured. Not one man or woman within my parish of Wardlaw, after reading the catalogue, was missed but John Mackeanire, who was seen to go hastily through Kingily and over the burn, as the people were convening for trial, and so escaped. He was seen and known at the Bridge end of Inverness, buying ground tobacco in papers, and so away through Strathnairn, and over the bridge of Dulce in to Strathspey; and no account of him for two years.

"John Mackeanvore, the capital murtherer, being in the pit at Inverness, laid fast in the stocks, continued there but about a fortnight, and both his feet down from the ancles dropt off as if by amputation. When he is brought forth he had a foot in every hand like a shoe last, cursing and imprecating, and praying God to revenge his cruel usage; so that many condemned the judge as too severe, and seemed to vindicate this villain, who is carried away in a sledge through the streets and over the bridge home to his own house in Finask, where his wife and friends attend him; falling in a fever is every Sabbath prayed for as for death, and that God w^d discover this murther. . . . In fine, I myself out of charity, cured this John Mackeanvore's wounds, untill at last his stumps were as strong as men's fists, without feet; and a contribution made for buying him a horse, and goes up and down the country confidently as an innocent, begging, and no account of John M'Keanire, who is reputed by all men to be the murtherer, having run for it as guilty; and we are in suspense for two years; the land of Finask (interim patitur justus) blasted upon, neither crop nor cattle thrive: Innocuus clamat sanguis; (innocent) blood cries." [64]

In the Isle of Man it is unlucky to let blood, especially that of a king or person of high rank, fall on the ground. Moore [65] states: "It is remembered to this day that when Iliam Dhone, William Christian, was shot at Hango Hill in 1662, blankets were spread where he stood, so that not one drop of his blood should touch the earth." It is thought that this may have some sacrificial meaning; the intent of the act springs from the idea of the soul in the blood.

For the wide-spread character of this belief elsewhere, the reader need only turn to Scott's Fair Maid of Perth (c. 23) with his note on the case which came before the High Court of Justiciary at Edinburgh in 1688; to the Lay of the Niblungs, where by this ordeal Kriemhild fastened upon Hagan the guilt of murdering her husband Siegfried; [66] in the sixteenth century Christian II. of Denmark, by commanding those present to place their right hand on the breast of the slain, brought about the detection and confession of the murderer, who was at once beheaded. [67]

An analogous practice is that of swearing on the skull, of which a case is reported at a recent criminal trial in Germany. [68]

Alongside of the blood or body-essence observation falls to be directed to the breath, likewise an essence. The soul is held to be especially in the breath. Breath has long ago been supposed to be the only part of man which will survive him. [69] Breathing accompanies life. An old Highland expression I have heard used by one lamenting a mother's death signifies: 'her breath is not before me'; [70] at death I have heard it said that the soul left the body in the form of a white vapour or smoke, [71]—expressions paralleled elsewhere, as among the Slavs. [72] The regular Highland expression for 'yielding the ghost, giving up the breath in death' is: 'thug e suas an deò.' [73] The Indo-European root of deò signifies 'to breathe': we may perhaps infer from the connotation of the various cognates that the transition of meanings would have been in the following series: breath, soul, soul of the dead, daimon, god. From the same root is the Gaulish dusios, 'daemon immundus, incubus; nightmare'; these Gaulish dusii were impure demons believed to have commerce with mortals, and are referred to by St. Augustine. We see thus that the root in one case yields a word restricted in meaning to the personal breath or soul, whereas in other tongues it connotes a demon, or, as with the Greeks, the god-soul, in its final sense God. When the Highlanders speak of the 'double,' the word is samhl, samhla, a word of like origin with G. samhuil, 'likeness, like,' cognate with Latin similis, English same: the 'double ' is vaguely described as a semi-transparency in which the chief features of one dying or dead are recognisable by the eye: physiologists might regard the 'double' as due to optical illusion. As a fact it is firmly believed that a ghost may be seen; I recollect a case where a woman went out one moonlit night to draw water from the well: on looking behind her she saw her own image or ghost (samhl) covered by a winding sheet, with the face veiled. This may be read by physiologists under the idea of the soul-image, or memory-image personified.

Any collection of instances of Second-Sight will give numerous cases where an apparition (taibhse) or vision has been thought to have been seen, and to the imagination these phantoms are real. They are, as the root of taibhse implies, things which 'show or speak,' with the folk-belief reservation that such ghosts cannot speak until they are first spoken to. As regards speech, the control remains with man. Through touch, however, they reveal themselves as dangerous; when parting with one they may leave a blue mark on the body, and as a precaution when travelling at night one must keep to the side and away from the middle of the highway so as not to obstruct their path. There may, according to folk-thought, be even a procession of ghosts as in phantom funerals. The ear no less than the eye is appealed to; it is a firm belief, or was in my childhood, that the shrieking of ghosts may be heard: when the ghost crossed over water it shrieked, or gave a yell, resounding through the rocks and woods, which was termed sgal, a word akin to the German schallen, 'to sound.' I heard it said of a ghost's yell on the way to a cemetery: bha a sgal a toirt fuaim air na creigean 's e 'tighinn sīos Āilean-an-Uchd, i.e. its shriek was resounding through the rocks as it was coming down Āilean-an-Uchd (the Mead or Green of the Brae, Brae-field). Another phrase is: ghoir an tāsc [74] = the ghost yelled. Besides deō, [75] which is the more spiritual aspect of the breath, or the breath as conjoined to the soul, there is another word anail, breath, Old Irish anál, Welsh anadl, anal, from a root an, to breathe; Gothic anan, to breathe; Sanskrit anila, wind. Differentiated therefrom is G. anam, soul; Old Irish anim (dative anmin), Cornish enef, Breton ene, plural anaoun, 'the souls, the dead'; cognate with Latin animus, anima, Greek ἄνεμος, 'wind.' Thus, by abstraction from the actual visible warm breath (deō) and the agent of the breath (anail), one attains to the idea anam (or soul), which we attain to consciousness of through the body.

It is the essence of man that he came to think of self as something different from the body: how man came first to think and speak of himself as something different from the body is an improper question to put. From the side of body our being is mortal: hence fitly spoken of in Gadhelic as duine, 'man,' a word cognate with Greek θνητός, 'mortal'; English dwine. As sentient, percipient, thinking agent, he is anam, 'soul,' the energy which discovers itself in the breath, the vital motion, the inner impulse which in our consciousness is given us in breath. Here it is of interest to compare with L. anima, G. anam, Gr. anemos, 'wind,' the force of the Sanskrit ásu, 'the breath of life in men and animals,' cognate with Norse anses, souls of ancestors worshipped as gods, meeting us in the Asen, the highest Norse gods, and in the Anglo-Saxon ése, the lower spiritual beings, the elves. Parallel in concept, though from a different root, is the meaning discoverable in English soul; German Seele, Gothic saiwala, which Persson [76] equates with Old Bulgarian si-la, force, power; Lithuanian sy-là, force, power; Prussian sei-lin, zeal, industry, exertion, effort; plural sei-lins, mind; seilisku, devotion; no-sei-lis, spirit: even were the Lithuanian and Prussian loaned from Slavonic, the roots sei̯, sai̯, si, convey the idea 'set in motion, let go.' When the energy, the inner impulse in the breath had departed, people could not but feel that all had gone, and thus the breath, the soul-in-the-breath, the inner-impulse-in-the-breath supplied the material which thought came to examine further in course of time. The soul was named from a something which it possesses, as an attribute in common with a function of the body. When death ensues one of the phrases is: shiubhail e, 'he went off,' the word siubhal being used usually for 'walking,' and cognate with Welsh chwyfu, 'move, stir,' thus amounting to 'he moved off, he stirred,' and in keeping with the parallel phrase chaochail e, 'he changed,' i.e. = he died, a current Highland expression.

The transition from breath-impulse to the divine through the idea of breath, soul, soul of the dead, daimon, God, may be made by a different path of thought. Just as soul is always given us with consciousness of the body, and is thus descriptively the idea of the body, so is also the world-body, and especially are the shining heavens prominent as a part thereof: thus is the Gadhelic Dia, 'God,' cognate with Latin Deus (met with also in Jupiter), Norse Tiw, 'the war-god,' tívar, 'gods'; Sanskrit devá, Greek δῖος, 'divine'; Zeus, who in Greek has various epithets, as at Dodona, where the official title was Ζεύσ Νάϊος, 'the stream god'; at Sidon θαλάσσιος, according to Hesychius, whence it follows that he was there a sea-god; Pausanias states that Aeschylus, son of Euphorion, applies the name of Zeus also to the god who dwells in the sea,—all which illustrate local transitions to sea-god from the original sky-god, the bright shining heavens. The Germanic races which, as we have seen, use a different root to express 'soul ' from that used in Celtic,—although the concept in both seems to embrace the common element of 'motion,'—have also a different root to express that of God, German Gott. According to the late W. Thomsen, of Copenhagen, the name means 'He to whom sacrifice is made, He who is worshipped'; Professor Höffding [77] thinks of a relationship between the root in God and that in giessen, 'to pour,' with Greek χέειν whose root χυ is taken as cognate with Sanskrit hu, whence huta, 'sacrificed,' also 'he to whom sacrifices are made.' A proto-Indo-European form for God, *ghutom, Schrader has defined as 'the divine element called forth by a charm from the deified phenomena,' and this word is taken as cognate with Sanskrit, hutá, 'called,' Avesta zavaiti, 'he curses '; Lithuanian zawėti, 'to charm.' [78] This would harmonise with the derivation of religio, 'religion,' from L. religare, 'to bind,' in the sense of what a man binds on the deity acknowleged by him.

Both paths are animistic, i.e. they read phenomena in terms of the soul. Both acknowledge the worship of spirits: the Latins worshipped the mânes, a word cognate with the Old Latin mânus, 'good,' hence 'the good spirits' of ancestors; the Celts worshipped the sīde, [79] known also as na daoine maith, 'the good people'—all vaguely subordinated to the ancestral spirit, God. All that is the work of and under the protection of so exalted a power is to the Celt holy or naomh; Early Irish nóem, nóeb, which includes perhaps the idea of what is beautiful, whether the word be cognate with Old Persian naiba, 'beautiful,' or as Bezzenberger less probably suggests, with Lettic naigs, 'quite beautiful.'

It will be sufficient provisionally to describe the chief forms of soul-cult, not forgetting the existence of various modifications and transitions, as:

1. Primitive Animism, which includes most primitive phases. Here account is taken of all phases of the body-soul and of the shadow-soul. The recognition of 'soul' as in the various bodily parts has been treated of

above; the shadow-soul has to be added. The shadow (faileas) is at this stage in intimate association with the soul. As a development of this thought is the danger of allowing one's likeness to be taken: I have known old people who had great aversion to having their likeness taken: it felt to them as if their souls were being abstracted, and any harm done to the likeness might result in harm to the person. On a par are all practices founded on the belief in evil influences from the magic of the living (witchcraft). The sorcerer, in Manx termed by the native designation fear obaidh, has soul-powers ascribed to him whereby he is held to cause illness, madness, death. Rites such as those connected with the 'clay-body' (corp criadh) and with turning of the heart in lead, and spells of all kinds are in vogue; the 'word' is all-powerful; rites such as touching the corpse and placing of water on the hearth after a death (as was done in Tiree, according to my authority, about 60 years ago), and perhaps the belief in the grave-guardian or literally the 'churchyard watch' (an fhaire chlaidh), indicate that religious cult was concerned chiefly with means of protection against the souls of the dead who could 'come back' (tathaich) and as revenants work their evil will. Under this idea, and the cult to be inferred, one might subsume the rites connected with the 'sin-eater' in Wales, springing out of that of eating in common with the deceased; more widely, all forms of communion, the earliest forms of sacrifice.

2. Animalism and Manism, of which Totemism is but a definite grade arising out of sympathetic association. The beliefs centre in the idea of the external soul; these will be treated of in the next chapter. So far as rites arise, at the outset the animal is in the foreground. The animal is on a par, though as a rule above man. Animal descent is inferable from certain personal and tribal names. The favour or displeasure of the animal is kept before the thought, and thus arises the cult of various particular animals, which may figure as protecting spirits. Of the Totemistic system, which is widely traceable among the tribes of Australia, Africa and America, we could hardly expect to find clear survivals among the Aryan family. For the Aryans I am prepared to discard Totemism altogether. Mr. Frazer has lately inclined to deduce that system from a savage theory of conception, which is too abstract. Its essence lies in sympathetic association, which allows of a tribe having regard to some mutual help and protection it may have come to believe as real between itself and some animal. Thus in the Highlands a serpent was thought of as incapable of doing harm to a true member of the clan Iver,—parallel to the immunity from snakes claimed by a snake clan (Ophiogenes) in Cyprus. As animal kinship is the essence of Totemism, and

not its later social organisation, I submit in dealing with the Aryans that Animalism shading into Manism represents a phase of social belief. The feeling of a tribe's kinship with certain animals need not have been arrived at among all races in the same way.

The serpent, the deer, the horse, the wolf, are all in this category; e.g. a Welsh belief seems to have been that all lizards were formerly women; [80] every farmhouse had two snakes: "They never appeared, until just before the death of the master or mistress of the house; then the snake died." Here may be recalled the rite of pounding the embers from a peat fire in one's stocking at the threshold, on the outer door-step, on St. Bride's day, [81]—the operant finally saying, "I shall not injure the serpent nor shall the serpent injure me." The old Lochaber hunter, Domhnull Mac Fhionnlaidh, was buried at his request in the skin of the last deer slain by him. [82] And quite lately, in a Highland Deer Forest, a case came to my notice of a workman who, when engaged on repairing a cottage, sat down to take his meal outside at mid-day when a hind passed by, narrowly scanned him, and having entered the house went up the stair and refused to be ejected, with the result that the man took fright and came out for aid, expressing himself to the effect that it was the spirit of a former occupant, now deceased, that had come back in deer guise.

This was no totemistic death ceremony, but it shows a subtle sympathy with the deer; the stag has always been a symbol of delight and of enjoyment. It is thus far parallel to the Black Shoulder (Buffalo) clan of the Omahas wrapping a dying clansman in a buffalo robe with the hair out, his face painted with the clan mark, and thus addressed by friends: "You are going to the animals (the buffaloes). You are going to rejoin your ancestors."

That instance of belief in transmigration occurred last year. At this stage of thought certain tribes may have one animal which they tacitly own as ancestral spirit. By the use of any animal name as an emblem of kinship, the individual would indicate to what tribal community he belonged; tribal names such as that of the Ossorians in Ireland allow us to infer the former existence of such a belief among the Celts: "The descendants of the wolf are in Ossory." The treatment must be left for the following chapter.

The second phase of this stage of thought would be a cult of human ancestors, specially of tribal chiefs and clan-heroes: this is Manism or

Ancestor Worship proper, culminating in hero worship. It is a subject for future investigation; it is to be noted that the characteristics pertaining to a particular clan or tribal community, which mark ancestor worship, will have fallen very much to the background if they can be at all inferred among the Celts; the relations emphasised will be found pertaining to mythologic concepts and to the Nature-Myth. For, as modifications and transitions in behalf are constant, ancestor worship gets partly transcended. But in Manism the guardian spirit has its specific influence on the tribal consciousness. I recollect Aoibhell of Craig Liath, the guardian spirit of the Dal Caiss, mentioned in the narrative concerning Brian Boru in the Wars of the Gaedhel and the Gall; there is also Mag Molach or Hairy Hand, and Bodach An Dūin of Rothiemurchus, as well as the more familiar belief in the Brownie which renders offices of help in some houses,—a feeble survival of early phases of cult. The central thought is that of Guardian Spirit and comes out in Macrimmon's Lament:

Dh'iath ceō nan stūc mu aodann Chuilinn
Is sheinn a bhean-shīdh' a torman mulaid.

i.e. "The mist has enfolded the peaks of the Coolin and the Banshee has sounded her wail of sorrow." In the Highlands of old the ghosts flitted about if the coronach or funeral threnody were unsung; the other side is, when the banshee calls she sings the spirit home. In some houses still a soft low music is heard at death.

3. Daimonism. Here daimonic influences are recognised wherein there is individual consciousness connecting the thought of guardian spirit with localities. From the rites followed at Loch Mo-Nāir, [83] Strathnaver, one may infer a former belief in a guardian spirit presiding over healing; generally at sacred wells the later Christian saints have succeeded to, and supplanted the memories of, the pre-Christian guardian spirits. There are spirits of localities, and among the Celts of Gaul we find traces of such as daimons protecting and avenging thermal springs, agriculture and commerce. Irish mythology has instances to show, e.g. Dian Cecht, as to whom compare Rhŷs's Hibbert Lectures on Celtic Heathendom. Primitive soul-concepts begin to be lost sight of and the qualities of the demons or daimons correspond to those of individual souls: the result is that Water-, Wind-, Vegetation- or Local Spirits, as met with in the Dindshenchus or stories of Place-Names, all border on the Nature Myth, and personify some aspect of

Nature as such. For example, the Highland stories of Cailleach Bhearra, the Old Woman of Beare, of whom later.

To return now: with the idea of what is tabu or prohibited, or bound under 'restrictions' (fo gheasa), there is connected fear, the fear of breaking the magic word, fear also before the working of demonic powers. In the totem-animals, which a universal survey of comparative human beliefs leads us to subsume as a phase of Manism, primitive man saw the souls of persons, of ancestors migrated. Rites wherein survivals of this exist may be expected to issue in a code which puts the individual on his guard against angering the spirits. My forest friend inferred a 'spirit' in the hind, and felt he was forbidden from repairing the old house for the successor. To another individual's consciousness the spirit might have been in a tree or bird, or even house. It is the sympathetic association of the moment that counts.

One of my acquaintances was suddenly seized by great hunger after passing a certain house: he came up to an old woman, who remarked on his pallid looks: "You have passed a house where people sat and partook of food without having asked a blessing." The individual confessed having passed such and such a house; then his old friend gave him a small piece of bread which she blessed; he partook, and the ravenous craving disappeared.

Or take the case of a boy who goes to an evening's entertainment in Highland hamlets, where he hears lots of ghost stories; he stays until it is late and very dark; if he must come home alone and have to pass lonely roads and places shadowed with trees, or streams where he has heard it said at the céilidh that dogs were seen which tore such and such folks in former times to death, the chances are that he will see more than is good for him: sympathetic association renders this inevitable, and the conditions being favourable most lads will experience a presence that is uncanny, a feeling of the eerie. How much more in earlier ages when every birth revealed a 'return'; if raising of the name (togail an ainm) be still reckoned as of import, as I know it to be, much more is the reality of life itself: the child is seen to resemble not its immediate parents but some grandparents or other relative or ancestor: how account for this? Nature is believed as full of spirits: it is not death that needs accounting for, it is life itself: the mother forms her own inferences wherever she may chance to experience the feeling of quickening, and readily forms a sympathetic association with some object or other at the place and time. A spirit part of some ancestor, she believes, has entered her: a soul has become incarnate.

This would in early ages have been the explanation on the male side of what now exists but in faint survival. I have known an instance, and I have heard of two more, all far apart, where at the birth of a baby the husband was believed to suffer the pains of childbed. In one case the husband was known to turn ill. I believe that such a psychical peculiarity, though very rare, and of great difficulty to verify, is traceable to the idea of a spirit-part (or man-soul) leaving the parent and being thought of as found in the child; the latter's gain was the father's loss. I am absolutely sure of this belief having been known in the Highlands within my own knowledge; it was explained from a power ascribed to certain wise mid-wives of transferring the mother's pains to the father. I rather think it is parallel to a belief concerning the first-born in the Punjab: if a son, his father is said to be born again in him, and he is supposed to die at the child's birth; in certain Khatri sections his funeral rites are actually performed in the fifth month of the mother's pregnancy. Rites now connected with male childbed are known as the couvade. Only dim reflections thereof are met with among the Celts. For parts of Ireland it is on record that a woman before childbirth occasionally wears the coat of the father of the expected child with the idea that the father should then share in the pains of birth. The physician who reports it notes that the father is carefully kept out of the way on these occasions, and that "women in childbirth often wear the trousers of the father of the child round the neck, the effect of which is supposed to be the lightening of the pains of labour. I have myself seen a case of this in Dublin, about two years ago." [84]

In Man a wife must keep her husband's trousers beside her in bed to prevent her infant being carried off by the fairies (Moore, 157). There are only very faint survivals apparently in Britain so far as known. But Dr. Norris F. Davey reports in the British Medical Journal for 26th Sept., 1891, p. 725, thus: ". . . There was a doubt as to the date of conception, but the husband confidently confirmed the date of quickening because 'he felt so bad himself at that time.' He was very much hurt when I ridiculed such an idea, and said, 'You may laugh, doctor, but I always feel bad when that happens without my wife saying anything about it; and why shouldn't I, as I am the father?' This civilised savage (who, I think, came from Wiltshire) was evidently a firm believer in the occult link, but it is not an Essex belief, as I never met with any similar fancy during the thirty-eight years' experience in that county."

Attempts to shift the pains of childbirth from the mother to the father have been instanced by Mr. Frazer[85] from Ireland, Scotland, France, Germany and Esthonia. For resorting to such enchantments Eufame Macalyne was burned alive on the Castle-hill at Edinburgh in 1591. When James VI. was born, a lady of rank, Lady Reirres, complained "that she was never so troubled with no bairn that ever she bare, for the Lady Athole had cast all the pain of her child-birth upon her." At Langholm, in Dumfriesshire, in 1772, Pennant found a belief that "the midwives had power of transferring part of the primeval curse bestowed on our great first mother, from the good wife to her husband. I saw the reputed offspring of such a labour; who kindly came into the world without giving her mother the least uneasiness, while the poor husband was roaring with agony in his uncouth and unnatural pains."

Ling Roth quotes from a 'well-known Professor of Philosophy,' who wrote to Timehri, ii. p. 160: "If ever you make out the couvade, I suspect you will find that its first origin was a real sympathy between husband and wife. I could tell you (if I had space) one or two very odd stories, where, during pregnancy, the husband, at a distance, was invariably affected by sickness—vomiting in one case. Such things are laughed at by the scientific, but if testimony goes for anything (and perhaps it does not), they are well established." The then editor of Timehri, iii. p. 149, speaking of this supposed real physico-sympathetic connection between a man and his wife, extracts the following from the Academy: "In Mr. York-Powell's interesting and able review of Grimm's Teutonic Mythology (Academy, Feb. 23), reference is made to the universal belief among our English and Irish peasantry 'that a man will suffer from such ills as are wont to accompany pregnancy, nausea, neuralgia, and the like, if his wife be lucky enough to escape them.' Just to show that folklore is in many cases but a too free and illogical argument based on facts, I may perhaps be allowed to say that I am to-day acquainted with three persons, one living in Sussex, one in London, and one in Northants, who invariably suffer from neuralgia or vomiting when their wives are enceinte, the ladies themselves having a very happy time of it."

The folk-belief in question is not, however, due to a too hasty generalisation from those coincident ills York-Powell specifies. It is an aberrant form of reasoning, but for the idea which grounds the belief one can adduce parallels: the Central Australian tribes believe that birth is a re-incarnation of a spirit-part—that conception results from the entrance of a spirit-part. [86] The Irish survival of wearing the trousers of the father can surely be only a relic of an earlier rite, wherein the father was credited with having birth-pains, and may be paralleled among non-Aryans from S. India.

In southern India, where Telugu is spoken, the wandering Erukala-vandhu observe the custom. The Rev. John Cain writes in the Indian Antiquary for May, 1874 (p. 151): "Directly the woman feels the birth-pangs she informs her husband, who immediately takes some of her clothes, puts them on, places on his forehead the mark which the women usually place on theirs, retires into a dark room, where there is only a very dim lamp, and lies down on the bed, covering himself with a long cloth. When the child is born, it is washed and placed on the cot beside the father; assafoetida, jaggery, and other articles are then given, not to the mother, but to the father. During the days of ceremonial uncleanness the man is treated as the other Hindus treat their women on such occasions. He is not allowed to leave his bed, but has everything needful brought to him."

Tylor [87] shows that it exists among the Dravidians, though not known as an Aryan Hindoo practice: a man at the birth of his first-born son or daughter by the chief wife, or for any son afterwards, will retire to bed for a lunar month, living principally on a rice diet, abstaining from exciting food and from smoking; at the end of the month he bathes, puts on a fresh dress, and gives his friends a feast. Accompanying the couvade, we find restrictions as to occupation, as to diet (even fasting), up to the time the navel string falls off, or longer. The rite implies religious scruple from the outset; there is more even than sympathetic association with the feebleness of child-life; so far it implies affection and self-sacrifice for the young life, and acknowledges succession through the father, and tends towards conjugal fidelity, though not strictly restricted to monogamy. Far from being a farce as such, it implicates some postulates of civilisation, and from the first it implies a religious theory embodied in rite. When it arises it is never felt as fiction or symbolic pretence: it is as a survival, not merely a sign and record of the change from maternal to paternal society, but a dim foreshadowing of future science, the knowledge of the real actuality of fatherhood. Couvade is a rite or custom that implicates some explanation of the introduction of life into the world. It implies sympathetic magic, as when a father diets himself from instinctive physical sympathy with the new-born infant; or by simulating child-birth it relieves the real mother by magical transference of pain. [88]

A digression may be allowed here. If there be a rite to implicate some theory of the introduction of life, such as that when you are born you are a spirit-part of some ancestor, would not a rite be necessitated to show that death, or the extinction of life, is due to the spirit or spirit-part of an ancestor having assumed another form? Is an ancestor thought of as being in the last dead, and is the last dead thought of as being called to defend his people at the place of burial until the next death? Is not what was ancestral spirit-part at birth not likely to be an ancestral spirit-part at death; and is not the last buried the guardian spirit, perhaps awaiting re-incorporation? Would not the conception of An Fhaire Chlaidh, the belief that the soul of the last buried keeps watch until the next funeral comes to the churchyard and is grave-guardian, fall in with such a view? Instances from the Highlands will be given in the fourth chapter (cf. p. 35 as to 'sitting with the dead').

The belief that even the bones of the dead could be a source of paternity is traceable in the Highlands. Sir Walter Scott, in his notes [89] to Canto III. of the Lady of the Lake, states that it was the account in the Laird of Macfarlane's Manuscript that suggested to him the idea of Brian the Hermit, 'bred between the living and the dead'; and the late Rev. A. Clerk, LL.D., minister of Kilmallie, who speaks of the tale as "the above probable story (!) of his (i.e. the child's) paternity," states that "this account of him is still preserved in the traditions of the place," that "the tradition still preserved in the country agrees exactly with the account given by the old Laird, representing the Gille Dubh (Black Lad) as an able and devout man, totally different from the savage seer depicted in the poem." [90] Dr. Clerk writes the name as Gille Dubh mac 'Ille Chnàmhlaich, or the Black Child, Son of the Bones, "for such, unpronounceable as it appears, is the true designation; and though the story may be familiar to many, we give the substance of it here as connected with the locality." I rather think cnàmhlach conveys the sense of mouldering embers of fire, as in the phrase cnàmhlach theine, but in either case the paternity is attributed to the dead. To this child in later life was attributed the building of the first church at Kilmallie, which simply means that the spot was sacred ere the introduction of Christianity. There are large beech trees near now; in 1746 the ash tree burnt down at Kilmallie was the largest and most remarkable in Scotland, being no less than 58 feet in circumference. This gives additional presumption of ancient sanctity.

Dr. Clerk tells how the young people of Corpach and of Annat (i.e. mother-church)—two neighbouring farms—were watching the cattle in the fold. "The place was a small hill a little to the west of the present church, close to the public road, and conspicuous from a clump of Scotch fir covering its summit. It shews some faint traces of its having been fortified as a stronghold, and its name, Cnocna-Faobh, or the Hill of Spoils, tells of its having been the scene of strife and of bloodshed. At the period in question it was strewn with the bones of the slain, left there to bleach under summer's sun and winter's snow, which proves that the conflict was between parties animated by the deadliest hate toward each other; for rarely indeed was such dishonour shewn to the dead in the Highlands." From this point I crave leave to quote the Laird of Macfarlane's [91] words: "The people report of a battell focht in old tymes, hard by thar Church, and how long after, hirds feeding ther cattell in that place, in a cold season, made a fyre of dead men's bones ther scattered, who being all removed except one mayd who took up her cloaths and uncovered hirself sum part here, a sudden whirlwind threw sum of the ashes in her privie member. Whereupon she conceaved and bore a sone called Gillie dowmak Chravo-lick, that is to say the black chyld sone to the bones, who after becam learned and relligious and built this Churche which now standeth in Kilmaillie."

The figure of Brian, whose story illustrates Parthenogenesis or Virgin Birth, goes back on Celtic tradition, wherein he figures as a demi-god. He is a being to whom entreaty is made; he is referred to by a Badenoch poet, Lachlan Macpherson of Strathmashie, who was born about 1723. In a poem humorously descriptive of a certain old gentleman's wedding, he says:

When all had assembled,
They of Brian entreated
That all might survive till their locks
Were grey as the bridegroom's.

The original of which is:

Nuair a thainig iad a nīos
Rinn iad achanaich ri Brīan

Iad a bhi uile cho lìath
Ri cìabhag fhir na bainnse.
   (Mackenzie's Sar-Obair Nam Bard, p. 263.)

Another song of about the reign of James VI., and composed by his stepmother to Domhull Gorm Macdonald, speaks of Brian in terms which put him alongside of Cuchulainn, Ossian, Oscar; and in a context, where the strength of sea and sun are invoked, so much so that Miss Tolmie notes Brian as signifying 'Divine Power.' [92]

A Highland sleep-blessing is to the following effect:

I lie down to-night with mild Mary and her son,
With Michael the bright-white, and with Bride beneath her mantle.
I lie down with God, and may God lie down with me;
I shall not lie down with Briain, and Briain shall not lie down with me. [93]

Though similar sleep-blessings are current in Ireland, Dr. Douglas Hyde [94] remarks that he has never elsewhere heard or seen 'this very curious expression,' —Briain, which now-a-days connotes something similar to Satan. Though apparently forgotten in Ireland, it is not yet extinct in the Isles. It there bears the force of "angel, archangel, god, divinity, hence god of evil; a term of exclamation. A bhriain = thou god; a bhriain Mhìcheil = thou god Michael." [95] The name Brian is met with in a poem where St. Michael, as the Gaelic Neptune and patron of the sea, is spoken of as Brian Michael; in other words, St. Michael, venerated among the Celts, has taken the place of the deity Brian.

Thou wert the warrior of courage
Going on the journey of prophecy;
Thou wouldst not travel on a cripple,
Thou didst take the steed of Brian Michael,
He was without bit in his mouth,
Thou didst ride him on the wing,
Thou didst leap over the knowledge of Nature. [96]

Brian seems to have been in part a sea-god, whose place was latterly taken by St. Michael, Michael of the white steeds, who subdued the dragon. But perhaps he was not always thought of in this aspect any more than the

Hellenic Zeus, who is a stream-god (Νάϊος) at Dodona and a water-god with the epithet θαλάσσιος at Sidon, instead of his usual place as a sky-god.

The whole figure of Brian—the Michael of pre-Christian times—is rooted in Old Celtic thought;[97] he with his two brothers Iuchar and Uar belong to the Tuatha De Danaan as gods of knowledge, of art and of poetry. Brian, Iuchar (or, in its longer form, Iucharba) and Uar are three aspects of the same deity,—a feature that is common in many countries where a deity is typified as a triad arising from psychic conditions of thought. Together, according to the Dialogue of the Two Sages, they beget an only son, whose name Ecne means knowledge, letters, poetry. Dana, elsewhere called Brigit, is the mother of these three gods or aspects of god-life, and she was wife of Bress, king of the Fornorians, but by birth she belonged to the divine race, her father being the Dagda. The Book of the Invasions speaks of Donand as their mother: "Donand, daughter of the same Delbaeth, that is to say, the mother of the three last, to wit: Brian, Iucharba and Iuchair." These were the three gods of danu, of fate, or, if we render it otherwise, of literature and art. Just as the cult of the goddess Brigit, a name in root cognate with the Continental name Burgundy, was in large measure transferred to the Christian St. Brigit, on whose altar at Kildare there burned perpetual fire, so the cult of Brian, the god, was transferred to St. Michael; just as Brigit was both goddess and female file, 'poet or seer,' so Brian and his brothers Iuchar and Uar are gods of knowledge, art and poetry. Brian, accordingly, is a seer. Brian is a son of Tuireann by Brigit; both mother and son are eminent in knowledge: Brian and his brothers have one son in common, viz. Ecna, i.e. knowledge. The same mythic idea is attempted to be expressed by three synonyms. The older form seems to have been Brión, as in the Wooing of Emer (Tochmarc Émire), a form made into Brian in the Fate of the Children of Tuirenn.[98] The root idea may be seen in brī, dignity, esteem, worth, ideas expressing a sense of what is exalted, hence 'born from on high.' At times he figures as Fortune, if not as Providence. Ossian in a lullaby to his mother is made to say:

If thou art my mother, and thou a deer
Arise ere sun arise on thee;

May Fortune (Providence) preserve thee from hoarseness-of-breathing [99]
Ere thy voice thy sweetheart hear. [100]

Mr. Campbell's variant is rendered by him thus:

"If Brian would take from me his murmuring, before my sweetheart will hear my voice." But the force of the first clause is: "O that Brian would check the srannan (hoarse breathing) of me," i.e. "may B. restrain from me the murmuring," being a wish that Brian, the fairy god, would keep her from making any noise by which her presence would become known to Fionn. Ossian's advice to his mother, in her animal-form of deer, that she should get up before sunrise, implies that otherwise she was liable to be shot by hunters; to be up ere sunrise was a sort of taboo comparable to some of the restrictions of the Early Irish kings in the Book of Rights.

Srannan a' bhāis, 'the rattle of death,' is not so strong a phrase as an cloicheir, the expression for the death-rattle. Since Brian figures as Fortune, we need not be surprised at meeting him as the author of good counsel. Gillies's Collection of Gadhelic Poetry (Perth, 1786) gives The Wise Man's Advice to his Son, maxims largely proverbial in the Highlands and partly current in Ireland, as we see from the lines given at the end of Nicolson's edition of the Proverbs, as well as from Bourke's Irish Grammar. The lines have wisdom, good humour and pithiness in the original, and I may give a literal rendering of some, which are in keeping with his character as a god of wisdom:

Counsel Brian did give to me
Self-minded not to be;
Nor go into fray nor fight
Unless, I thought, I would come back in life.
Another counsel he gave
Which, methinks, was none behind:
  Though mine were the world's wealth
  Not to set it against mine honour.
Of frequenting the Temple be mindful,
Fix not thy purpose on evil:
Let not this world's pelf
Cause thee to perjure thy soul.
If of a weakling thou hast a foolish report
Put not thine [101] thereto;
Be not surety in a lie—
Let that tale pass bye.
Affable and kind be to thy friend,
With a stranger shun a quarrel;

Say not thou wilt refuse the right
Nor seek nor refuse honour.
In thy palms squeeze not the thorn,
To thy foe thy distress make not known.
A beast of venom never willingly waken,
—A knife's edge in thy flesh.
Be not over fiery nor fierce,
Without a staff frequent not the stream;
Let aught not escape thy lips
That will earn thee reproach.
The fierceness of fellow despise not;
Of boiling fluid sip not a drop,
A clean sharp-edgèd razor-blade
When thou see'st, tread softly by.
Haughty-minded be not; nor self disparage,
Spend not on trifles thy goods.
For folly's sake stir not strife
Nor refuse to fight when it needs be.
Of a trifling flaw be not over-watchful;
Oppress not the poor;
Nor praise nor dispraise the worthless
Until the faultless sage is found.
Dear one, for thy youth sufficeth,
Threap not in a matter disputed;
Thy character to coarse jest expose not
Nor groundless prefer thy complaint.

The latter-day reports indicate clearly that Brian's birth is one of parthenogenesis: possibly an earlier age may not have distinguished this from the action of the Dusii, the incubi which were thought of as consorting with mortals. [102] A parallel belief is met with among the Bretons. My reference is in Keightley (p. 441), who quotes W. Grimm: "In the ruins of Tresmalonen dwell the Courils. They are of a malignant disposition, but great lovers of dancing. At night they sport among the druidical monuments. The unfortunate shepherd that approaches them must dance their rounds with them till cock-crow; and the instances are not few of persons thus ensnared who have been found next morning dead with exhaustion and fatigue. Woe also to the ill-fated maiden who draws near the Couril dance! nine months after the family counts one more. Yet so great is the power and cunning of the Dwarfs that the young stranger bears no resemblance to them, but they impart to it the features of some lad of the village."

But the Kilmaillie story is the more primitive one, as it points to belief in the Virgin Birth. We recall Hera who conceived Hephaistos simply by inhaling the wind; the maiden Wenonah of Longfellow's poem who was quickened by the west wind and bore Michabo (i.e. Hiawatha); the virgin Ilmatar fructified by the east wind gave birth to the Finnish Väinämöinen. Mohammedan tradition spoke of a preadamite race of women who conceived daughters by the wind; the Arunta tribes of Australia hold that a storm from the west brings child-germs. These are only partial parallels, for in the Highland story it is the wind, but the wind reinforced by the bones of the dead. In short, there is ancestral virtue in Brian's birth quite as much as was associated with the birth of Servius Tullius at Rome, where the father was deemed to have been the household Lar. From Irish literature instances of supernatural birth have been given in Meyer and Nutt's Voyage of Bran the Son of Febail, and I must not further enter on the theme here. Even a star is sometimes conceived as fructifying: St. Aidan or Maedoc was born of a star which fell into his mother's mouth as she slept. [103] Commonly at this stage of thought fructification is regarded as due to the swallowing of a worm: the births of Conchobar and of Cuchulainn were accounted for by their mothers having swallowed worms in the draught. Most closely associated is the idea of the Birth-Token. In the Breton story of the King of the Fishes we meet with a poor and childless fisherman who spares the life of a fish with scales of gold, which his wife desires to eat. When re-caught, the fish asks that its head be given her, and the scales buried in the garden: the fish promises that to the wife would be born three children with beautiful stars on their foreheads, while from the scales would grow three rose-trees, one of which was to belong to each of the boys and be his life-token, and when the boy was in danger of death his tree should wither. Variants assign parts of the fish to the fisherman's mare and bitch, which bring forth young to the number of the children. [104] In the Highlands we meet with the same story: here the fish tells the fisher: "Thou shalt let no man split me, but do it thyself. Thou shalt put into the pot but a morsel of my liver and a bit of my heart to boil for thyself, and for thy wife, and for thy mare, and for thy dog to eat. Three bones thou wilt find at the side of my head. Go out and bury them in the garden. Thy wife will bear three sons. Thy mare will cast three foals. Thy dog will litter three whelps. When they are born dig up my bones and keep them. Three trees will sprout where the bones are buried, and they will be in leaf and budding, in sap and growing, summer and winter, spring and autumn, every day for ever, so long as the clan shall live. They will droop or wither or die as they do." [105]

With these life-tokens thought has already made the transition to the idea of the external soul.

THE WANDERINGS OF PSYCHE

IT is a primitive idea that the soul can leave the body. As separable soul [106] it may take manifold forms. A Breton tale tells of a giant's life as being in an egg, in a dove, in a hare, in a wolf, which lives in a coffer at the bottom of the sea. On Gadhelic ground we meet with it in the young king of Easaidh Ruadh, where the giant's soul is spoken of as, first, in the Bonnach stone, then in the threshold. "There is a flagstone under the threshold. There is a wether under the flag. There is a duck in the wether's belly, and an egg in the belly of the duck, and it is in the egg that my soul is." The king in his pursuit of his lady-love, taken captive by the giant, had the assistance of a dog, a falcon, and an otter. The dog pulled out the wether; the falcon caught the duck as it flew away; and the otter recovered the egg from the ocean into which it had rolled. Thereafter he had but to crush the egg and end the giant's life. Parallel to this is the case of the sea-beast who captures the king's daughter in Campbell's tale of 'The Sea-Maiden': the soul of the beast is in an egg, in a trout, in a hoodie, in a hind, which lives in an island in a loch.

Next, the external-soul may be regarded as present in an object intimately associated with a man, as, for instance, the ancestral sword.

The Highland oath upon the dirk is referred to in the legends of Strathisla, [107] the Strathylefe [108] of the charter of King William of Scotland. The 'Sick-Bed of Cuchulainn,' an ancient Gadhelic tale, says expressly that, of old, demons were wont to speak to men from out of their weapons: the consequence was that, if men swore false oaths, their swords became turned, or turned themselves against them. [109] The Gadhelic asseveration [110]—by thy father's hand and by thy grandfather's hand and by thine own two hands supporting them—has reference ultimately to the sword. The custom is parallel to that in Aeschylus, who makes a hero swear by his sword. [111] One recalls the familiar spirit which Paracelsus kept imprisoned in the pummel of his sword as in the portrait of Lumley Castle, and of which Butler in Hudibras speaks:

Bombastus kept a devil's bird

Shut in the plummel of his sword,
That taught him all the cunning pranks
Of past and future mountebanks.

In the modern Scottish oath with uplifted hand both judge and witness appeal to the Deity, as did the Greeks when they lifted up their hand at sacrifice, as did Aaron when he lifted up his hand towards the people. But the Gadhelic tradition leads back to an earlier world, and recurs likewise in the word for oath, [112] which was originally taken in presence of the relics. Keating (vol. iii. 53) tells of one whose head fell off at the fair of Taillte for having sworn falsely by the hand of Ciaran. And Spenser for his time says: "The Irish use now to sweare by their lord's hand, and to forsweare it they hold it more criminal than to sweare by God." [113]

The external-soul may meet us as a little spectre (fuatharlan) or moth. This I have heard spoken of as a soul-form. And for the more general belief let me adduce what Pennant states:

"The belief in spectres still exists; of which I had a remarkable proof while I was in the county of Breadalbane. A poor visionary, who had been working in his cabbage garden, imagined that he was raised suddenly into the air, and conveyed over a wall into an adjacent corn-field: that he found himself surrounded by a crowd of men and women, many of whom he knew to have been dead some years, and who appeared to him skimming over the tops of the unbended corn, and mingling together like bees going to hive: that they spoke an unknown language and with a hollow sound: that they very roughly pushed him to and fro; but on his uttering the name of God, all vanished but a female sprite, who, seizing him by the shoulder, obliged him to premise an assignation, at that very hour, that day sevennight: that he then found that his hair was all tied in double knots, and that he had almost lost the use of his speech: that he kept his word with the spectre, whom he soon saw come floating through the air towards him: that he spoke to her, but she told him at that time she was in too much haste to attend to him, but bid him go away, and no harm should befall him; and so the affair rested when I left the country." [114]

An authentic instance given by a friend is that of M. A., a solicitor in Edinburgh, about seventy years ago; he saw a moth flitting round the table suddenly wing its flight to a neighbouring room. Where is it gone? he called, and added that it was a soul-spirit haunting the place, and a sign of death.

This, is but another case of the soul taking a form somewhat analogous to that of the butterfly-soul. In Wales aged people used to say that white moths were the souls of the dead who in this form were allowed to take farewell of the earth. When any kind of moth fluttered around a candle, people said somebody was dying, and the soul was passing (Trevelyan, 307).

The soul is at times thought to assume the form of a butterfly, dearbadan Dé, tarmachan Dé being the Highland names; they are in part god-names. The Irish féiliocán the Manx follican, 'butterfly,' do not show the god-soul in the name, but there is an Irish legend as to a priest who came to disbelieve that men had souls. "Who ever saw a soul?" he would say. "If you can show me one I will believe." All the king's sons were on his side, but at last a mysterious child comes on the scene and shows him that if we have life though we cannot see it, we may also have a soul though it is invisible. He had met at last one who believed, and having told the child his story he bade him watch, "for a living thing will soar up from my body as I die, and you will then know that my soul has ascended into the presence of God." This was to be a sign that his previous teaching was a lie. His death is then described, and when his agony seemed to cease, the child, who was watching, "saw a beautiful living creature, with four snow-white wings, mount from the dead man's body into the air, and go fluttering round his head. So he ran to bring the scholars; and when they all knew it was the soul of their master, they watched with wonder and awe. until it passed from sight into the clouds. And this was the first butterfly that was ever seen in Ireland; and now all men know that the butterflies are the souls of the dead waiting for the moment when they may enter Purgatory, and so pass through torture to purification and peace." But the schools of Ireland were quite deserted after that time, for people said, what is the use of going so far to learn when the wisest man in all Ireland did not know if he had a soul till he was near losing it; and was only saved at last through the simple belief of a little child? [115]

In Brittany souls are frequently thought of as in butterfly form; but there the soul, on leaving the body, is often held to take the form of a fly, sometimes that of a raven. [116] There is here, and in what is said of the moth, much that reminds of what Ralston (Songs of the Russian People,

118) tells of the Slays: "The butterfly seems to have been universally accepted by the Slavonians as an emblem of the soul. In the Government of Yaroslav one of its names is dushichka, a caressing diminutive of dusha, the soul. In that of Kherson it is believed that if the usual alms are not distributed at a funeral, the dead man's soul will reveal itself to his relatives in the form of a moth flying about the flame of a candle. The day after receiving such a warning visit, they call together the poor and distribute food among them. In Bohemia tradition says that if the first butterfly a man sees in the spring is a white one, he is destined to die within the year. The Servians believe that the soul of a witch often leaves her body while she is asleep and flies abroad in the shape of a butterfly. If during its absence her body be turned round, so that her feet are placed where her head was before, the soul-butterfly will not be able to find her mouth, and so she will be shut out, from her body. Thereupon the witch will die."

With this one might compare the belief in the Cotswolds in the Death's Head Moth as an harbinger of death, while in the Midlands the bat is regarded with awe,—both possibly old British.

The idea of the soul as in bee-form is familiar; for this reason the habit prevailed in some places of veiling the hive in crape, as if to notify them of a death in the household. I remember the case of I. B., who, when his brother died, put the bees into mourning.[117] The late Rev. Dr. Forsyth, minister of Abernethy, recorded the following tradition in his earlier days when minister at Dornoch,—a legend which illustrates also the ideas of the soul-bridge and of the tree as taken to witness: "Once upon a time there were two men travelling together on foot along Speyside. The elder one of the two grew weary, and they sat down to rest under a tree, having drunk of a little stream that ran below them. The wearied man soon fell asleep, and his companion sat watching the larks singing above the furze-bushes and the dimpling and purling of the burn. He heard his fellow-traveller groaning and muttering in a restless sleep, and he soon after saw creep out of his mouth an insect like a bee, only wanting its wings. This bee crawled along the man's clothes and down on the sod till it came to the brook, which it could neither fly over nor swim. It aye turned back and back, and aye tried it again, till the waking man, letting it creep on his sword, helped it across. It then went on two hundred yards or more and disappeared in a small cairn. Presently the sleeper came to himself and told his friend that he had a strange dream: a 'wee wee crayterie no bigger nor a bee' had told him of a hidden treasure, and had promised to show it to him. It had seemed to him as if the creature came out of his mouth, had crossed the burn by his comrade's help, and had gone out of sight in a cairn. The watcher (who had had time to follow the bee to the cairn just hid by a rising ground, and not more than two hundred yards off) laughed at the story, but the elder man said that it must be true, and declared his mind to seek the cairn and its contents. High words followed, and the younger, drawing his sword, slew the man who had dreamt the dream of gold. The victim with his last breath upbraided the other with treachery, and took the tree, under which he had slept and now lay, to witness that he had been foully murdered. The murderer dug out the cairn and found the treasure, gold and silver and silver arm-pieces, and became a gay rich man, but 'aye where he went men saw a tree abuve him and behind him, aye walking where he walked, and staying where he stayed. An' for all his gear he neuer got a friend to bide wi' him, nor a lass to mary him. At last he was ouer weary of it all, and went to the priest and telled him the way of it, and made a restitution to the dead man's folk, and that was good to him whatever; but he didna live lang syne.'" [118]

Hugh Miller, in My Schools and Schoolmasters (ch. vi.), records a story told him by his cousin at Gruids, Sutherland. He communicated to me, says Miller, a tradition illustrative of the Celtic theory of dreaming, of which I have since often thought. "Two young men had been spending the early portion of a warm summer day in exactly such a scene as that in which he communicated the anecdote. There was an ancient ruin beside them, separated, however, from the mossy bank on which they sat, by a slender runnel, across which there lay, immediately over a miniature cascade, a few withered grass stalks. Overcome by the heat of the day, one of the young men fell asleep; his companion watched drowsily beside him; when all at once the watcher was aroused to attention by seeing a little indistinct form, scarce larger than a humble-bee, issue from the mouth of the sleeping man, and, leaping upon the moss, move downwards to the runnel, which it crossed along the withered grass stalks, and then disappeared amid the interstices of the ruin. Alarmed by what he saw, the watcher hastily shook his companion by the shoulder, and awoke him; though, with all his haste, the little cloud-like creature, still more rapid in its movements, issued from the interstice into which it had gone, and, flying across the runnel, instead of creeping along the grass stalks and over the sward, as before, it re-entered the mouth of the sleeper, just as he was in the act of awakening. 'What is the matter with you?' said the watcher, greatly alarmed,—'What ails you?' 'Nothing ails me,' replied the other; 'but you have robbed me of a most delightful dream. I dreamed I was walking through a fine rich country, and came at length to the shores of a noble river; and, just where the clear water went thundering down a precipice, there was a bridge all of silver, which I crossed; and then, entering a noble palace, on the opposite side, I saw great heaps of gold and jewels, and I was just going to load myself with treasure, when you rudely awoke me, and I lost all.' I know not what the asserters of the clairvoyant faculty may think of the story; but I rather believe I have occasionally seen them make use of anecdotes that did not rest on evidence a great deal more solid than the Highland legend, and that illustrated not much more clearly the philosophy of the phenomena with which they profess to deal."

This is exactly the story in King Gunthram's Dream; it portrays an aspect of the external soul:

These Highland stories have a strange similarity to that in the Latin of Paul the Deacon (720-790 A.D.). "It befell one day that Gunthram, King of the Franks, went hunting in a forest, and, as often happens, his companions were scattered, and he himself left alone with one loyal attendant. He was overcome with sleep, and slept with his head resting on his retainer's knees. As the king slept, the other in whose lap he lay, saw a small creature like a lizard come out of his mouth and look for some way to cross a slender stream of water that was running near. He drew his sword from the sheath and laid it across the water, and the little reptile went over it to the other side, and disappeared in a hole in the hill. It returned not long after, and came back over the sword and into the king's mouth. When Gunthram awoke he described a wonderful vision. It seemed in his dream that he had crossed a river on an iron bridge and entered a mountain where he found a great treasure of gold. Then the squire told him what he had seen while the king was asleep.

Search was made in the place, and great heaps of ancient gold discovered there. Of this the king had a paten made of great size and weight adorned with precious stones which he intended to have sent to the Holy Sepulchre in Jerusalem, but he was prevented, and placed it on the shrine of St. Marcellus at Chalons, the capital of his kingdom, where it is to this day."

Ere passing from this, I may add another curious story from the same source as illustrating a parallel belief as well as transformation. Cunincpert, King of the Lombards, was standing at the window of the palace in Pavia, consulting with his marshal (marhyaiz, i.e. the groom who bits and bridles the horse) how to remove his enemies Aldo and Grauso. A large fly settled on the window sill before him; the king made a blow at it with his dagger, but only cut off a leg. Meantime, Aldo and Grauso were coming to the palace, ignorant of the king's designs against them. When they were at the church of St. Romanus near the palace, there met them a one-legged man, who said to them that if they went to Cunincpert he would kill them. They were filled with terror at this, and took refuge behind the altar in the church: this was told to the king. Then C. blamed his marshal for publishing his intention. But the marshal answered: "My lord king, thou knowest that since this was spoken of in counsel I have not departed from thy presence; and how could I tell it to any one?" Then the king sent to Aldo and Grauso asking why they had fled to sanctuary. They answered: "Because it was declared to us that our Lord the king would have put us to death." Again the king sent to ask them who had given them these tidings, affirming that unless they told they should never have grace. Then they sent to the king to say that a lame man had met them, wanting a foot, and with a wooden leg, who had warned them of destruction. Then the king saw that the fly whose foot he had cut off was an evil spirit, and had discovered his secret. He brought away Aldo and Grauso from their refuge, and forgave them, and took them into his favour.

The nearest parallel is in a Breton story where the soul is seen as an insect. Pezr Nicol was a man, and he died. His friend, Yvon Peuker, saw a fly come out of the dying man's mouth, a shadowy fly,—with gauzy wings, something like the ephemeral insects that hover over streams at eventide. It dipped its feet in a basin of milk, flew round the room and vanished. When it re-appeared it settled on the corpse, and there remained, allowing itself to be shut in the coffin with the dead man. Peuker saw it again when they reached the churchyard, and understood then that it must be the soul of Pezr Nicol. The insect soon flew to a marsh not far from the farm on which Pezr Nicol dwelt during his life. Then it perched upon a thorn-bush.

"Poor little fly! what do you do here?" asked the good Peuker.

"You can see me, then?"

"I see you certainly since I am speaking to you. Tell me, are you not the soul of the departed Pezr Nicol, who was my best friend on earth?"

"Yes. This is the place where God wills me to be for my expiation, and I have to remain here five hundred years. God must regard you with great favour, having permitted you to recognise my soul under this form."

The soul then explains the dipping of the feet in milk as an act of cleansing ere appearing before the Judge, and explains his flitting about as a bidding farewell to the farm-implements and animals, and his being shut in the coffin as an obligation to remain with the body until God gave sentence. [119]

The belief in the bird-soul was well known in the Highlands. To illustrate: A farmer was coming home from Inverness to Buntait when at a weird part of the way his mare got uncontrollable and ran up with him to where was a waterfall (eas). Whereupon he swooned and fell off. On recovering he found his way home and was amazed at finding his mare tied in the stable, not knowing how it happened, for nobody confessed to having tied her. Soon after he hurt himself in moving a heavy box of oats at the farm of Shewglie; a plough or two broke thereafter at the spring-work, always a bad omen. Getting more unwell, he said to his wife the night before his death: "What a beautiful bird I heard singing by my bedside to-night." "I well believe it," she replied. To which he answered: "It was my ghost; I cannot live long." He it was who composed the song containing the verse:

Chan è do ghug ūg tha air m'aire
ach m'uireasbhuidh mór tha mi 'gearain
'S mu'n tig thu-sa rithist, a bhròineag
bidh mise an ciste-bhòrd nan tarrung.

i.e. ''Tis not thy "guck-ook" (or sad cry) that I heed; 'tis my deep need that is my plaint; ere thou comest again, O sad one! I shall be a-nailed in the coffin.'

In St. Kilda the cuckoo is a bird of ill omen (cf. Glasgow Herald, June 10, 1910). A common bye-name for it over the Highlands is bradag, 'rascal,' from its neglect of its young: to express contempt or ill-luck there is the phrase: 'chac a chuthag air' = 'the cuckoo "dropped" on him.' It is a bird of augury: 'chuala mi chuthag gun bhiadh am bhroinn . . . s dh'aithnich mi féin nach rachadh a bhliadhna leam' = 'I heard the cuckoo while fasting (ere I took breakfast i.e.) . . . and I knew that the year would not go well with me.' It is unlucky in the Highlands to hear the first cuckoo of the season ere one has broken one's fast. In Mid-Wales there seems to be a trace of a belief that the cuckoo was once a beautiful lady who wept over her brother's death until she was changed into a bird (Trevelyan, 109). With this last falls to be compared the Slavic belief that the cuckoo is a transformed girl who mourned too much for her lost lover.

It is curious that in Anglo-Saxon lyrics of the eighth century the cuckoo is a bird of sorrow, filling the heart with care—which may be due to Celtic influence, as it is an idea alien to Germanic literature, though I cannot prove this by citing old references as yet. The Breton fishers near St. Malo not so long ago spoke of it as 'parent,' and thought of it as a good augury for fishing: at St. Jacut the first boat that hears the cuckoo casts out a rayfish as offering: the sailors of St. Cast, if they hear it sing when embarking, light a pipe in its honour. In Friesland, Lithuania, and south-east of the Urals there are dances in honour of the cuckoo, which have been regarded as remnants of a totem-dance in Europe.[120] The Highland song by Dr. Maclachlan of Rahoy speaks of the cuckoo as dispelling sorrow—'s to thogadh bròn om chridhe, i.e. "tis thou wouldst raise grief from mine heart'—but this is quite modern, and the whole song reproduces loosely the feeling of a poem in English which speaks of the bird thus:

Thou hast no sorrow in thy song
Nor winter in thy year!

In some of the Celtic areas of old the feeling would have been the reverse.

I take the following from Miss Dempster of Skibo's collection in a document among the Campbell of Islay Manuscripts in the Advocates' Library: "Some days before the death of Dr. Bethune, sometime minister of the parish of Dornoch (1816), a large cormorant was observed sitting on the steeple of the parish church—the whole town took this as a sign that the incumbent was not long for this world. One of the same birds was seen flying and lighting on parts of the building in 185? the vulgar predicted from this a similar result, and the event justified the saying, for the then clergyman sickened and died after a short illness.

A common proverb associates the magpie with death, but if two come to a house it portends a wedding.[121] The raven is equally a bird of omen, raven-knowledge[122] or wisdom being proverbial; I find it referred to in a poem in the 'Massacre of the Rosses,' and quite recently in a poem in memory of Louisa MacDougall of MacDougall by the clan bard to whom the raven is symbolic of the prowess and valour of the descendants of Conn and Somerled:

Cumha Cholla is Chuinn
'S cumha Shomhairle mhòir chruinn
Bu tric fitheach air luing 's air bord.

The Isle of Man has similar beliefs. As to the magpie they say:

One for sorrow, two for death,
Three for a wedding and four for a birth.

Ravens, too, are uncanny, because they were originally Odin's messengers, suggests Mr. Moore, but perhaps the parallel Norse belief is only a coincidence.

In Wales the eagle was of old a bird of divination. "The descendants of a person who had eaten eagles' flesh to the ninth generation possessed the gift of second sight." The eagles of Snowdon were regarded as oracles; chained eagles were supposed to guard the resting-place of King Arthur. When high winds prevailed the saying was, "the eagles are breeding whirlwinds on Snowdon" (Trevelyan, 81-82). One recalls the Roman service of the consecratio (Herodian, iv. 2), where the eagle that rose from the pyre symbolised the soul of the Emperor, the eagle-god. The eagle of the legions was a fetich to the common soldier, who anointed it and prepared a sacellum for it in the camp (Pliny, Hist. Nat. xiii. 23). The fire-stealer Prometheus is an eagle-god; from a divine eagle some royal families of old fabled their descent (v. Reinach, Cultes, Mythes et Religions, iii. p. 78). The witches (doiteagan) of Mull in legend are said to assume raven form, and in this guise raise a tempest and croak maledictions on the Lochlin princess associated in Mull story with the disaster [123] to a vessel from Spain.

The soul in swan form is best evidenced by the Fate of the Children of Lir, a tragic story of great pathos wherein human beings are transformed into swans at the bidding of a cruel stepmother. It is easily accessible in Joyce's Old Gaelic Romances. The metamorphoses of the three daughters of Lir, the sea-god, is but a return to their primitive estate. In its basic idea one may compare Zeus and his wooing of Leda, a legend which goes back to an early age when some Greek tribe had for goddess a swan which they thought of as of near kin to mortals. With the rise of thought such gods in animal form give place to gods in human form.

In St. Kilda (Gaelic, 'Hirt, Hiort') this phase of belief appears as 'the ghost-bird.' The last British specimen of the Great Auk was captured there on Stac-an-Armuinn between 1830 and 1835. "It was described as being about the size of a year-old lamb, with a head like a razor-bill, and short wings, so that it could not fly. The men caught the bird, tied a rope to its leg, and kept it for two or three days. The extraordinary appearance of the bird impressed the men so much that they thought it was a ghost, and looked upon it as the cause of the bad weather they were experiencing. They, therefore, killed the poor bird, and threw it at the back of the house, covering it with stones. It has ever since gone by the name of the 'ghost-bird.'" [124]

The sapient islanders of the Hebrides would thus seem to have been at the same level of belief with those Greeks who believed that the soul left the body in the form of a bird. [125]

Here, I think, one should place Cuchulainn's bird-of-valour, which symbolises not merely the hero's fury, but the transmission of the ancestral god-soul, symbolised among other peoples by the eagle-tipped sceptre, handed down from king to king, as well as by the eagle portrayed on standards, which goes back on the belief that the soul of a monarch once upon a time appeared as an eagle, and in this form watched over the fortunes of empire. The standard transmits the virtue of the ancestral hero; the soul of the slain king is magically transmitted to his successor. It springs from Manism, or the worship of manes or spirits, comprehensive of all forms of totemism to which there are early references in Gadhelic saga. Thus the mother of Conaire Mōr learns that her son must not kill birds. Once he saw great white-speckled birds of unusual size and beauty coming towards him. He pursues them until his horses were tired. The birds would go a spear-cast before him, and would not go any further. He pursued them out to sea and overcame them. The birds quit their bird-skins and turn upon him with spears and swords. One of them protects him and says: "I am Némglan, king of thy father's birds, and thou hast been forbidden to cast at birds, for here there is no one that should not be dear to thee because of his father and mother." [126] The violation of this Tabu led to Conaire's death. In the Cuchulainn saga there is the case of Dechtere and her attendant troop of bird-maidens.

In the traditions of the Cymry birds appear as instruments of divination to diagnose royal blood. The bird-soul is here the ancestral-soul. According to Giraldus Cambrensis it happened that in the time of Henry I. Gruffydd ap Rhys ap Tudor, who, although he only held of the king one commote, namely, a fourth part of the cantref of Caio, yet was reputed as lord in Deheubarth, was returning from court by way of Llangorse Lake, in Brecknockshire, with Milo, Earl of Hereford, and Lord of Brecknock, and Payn Fitz John, who then held Ewyas, two of the king's secretaries and privy councillors. It was winter, and the lake was covered with water-fowl of various kinds. Seeing them, Milo, partly in joke, said to Gruffydd: "It is an old saying in Wales that if the natural prince of Wales, coming to this lake, command the birds upon it to sing, they will all immediately sing." Gruffydd replied: "Do you, therefore, who now bear sway in this country, command them first." Both Milo and Payn having made the attempt in vain, Gruffydd dismounted from his horse, fell on his knees with his face to the east, and after devout prayers to God, stood up, and making the sign of the Cross on his forehead and face, cried aloud: "Almighty and all-knowing God, Lord Jesus Christ, show forth here to-day thy power! If thou hast made me lineally to descend from the natural princes of Wales I command these birds in thy name to declare it." Forthwith all the birds, according to their kind, beating the air with outstretched wings, began altogether to sing and proclaim it. No wonder that all who were present were amazed and confounded, and that Milo and Payn reported it to the king, who is said to have taken it philosophically enough. "By the death of Christ" (his customary oath), he replied, "it is not so much to be wondered at. For although by our great power we may impose injustice and violence upon these people, yet they are nevertheless known to have the hereditary right to the country." [127]

In Scotland there was a saying that the robin "had a drop of God's blood in its veins, and that therefore to kill or hurt it was a sin, and that some evil would befall any one who did so; and, conversely, any kindness done to poor robin would be repaid in some fashion. Boys did not dare to harry a robin's nest." The yellow-hammer and the swallow were said, each, "to have a drop of the Devil's blood in its veins; so the yellow-hammer was 'remorselessly harried,' and the swallow 'was feared and therefore let alone.'" [128] Here is an illustration of the blood of the gods communicated to earthly organisms.

One may infer from many references that the Druids practised augury from the cries of birds. In an ancient poem ascribed to St. Columba, he says, alluding to the omens of the Druids:

I reverence not the voices of birds,
Nor sneezing, nor any charm in the wide world.
My Druid is Christ the Son of God.

A Latin Life of St. Moling has it that the wren is a bird of augury: magus avium, eo quod aliquibus praebet augurium; the Pseudo-Cormac Glossary explains it as drui-en, a druid bird. In Gaelic dreathan (donn) is used for 'wren'; Stokes [129] gives dreoan, from *dreo = W. dryw, 'wren; also druid, soothsayer,' from proto-Celtic *drevo, cognate with German treu, E. true. It seems to me that this derivation has much to support it in the folk-lore concerning it as a bird of soothsaying; the druid of birds.

O'Curry says the Druids divined from the chirping of tame wrens.

The wren has a drop of God's blood, in the folk-belief of some Highland districts. He is king of birds, a dignity attained to according to West Highland tradition by his having secreted himself above the eagle that soared high above all other birds, whereupon the wren flew a little upwards and cried: "Birds, behold your king." He was accordingly elected king in the assembly of birds. Yet the Manx custom of 'hunting the wren' shows that once a year it was ceremoniously slain, and its feathers distributed so as to communicate divine virtue. Without a dead wren to protect them the Manx fishermen would not once upon a time go to sea. It was a 'fairy' of uncommon beauty, says Bullock in his History of the Isle of Man, that used to unduly entice the men to sea, where they perished, and on being hunted down by a knight-errant she was only able to escape by assuming the form of a wren. A spell brought it to pass that every New Year the wicked 'fairy' had to take wren-form, and ultimately perish by a human hand. The feathers of the killed wren were preserved with religious care as an effectual preservation from shipwreck for one year; every person met with had to purchase a feather and to wear it in their hats for the day. Formerly the naked body was interred with great solemnity in a secluded corner of the churchyard, and the evening concluded with all manner of sports.

Possibly it was but a coincidence that the stoning of the wren took place on St. Stephen's Day, for Waldron, speaking of an earlier time, says "On the 24th of December, towards evening, all the servants in general have a holiday; they go not to bed all night, but ramble about till the bells ring in all the churches, which is at 12 o'clock; prayer being over, they go to hunt the wren, and after having found one of these poor birds, they kill her and lay her on a bier with the utmost solemnity, bringing her to the parish church, and burying her with a whimsical kind of solemnity, singing dirges over her in the Manx language, which they call her knell, after which Xmas begins." [130] The divinity of the wren as protecting spirit is here indicated; the slaughter is a rite of sacrifice to attain communion with the divine, here held to be a malific power.

In West Sutherland I ascertained that some of the fishermen formerly held it was unlucky to kill a gull, for gulls were the souls of the deceased. Perhaps the idea of the isle or paradise of birds, as in the legend of St. Brendan, was founded on the belief of the soul in bird-form. Nothing has taken firmer hold of the Gadhelic mind than the Fate of the Children of Lir, who were turned into swans at the instance of their cruel stepmother, but they retained their souls, as is witnessed by their having ascribed to them the knowledge of their own Gadhelic music and their Gadhelic speech. Further, in the Highlands it used to be said that the earth placed over spots where a murder had been committed was wont to be disturbed by birds at night, which recalls to one the old Arab belief that the blood of a murdered man turned into an accusing bird till vengeance was taken for the dead. An Irish tradition in Keating [131] tells of a queen and her handmaid who were turned into two herons at the word of Columcille. Another tells of Aoife in the form of a crane that belonged to the sea-god, Manannán. [132]

Birds are credited with a speech of their own. Such was the lapwing's cry: Mhurchaidh bhig! na creach mo nid (sic), i.e. 'little Murdoch, harry not my nest.' All such ascriptions of speech to birds are attempts to give renderings in human language of the cries of the various birds. Though many and varied they need not here detain us.

For parallels where this belief has assumed a developed form one may point to the Dove Cult of primitive Greece, where sacred doves are associated with a sepulchral cult. It was the favourite shape in which the spirit of the departed was imagined to haunt its last resting-place. An early Indian code requires that upon the occasion of a sacrifice a fragment of the offering to the departed spirits should also be thrown to the birds, "because we are taught that our fathers glide along, taking the form of birds." [133]

Here comes the transition to the Language of Animals.

(a) The last words said by the cow were: Na buail do bhas orm = 'do not smite me with your palm.' It was not right that the blessed creature, the cow, should be struck by 'the flesh of the sinner.' If one had only a stick three inches long he should use it in driving the cow instead of striking her with his hand. Can this be a survival of a religious precept? Cf. the sacred cow of the Hindoos.

(b) The last words spoken by the horse were:

Na greas le bruthach mi
Na buail an aghaidh leothaid mi
Nuair a gheibh thu air an réidhleach mi na caomhain mi
Biadhaidh gu math mi nuair a théid mi dhachaidh.

i. e. 'Hurry me not down a brae, nor force (lit. strike) me up an incline; on the level do not spare me; feed me well on going home!'

(c) When sheep had language, as all animals once had, it is said that the last thing spoken by a sheep was a request that its bones should never be burned. Since that time it is not considered right to throw a bone of a sheep into the fire, and any person doing so is checked. One may infer that in pre-Christian rites the sheep was burnt in sacrifice. Cf. the sacrifices to Crom Cruach.

Cattle are so deeply loved that in the Highlands certain names run in the breed from generation to generation; cattle-names may be very old, as also cattle calls, e.g. pruch, a call to cows only, with meaning 'come here'; to calves the call is, pruicidh; also pru-dhé, pru-dhé, pru-dhé.

Numerous traces of animal worship existed among the Gauls. The tribal names Taurisci, Brannovices, Eburones point respectively to a veneration of the Bull, the Raven, the Boar, among peoples who probably once traced their descent from them. Place-names like Tarvisium, 'Bulltown (?)'; Lugudunum, 'Raven-Fort'; personal names like Deiotarus, 'the divine bull ';

Artogenos, 'the descendant of the bear,' point in the same direction. The boar was also sacred, as may be inferred from emblems on coins. The mare-goddess Epona had its parallel in the male horse-god Rudiobus, of which an image in bronze, showing no rider, has been found near Orleans, along with figures of boars and of a stag. [134]

So closely was the association between man and cattle felt in former times that we come across cases of 'animal-fasting,' like as we meet with the equally archaic though different idea of 'fasting on a person' in the Brehon Laws. The fasting of cattle as well as of human beings is spoken of in Adamnan's Second Vision, translated by Stokes from the Lebar Breac. He notes: "That calves were sometimes made to fast in Ireland after a chieftain's death appears from a poem in the Cogadh Gaedel re Gallaibh (ed. Todd, p. 100), two lines of which mean: 'Though calves are not suffered to go to the cows in lamentation for noble Mahon.' The practice may possibly, Dr. Todd suggests, have been suggested by Jonah iii. 7. But it rather seems a result of the belief in the souls of animals, and of the tendency to treat them as human, which are found in every race at a certain stage of its culture." [135] In Ireland the local saints were believed to guard the lives of certain kinds of animals. St. Colman's teal could neither be killed nor injured; St. Brendan provided an asylum for stags, wild boars and hares; St. Beanus protected his cranes and the grouse which bred upon the Ulster mountains. [136]

The local saints often took the place of the old gods. Caesar's statement [137] shows us that to the ancient Britons hare, goose and domestic fowl were taboo. Giraldus gives a story of the loathing shown by the Irish chieftains on being offered a dish of roasted crane. [138] The hare often figures in folk-belief. Thus Boudicca, the queen-heroine of the ancient Britons, loosed a hare from her robe, observed its movements as a kind of omen, and when it turned propitiously the whole multitude rejoiced and shouted. [139] In Western Brittany not many years ago the peasantry could hardly endure its name; [140] such is the case in parts of Russia. The oldest Welsh laws allude to the magical character of the hare, which was thought to change its sex every month or year, and to be the companion of the witches who were believed to assume its shape. In one part of Wales the hares are called St. Monacella's lambs, and it is said that up to very recent times no one in the district would kill one. "When a hare was pursued by dogs it was believed that if any one cried 'God and St. Monacella be with thee!' it was sure to escape." [141]

To be fed on the hares of Naas was one of the prerogatives of the kings of Tara, [142] which means that to others it was forbidden. Shape-shifting or transformation into hare-form may fitly lead to the consideration of the theriomorphic soul or the soul in animal form.

(a) Transformation into hare-form.—This deeply-rooted belief has been current for ages, and is not yet extinct. Wherever witchcraft obtains any hold this belief is met with. I have personally heard of and known many women who were regarded as having the power of shifting themselves into hare-shape. It was most uncanny to see a hare pacing a thatched cottage in the gloaming, still more to see several of them capering at cross-roads. The belief is exemplified in many folk-tales, as in 'The Leeching of O'Céin's Leg,' where the gearraidh, 'hare,' is spoken of, the nearest Scottish form to the Irish geirrfhiadh, 'short-deer.' As a rule geārr is used for 'hare,' but maigheach also occurs from magh, 'plain,' i.e. 'campestris.' There are numerous stories in the Highlands of hares having been shot at with a gun having a 'silver six-pence,' the creature shot being reputed to be some local witch afterwards found suffering of secret wounds. The transformation of witches into hare-form is the chief Highland characteristic, which tallies with the Isle of Man account. [143] It enters into Welsh folk-lore, but it is rather the idea of augury that is emphasised. [144] In Brittany at Lannion [145] souls take the form of hares. Everywhere in Celtdom it is a creature of omen for expectant mothers who have their old rites to avert hare-lip. Its lore dates from British times, and is met with widely in England; a writer in the Oxford Times (2nd January, 1909) refers to the Phantom Hare thus: "In the Cotswold country the rustics declare that every seventh child of a seventh child possesses 'second sight,' and that the 'wraith,' or, as they call it, the 'bogy,' of a person about to die is always visible to such persons. An old woman told me here that he who should deceive a maid, or lead her astray, would be ever afterwards haunted by her 'bogy' in the shape of a hare. This, she declared, was invisible to all except the haunted one, and in the end the hare, by some means or other, caused the deceiver to die."

A memorandum made by Bishop White-Kennett about the hare, which we may regard as a token from what Caesar says regarding the hare, the cock and the goose, is here in point: "When one keepes a hare alive and feedeth him till he have occasion to eat him, if he telles before he kills him that he will do so, the hare will thereupon be found dead, having killed himself." Mr. Gomme points out that this respect is carried further at Biddenham, where, on the 22nd September, a little procession of villagers carried a white rabbit (a substitute for hare) decorated with scarlet ribbons through the village, singing a hymn in honour of St. Agatha. All the young unmarried women who chanced to meet the procession extended the first two fingers of the left hand pointing towards the rabbit, at the same time repeating the following doggerel:

Gustin, Gustin, lacks a bier,
Maidens, maidens, bury him here.

This ancient custom had for its object the reverential burying of a rabbit or hare.

Gregorson Campbell in his Witchcraft and Second-Sight in the Highlands and Isles of Scotland, gives tales wherein witches are credited with the power of appearing in the guise of sheep, hares, cats, rats, gulls, cormorants, whales. By far the most common belief is that of witches in hare-form; of this class. of story the saying holds: though not to be believed, it may be told (ged nach gabh e creidsinn, gabhaidh e innseadh). In this category is to be placed the tale of the Sutherland worthy as recently retold in the Northern Chronicle, from the old man's experience by Mr. D. M. Rose. The narrative is characteristic of its class. Mr. Rose says:

"Donald told me the story himself, and swore it was 'true as gospel.' Of course I was bound to believe him, and did not hurt the poor man's feelings by telling him that such yarns were common in half a dozen northern counties. In the days of his youth Donald had been sent to cut peaty away in hills at a spot far distant from any human habitation. About mid-day Donald sat down on the peat-bank to rest, but was startled at hearing weird sounds in his neighbourhood. He sprang to his feet and looked eagerly in every direction without discovering anything to account for the strange noise. He was about to resume his seat, when presently there came into view, over a small hillock, a monster hare with two black hounds in pursuit. As the beast was making straight for the spot where he stood, Donald grasped his 'spadarel,' and raising it aloft he brought it down on poor puss's back, severing her into two as she passed. Just fancy the horror of Donald when he gazed at the severed fragments. One part of puss was gradually transforming itself into the face and features of a neighbour's wife who had an uncanny reputation, while the other portion remained 'a hare.' Donald had such a 'sair fleg' that he bolted. After running a few paces he thought it prudent to recover his 'spadarel,' and was exceedingly astonished to find not the least trace of the dead bit of woman, hare or hounds! Donald was so thoroughly alarmed that he rushed homewards. His wife, who was absent, came hurrying in with the startling news that the neighbour's wife had been killed about the middle of the day, and that she had been at the house to see the body laid out. Donald at once sprang to his feet, although he felt as 'waik as a child,' a cold shiver ran down his back although there were 'big drops of swate' falling from his brow. At last Donald managed to ask his wife if the 'woman was in bittocks,' i.e. in pieces. 'What do you mean,' said his wife, 'the poor craitur went to the byre to milk the coos, and as she passed one of the shelties draive his two hind heels into the poor woman's side, and she didna live an hoor after that.' 'Thank the Lord,' says Donald, with a fervent sigh of relief, but he kept the story of his own 'experiences in memory for many a year'—not even revealing his tale to the wife of his bosom. Of course he had seen the soul of the witch trying to escape from the black hounds of Hades!"

A totem animal is a characteristic omen. Boudicca, the Queen of the Iceni, is said to have taken a hare from out her bosom, and to have drawn an augury therefrom as to the course of her attack upon the Roman army. In Northamptonshire if a hare run along a street it portends fire to some house near by. In 1648 Sir Thomas Browne says it was deemed unlucky when a hare crossed one's path: there were few over three-score that were not perplexed by it. In parts of Scotland the unluck due to meeting a hare did not extend after the next meal was taken. In north-east Scotland the name of the hare must not be pronounced at sea. One cannot but agree with Mr. Gomme's conclusion that a classification of the beliefs and customs connected with the hare takes us to every phase of totemistic belief, and that it is impossible to reject such a mass of cumulative evidence. [146]

Shape-shifting (dol ann an riochd) does not as such raise the question of reincarnation of the soul. Soul and body are not nicely differentiated at that stage. The good folks I have known who were held to assume the form of hares at will were thought of as doing so as complete natures: on regaining human-form, if wounded in their hare-form, they had the self-same wounds on the corresponding part of the body. Parallel is the Welsh case of Llew Llawgyffes who, on being wounded, assumed eagle-form, and was afterwards found in bird-form with the flesh putrefying from his wound. The eagle-form is not quite a case of the bird-soul: it belongs to the category of shape-shifting, and to a stage of thought which looks at body and soul as one. His wound is the cause of his death, just as the wounds got by certain hares are held to be the cause of a certain witch's death.

(b) Transformation into cat-form.—An Hebridean tale tells how there was once a wedding; and the folks went to it all but one young man. He was asked to the wedding too, but somehow he didn't go, but his mother went. He stretched himself in bed and lay awake. Three cats came in by a window. When they got in, seeing nobody in they changed into three girls. The young man saw them and knew them. They drank up his mother's milk. He looked at them and they noticed him looking. They besought him not to tell, and threatened that if he ever told it would be all the worse for him. They then left. His mother came back from the wedding and he at once told her what he saw. Some time after his mother and their mother had a quarrel, and his mother cast up to the other the shapes her daughters had taken. Not long after this when the young man was on an errand he was late of returning. A search was made for him, and he was found dead on the way.

With this compare the strange big cats in the Fled Bricrend, [147] an early Irish tale of the Cuchulainn saga. One night as their portion was assigned the heroes, three cats from the cave of Cruachan were let loose to attack them, i.e. three beasts of magic. Conall and Loigaire made for the rafters, having left their food with the beasts. In that wise they slept till the morrow. Cuchulainn fled not from his place from the beast which attacked him. But when it stretched its neck out for eating, Cuchulainn gave a blow with his sword on the beast's head, but the blade glided off as 'twere from stone. Then the cat set itself down. In the circumstances Cuchulainn neither ate nor slept. As soon as it was early morning the cats were gone.

Clearly these cats are representative of another-world power: and are thought of as one of the disguises under which the other-world magician tests the hero, one of a series of tests through which Curoi, such is the magician's name, awards the palm for bravery to Cuchulainn.

Early Irish is catt, Welsh cath, Gaulish, cattos: the tribal name in Clan Chattan (the Mackintoshes, with Cattanachs, Shaws, Davidsons, and other septs) and in Cataibh, Cataobh, 'Sutherland'; Diuc Chatt, Duke of Sutherland; the root survives in Caithness (Caitness being heard with old people), all pointing to a belief in animal kinship, as witnessed to by the idea of transformation.

(c) Transformation of a human being into mare-form,—"the horse being a blessed animal since our Saviour was born in a manger." Dornoch is noted in the annals of witchcraft in Scotland as the place where the last execution for that supposed crime took place. Witchcraft ceased to be a capital offence by Act of Parliament in 1736. The execution at Dornoch occurred in 1722. The victim was a woman, who, according to popular belief, turned her daughter into a pony by her magical arts and got the devil to shoe it. This belief was more than an unconscious reminiscence of the horse's shoe in the burgh crest. The traditional site of the execution is the part of Dornoch known as Littleton, where, in one of the gardens, a stone with 1722 deeply incised upon it marks the spot.

For illustration I translate a modern narrative from Tiree which exemplifies fairly recent belief:

"Once upon a time there were two young lads who had engaged to serve in the house of a great man. They had the same food and the same work, yet, in spite of all, one of them was strong, seemly and stout, while the other was daily declining,—and, what was exceeding strange, every morning he was very tired as if he were not getting half enough of food. This was causing great astonishment to every one, and especially to the lads themselves. They knew not what it meant nor what they should do. Thereupon the lad who was seemly and stout said: 'When we go to bed to-night you will take my place by the wall and I will go on the side where you are lying.' Thus they did. They went to bed, and he who was by the wall slept at once, but though the other went to bed he slept not; he kept awake to see what should happen. While he thus reflected, who should enter but his mistress with a horse-bridle in her hand. As soon as she came in she shook the bridle to his face, which she no sooner did than he sprang into horse-form (became a horse). She then took him out and put a saddle on him, and sprang on his back and rode off. At no length of time they reached a big house, and she sprang to the ground and opened a stable-door where were many horses besides. She tied him there and went off. Though he was in horse-form he had human consciousness, inasmuch as he was awake at the time she shook the bridle at him. Accordingly, when she went away he began to try whether he could take the bridle off with his fore-feet. At last he succeeded, which he no sooner did than he was a man as formerly. Then he caught the bridle and bethought him of contesting with his mistress when ever she returned.

"Shortly thereafter she came with many more women like unto her. When he saw his mistress he shook the bridle at her, as she had done to him, which he no sooner did than she all at once became a big beautiful mare. Then he took her out and saddled her, but instead of going home, what did he do but go to a smithy and roused the smith. He requested the smith to put four shoes on her. The smith replied that he would not at all do so, it was too late to do such a work. The lad said that he would give him anything, even a 'white' note (a pound sterling), provided he could have her shod. On hearing this the smith came out and kindled the fire, and in a short time the house-wife was shod. Then he made for home. On arriving he took the bridle off her and she was a woman as formerly. Thereupon he went to sleep. On the morrow great sorrow fell on the household, for the mistress was ill. And, what made everybody wonder, no one was allowed into her chamber to see her. As things were in such a case the lad came where his master was and requested to be permitted to see her. The master said no, that nobody was allowed to enter. The lad said that he must needs go. What with everything he did the lad got in where she was. As soon as she saw him she scowled at him. He enquired how she was. She was not willing to answer, but he said to her: 'Stretch out your plut (paw, hand),' which she would not do. He seized hold of her, pulled out her hand, and what was it but that she had a horse-shoe thereon, and on the other hand as well, likewise a horse-shoe on each foot. He looked at her and said: 'Well you know what this means and the dreadful work you were at. Now give me your troth that I shall never either see or hear of your being at this disgraceful work, and I will take off the shoes.' She pledged to him her word, and he removed the shoes, and all was well thereafter. In a short time the lean lanky fellow grew stout and strong, and everybody about the place had peace. Such, for you, is the tale of the famous witches."

The original, which I owe to the kindness of a Tiree man, the Rev. J. MacCallum, Manse of Assynt, is as follows:

"Bha aon uair ann dà ghille òg a bha air fasdadh ann an tigh duine mhóir. Bha iad air an aon bhiadh agus air an aon obair, ach an deidh gach nì bha fear dhiubh gu làidir, coltach, reamhar, agus bha fear eile dol air ais gach latha, agus nì bha glé iongantach bha e anabharrach sgìth a h-uile maduinn mar nach biodh e faighinn leth gu leòr do chadal. Bha so a' cur mòran iongantais air gach h-aon agus gu sònruichte orra féin. Cha robh fios aca dé bu chiall do no dé a dheanadh iad. An sin thubhairt esan a bha gu coltach, reamhar: "Nuair a théid sinn a luighe nochd théid thu-sa ann am àite-sa ris a bhalla agus théid mi-se air an taobh air a bheil thu-sa.' Rinn iad mar sin. Chaidh iad do'n leabaidh agus chaidil e-san a chaidh ris a' bhalla anns a mhionaid ach ged a chaidh a feur eile luighe cha do chaidil e. Dh'fhan e 'na dhùsgadh fiach dé thachradh. 'Nuair a bha e a' smuaintinn air na nithean so cò thàinig a steach ach a bhan-mhaighstir agus srian eich aice 'na làimh. Cho luath 'sa thainig i 'steach chrath i an t-srian m'a choinneamh agus cha bu luatha rinn i so na leum e-san 'na each. An sin thug i mach e agus chuir i diollaid air a dhruim. An sin leum i ga mharcachd agus dh'fhalbh i leis. Ann an ceann úine nach robh fada ràinig iad tigh mór agus thàinig i-se air làr agus dh'fhosgail i dorus stàbuill far an robh móran each eile. Cheangail i ann an sin e agus dh'fhalbh i. Ged a bha e-san 'na each bha fathast mothachadh duine aige a chionn gun robh e 'na dhùsgadh an uair a chrath i an t-srian ris. Mar sin 'nuair a dh'fhalbh i-se thòisich e-san air fiachuinn am b'urrainn dha an t-srian a thoirt dheth le 'chasan toisich. Mu dheireadh chaidh aige air so a dheanamh. Agus cho luatha 's a thachair so bha e 'na dhuine mar bha e roimhe. An sin rug e air an t-srian agus thubhairt e ris féin gum fiachadh e i ri a bhan-mhaighstir 'nuair a thigeadh i air a h-ais.

"Tachdan beag na dheidh sin thainig i féin agus móran de mhnathan eile a bha coltach rithe féin. 'Nuair chunnaic e-san a bhan-mhaighstir chrath e an t-srian rithe mar a rinn i-se rise-san agus cho luath 's a rinn e so leum i-se 'na cabal mór briagha. An sin thug e mach i agus chuir e oirre an dìollaid ach an àite dol dhachaigh 's e rinn e dol gu tigh gobhainn agus a chur air a chois. Dh'iarr e air a ghobhainn ceithir chruidhean a chur oirre. Thubhairt an gobhainn nach cuireadh gu dearbh, gu robh e ro an-moch air-son dol a dheanamh a leithid so de dh'obair. Thubhairt an gille gun tugadh e nì sam bith, eadhon not gheal ach na cruidhean fhaotainn oirre. 'Nuair a chual an gobhainn so thàinig e mach agus bheothaich e an teine agus ann an ùine bhig bha bean a' bhaile air a cruidheadh agus an sin ghabh e dhachaigh. 'Nuair a ráinig e an tigh thug e dhith an t-srian agus bhà i 'na bean mar a bha i roimhe. 'Na dheidh sin chaidh e-san a chadal. Air an là màireach bha bròn mór air an tigh sin oir bha bean an tighe [148] gu tinn. Agus ni a bha 'cur iongantais air gach h-aon cha robh neach sam bith air a ligeil a steach ga faicinn. 'Nuair a bha so mar so thàinig e-san, an gille, far an robh a mhaighstir agus thubhairt e e-san a ligeil a steach ga faicinn. Thubhairt am maighstir nach leigeadh, nach robh neach sam bith ri dol a steach ach thubhairt an gille gu feumadh e-san dol a steach. Leis a h-uile rud a bh'ann fhuair e steach far an robh i. Cho luath 's a chunnaic i e chas i sgreang oirre.

"Dh'fhoighneac e dhìth ciamar a bha i. Cha robh i air-son freagairt a thoirt dha ach thubhairt e-san rithe: Sin a mach do phluit. [149] Cha deanadh i so agus rug e oirre is thug e mach a làmh agus de a bha ann ach gun robh cruidh eich oirre agus air an laimh eile cuideachd, agus air gach cois. Sheall e oirre agus thubhairt e rithe: 'Tha fios agad gu math de is ciall da so agus de an obair uamhasach a bha thu 'deanamh. A nis thoir dhomh-sa t'fhacal nach faic agus nach cluinn mi iomradh ort gu bràth tuilleadh ris an obair mhaslach so agus bheir mi dhiot na cruidhean.' Thug i dhà a facal agus thug e-san dhìth na cruidhean agus bha gach nì gu math tuilleadh. Ann an úine bhig dh'fhàs an gille bha caol truagh gu leathan làidir agus bha sith aig gach neach mu'n tigh.

"Sin agaibh naigheachd nam buitsichean móra!"

It is to be remarked that a variant of this Tiree tale exists in Ireland, where it has quite recently been printed: Lúb Na Caillighe, narrated by Michael Mhag Ruaidhri, and edited with vocabulary by Mr. J. Lloyd. [150] The story is located at The Loop, a tiny hamlet in Ballymulligan townland, five miles to the east of Moneymore, Co. Derry. The location has been motived in part by the word Lúb, usually meaning 'a bend,' 'a curve,' having the secondary sense of 'quirk, trick.' Hence 'Lúb na Caillighe' means also 'the Hag's Trick,' 'the Old Wife's Trickery.' The Irish version is located in Ulster, the province which most abounded with wizardry and the black art, according to the Irish folk-tale. This may be a remnant of old tradition referring to some relics of primitive rites among the Picts of Ulidia of old. The secret was revealed to the lad by an old woman who lived with her daughter not far off from the farm where he was employed. The details further differ in that the Tiree version ascribes human reason to the lad while in horse-form, inasmuch as the bridle was shaken over him while awake. But the Ulster version has it: "If thou be asleep when the hag comes in, she will shake the bridle above thy head in bed, and through the might of her druidism thou wilt arise up towards her, and she will put the bridle on thee." This done, the Hag rides him during the night throughout the length and breadth of the land, which causes his feeling quite exhausted as he awakes from sleep in the morning. The plan advised by the wise woman friend in the Ulster version is that the lad is to keep awake by tightening a waxed flaxen cord around his big toe, so as to ward off all sleep. The Hag comes to his bed thrice, but finds him awake: the third time she goes off in high dudgeon, as it was near midnight; hence "it was no time for her to delay about it." Apparently, unless her bridle had worked its magic by that hour, she was left powerless, for the Hag retired to her bed where the lad, who went thither at cock-crow, found her fast asleep,—"her snoring would fetch deaf kine from the woods." He shook the bridle, which was at the head of the bed, over her, and the Hag became a mare. At daybreak, as he was returning, he came upon a smithy. He asks the smith to shoe the mare. The smith was in great haste, for he took them for fairy-folk from the hills, and he was not long about his work. On reaching the house he took her into her room, took off the bridle, when she resumed her woman-shape as before, save that she had shoes on her feet and hands, and she as dead as a herring, her blood being well-nigh shed through the steel nails in the shoes. He left her in that shape, and went to sleep himself. Her husband was good and just, and saw that her wizardry won her the deserts she merited. We do not hear that the shoes were taken off her as in the Tiree version. The Irish version adds that the lad finally married the daughter of her who instructed him how to cope with the Hag's wiles.

The only magic-bridle in living Highland folklore is that attributed to the Willox family: it has the gift of calling up in the water-pail for the purpose the apparition of the worker of the evil-magic; it makes the figure of the absent one present. The bridle or bit thereof was said to have been got from the water-horse. It is a relic of the bridle of Manannan's steed, the horse of the lord of ocean.

The Clan Leod are thought of as having a close connection with the horse. It is mentioned in the rhyme:

Siol nan Leòdach
Siol a' chapuill
Bhacaich spògaich
Bheathaicheadh air
Moll is fòlach
Air dubhadan dubh
Is gulm eòrna.

i.e. the progeny of Leod, the progeny of the horse, lame and awkward, fed on chaff and rank grass, on the black "beard of dried oats," and singed barley-straw. This curious rhyme points to the horse as held once in special esteem among this clan whose name is of Norwegian origin. The horse may have been to them an object of imitation, and in some ways a sort of ideal. A modern philosopher remarks on the English: "they have forgotten that they are horses though the fact remains. Do they not still worship their totem at their chief festivals, abstain from eating it, and pay more attention to its breeding than to their own." [151] The mythic Hengist and Horsa contain some such reference.

Gregorson Campbell states: [152] In the Hebrides a horse is supposed to have reference to the Clan Mac Leod. The surname of horses is Mac Leod, as the Coll bard said to the Skye bard:

 Often rode I with my bridle
 The race which you and your wife belong to.
 = Is tric a mharcaich mi le m' shréin
 An dream g'am bheil thu fhéin 's do bhean.

Under this phase of the theriomorphic soul I may include Morc Na Maighe of Lochaber tradition. Although I find O'Brien's Irish Dictionary gives morc as 'hog or swine,' it seems but a variant of marc, 'horse' (whence marcach, 'rider'), the word which gives his name to King Mark of Cornwall, who is fabled to have had horse's ears. The legend associates Morc Na Maighe with Caoilte, but belongs to a much more primitive strata of myth than the Féinn Cycle. She is credited with being on foot as swift as the lightning; Caoilte and the Morc have the speed of the venomous winter wind, but the Morc is swifter than Caoilte, the fleetest of the Féinn. In their contest she outran him. As the glens were filling and foretelling of the storms and the clouds were lowering Caoilte had recourse to the device of springing aloft and seizing hold of her by the mane, nor did she ever perceive he was hanging to her. At long last, as sun was setting, Morc Na Maighe lay down by the foot of an oak tree, worn out by the heat, and her breath visible as vapour or mist. Caoilte standing by her side taunts her with her speed being the slower because of her weariness. The impudent reply to her query if he is really there is that Caoilte is the better for that race-before-a-leap. He will now proceed and bids her fare-well.

"It is age that has sufficed for me," she said. "But I have had my own day and I hope now to go home (literally, I am not of a hope that I will not now go home)." There we have the death-sigh of an old order of mythic beings. "Happy wilt thou be, thou shaggy hairy ugly thing, if thy four feet keep pace with what thy two eyes see," said Caoilte on meeting her. In this legend we have to do with more than a mere personification of cloud shapes, with an aspect really of the theriomorphic soul. It belongs to an early stage of the process of belief which led to the forming of deities named Tarvos (the bull), Moccos (the pig), Epŏna (the goddess of horses), Damŏna (the goddess of cattle), Mullo (the ass), among the Gauls and to the ancient Britons having held the hen, the goose and the hare as taboo, as not to be killed or eaten.

THE WANDERINGS OF PSYCHE (PART 2)

THE foregoing brief summary, sufficient for my present purpose, is from living tradition. I give now the original Gaelic, which I owe to Mr. Kenneth Macleod, who kindly wrote down for me such incidents as he remembers, and states that he is not quite certain whether the Morc was an each-uisge or an each-coilleadh or a combination of both.

Rhys inclines to take the Irish Morc, corresponding to the Welsh March ab Meirchion, i.e. 'Steed son of Steeding,' as a sort of Irish Pluto. In the Book of Leinster (fol. 160[a]) Morc (Margg, Marg) figures as steward of the King of the Fomori. Marc is the name of one of the foes killed by Cuchulainn on the tain (Book of Dun Cow, 70[b]). Morc appears as (a) having horse's ears, (b) a king, (c) captain of a great fleet: he is horse-man, a monster sharing the qualities of both. [153]

The original runs:

"Morc Na Maighe.—Latha do Chaoilte 'na aonar anns a' Chreig ghuanaich, cluinnear farum-fad-as na fadhaide anns a' choillidh ghruamaich, agus gabhar a mach air a h-ionnsaidh. Cò thachair ris ach gum b' e Morc Na Maighe, agus i 'ga deisearadh fein an sùil na greine. 'Gum bu sheatha [154] duit fein, a Chaoilte,' ars' ise, 'ma bhrathas [155] tu air an Fheinn mus beir an cuan siar an nochd air a' ghrein.' ''S gum bu sheatha duit fein, a phiullagaich pheallagaich ghrainnde,' arsa Caoilte, 'ma chumas do cheithir chasan ris na chi do dhà shùil.' Bha sid air a cois le clise dhealan 's le fuaim thorrunn, agus thugar a' ghrian de Chaoilte. 'Tha Mactalla,' ars' ise, 'air luirg na fadhaide, agus bitheamaid-ne a nis air a luirg-san.' Mach a ghabh iad le cheile mar ghaoith ghuinich gheamhraidh, 's bha an ceum-toisich aig Caoilte. Bha na glinn a' lionadh 's bha na mill a' sìneadh, 's bha an ceum-toisich a nis aice-se. 'Is mòr do luathas, a mhuirc,' arsa Caoilte. 'Cha mhoillid e sin, a Chaoilte,' ars' ise, agus i toirt spreadhaidh eile aisde. 'Feuchaidh sinn ealaidh eile a nis,' arsa Caoilte ris fhein; 's thugar duibhleum as, 's beirear air mhuing oirre, agus cha tug ise an aire riamh gun robh e nis an crochadh rith. Mu dheireadh 's mu dhiu, aig dol fodha na gréine, laigh Morc Na Maighe aig bonn craoibh-dharraich, 's an teas 'ga ruighinn 's a h-anail ruith 'na ceo. 'Is moillid do luathas an sgìos, a mhuirc,' arsa Caoilte, 's e seasamh air a beulaibh. 'A bheil thu sin, a bheadagain?' ars' ise. 'Tha,' ars' esan; 'is fheairrde mi an roid ud—theid mi nis gu h-astar—slàn leat.' 'Is i an aois a dh' fhoghainn domh,' arsa Morc Na Maighe; 'ach bha mo latha fein agam—cha'n 'eil mi 'n dùil nach teid mi dhachaidh a nis.'"

(d) As regards fowl, I can only find few apposite references: Conaire the Great, who was held to be descended from a fowl, was interdicted from eating its flesh. [156] At 'Goose Fair' at Great Crosby, Lancashire, the goose was held as too sacred to eat. In parts of Scotland, too, there was a prejudice against eating the goose, [157] it being too sacred.

Another prejudice existed against white cows. Dalyell in his Darker Superstitions of Scotland mentions the existence of a prejudice against white cows,—which seem to have been held as consecrated animals. And I knew a man in the Highlands who could on no account eat pork: he would turn quite ill on being told that such was given him disguised in any form. I can but remind the reader of the sacredness and potency of swine's blood to cure warts, and of the story of Diarmud, whose life depended on that of the venomous boar. This last might admit of an explanation different from the preceding.

(e) The soul in deer-form.—In the earliest documents of the Ossianic cycle it is Finn and not Ossian who plays the role of poet. Yet, in the prose tales, dialogues and lyrical monologues are interspersed, and these verses are put in the mouth of the persons concerned just as if they were the poetical composers of the same. Windisch (Ir. Texte, i. 63) supposes that in this wise Ossian has developed into a poetic figure. The poems which, in the saga, were put into his mouth, came to be regarded as his work till they became gradually typical of a whole species of literature. In support of his hypotheses Windisch points out that the headings of the poems in point are to the effect: Ossīn or Finn cecinit,—a heading corresponding to the formula of the Cuchulainn cycle when poetical pieces are by way of dialogue and quasi-dramatically incorporated in the prose-tale, to wit: 'Conid and ro chāchain Conchobur inso' = 'Here Conchobair sung as follows.' From this to Auctor hujus Ossīn, the formula of the Book of Lismore, is but a small step. No one, too, who was not versed in poetic art could be admitted into the Fēinn, as Keating reports, but I have little doubt this was the invention of those poets of mediaeval times who wanted to glorify their office. I would in particular point out that the mediaeval craving after an etymology for the name Ossian came to strengthen the tendency just referred to. In modern times it is traditionally narrated that he had colg an fheidh, 'deer's hair' (fur, pile), upon his temple, and that in virtue of having this on a corner (oisinn) of his brow he was called 'Corner,' i.e. Oisein. Further, in the Book of the Fēinn one reads the tradition of 1870. "When Oisein was born in the mountains, it was so that if his mother licked him as deer licked their calves, he was to be a deer like his mother.

If not he was to be a man like Fionn his father. She had so much of the deer's nature in her that she began to lick the child, and she gave one sweep of her tongue to his temple. The deer's hair (colg an fheidh) grew on the corner of his brow at once. When his mother saw that, she had so much of the woman's nature left that she wished her son to be a man, she stopped licking him, and he grew up to be a man, and they called him Oisein (i.e. Angle or corner). He was the best bard in the world" (L. na F. p. 198).

In the above version Ossian is Cuchulainn's nephew, for his mother is the sister of Cuchulainn mac an Dualtaich, under spells (geasan). Fionn had been under a taboo that he would marry any female creature he might chance to meet. He fell in with a deer, and by putting his finger under his wisdom-tooth he knew the deer was an enchanted woman. Here we have the animal parentage of Ossian, of which account the above is but the afterglow. On the margin of the Book of Leinster (1160) there is the following reference to the mother of Ossian:

māthair Diarmata o'n Dāil
ingen churraig meic Chathāir
is blai derg de'n Bhanbai bhrais
māthair Ossine amnais
ticedh [sī] iricht eilte
i comdāil na dibeirge
codernad Ossine de
ri Blai ndeirg irricht eilte.
              LL. 164 marg. supp.

i.e. 'The mother of Diarmad, from Dāil, daughter of Currag mac Cathar; and Blai Derg, from the rushing Banba, the mother of the formidable Ossian. In a doe's shape she used to come and join the outlawed band, and thus it was that Ossian was begotten upon Blai Derg disguised as a doe' (cf. Sil. Gad. 522).

According to a Barra version Fionn's first wife Grainne, enchanted in the form of a hind, was mother to Ossian. It was a fairy sweetheart that put her under spells. The fairy sweethearts used always to be at that kind of work. It was on a pretty little green island which is called Eilean Sandraigh (or otherwise on a sea-rock in Loch-nan-Ceall, in Arasaig) that Ossian was born (Leabhar na Feinne, p. 199).

The soul in deer-form is met with in another story connected with Forsair Choir' an t-Sīdhe, 'The Forester of Fairy Corry.' I give it as told by the late Alexander Macpherson of Kingussie.

"The White Hind.—Somewhere in this Garden of Sleep (Kingussie Cemetery) hallowed by St. Columba, although no trace can now be found of the actual grave, there rests the dust of the celebrated forester of the Fairy Corry, a native of Cowal in Argyllshire. This hero was of a branch of the MacLeods of Raasay, and being fair-haired his descendants were called Clann Mhic-ille bhain—that is, children of the fair (literally white) haired man, who now call themselves by the surname of Whyte. The forester was universally believed to have had a Leannan-Sith (a fairy sweetheart), who followed him wherever he went.

"Mr. Duncan Whyte, of Glasgow, one of the eighth generation in direct descent from the forester, communicated to me in Gaelic sundry very interesting traditions which have come down regarding his famous ancestor. In the year 1644 the Earl of Montrose was in the field with an army on behalf of King Charles I.; while the Earl of Argyll had the chief command of the Covenanters' forces. Montrose was burning and pillaging in the north when Argyll received instructions to go in pursuit of him. The forester was in Argyll's army, and the fairy sweetheart, in the shape of a white hind, followed the troops wherever they went. While they were resting in the neighbourhood of Ruthven Castle, in Badenoch, some of the officers began to mock Argyll for allowing the hind to be always following the army. Their ridicule roused his wrath, and he commanded his men to fire at the hind. This was done without a particle of lead piercing her hair. Some observed that the forester was not firing, although pointing his gun at the hind like the rest, and he was accused to Argyll. He then received strict orders to fire at the hind. 'I will fire at your command, Argyll,' said the forester, 'but it will be the last shot that I shall ever fire,' and it happened as he said. Scarcely was the charge out of his gun when he fell dead on the field, The fairy gave a terrific scream and rose like a cloud of mist up the shoulder of the neighbouring mountain, and from that time was never seen following the army. It has been believed by every generation since that the fairy left a charm with the descendants of the forester, which shall stick to them to the twentieth generation." [158]

From Irish tradition I take the following example. It is the story of Oisin Born of A Doe in Cremlin (West Mayo):

"One fine sunny day the seven heavy battalions of Fionn encamped at the foot of Murrn, in the land of lakes; the son of Devvra sat on the top of a hill, looking over rocks and cliffs where there were only wild wolves and badgers: near him was Gaul, son of Morni. Fifty strong men had charge of the hounds in leash: the hounds running at liberty were put under care of the hunters of Leinster and of Munster.

"A hawk was making melodious sounds for the children of Ruanan who were led by Caoilte: the baying of the hounds in the woods drove the deer and wild beasts into the darkest shades and caves of the glens.

"A young doe rose up in the chase: Fionn, the active white-handed hero, saw her beauty; he gave vehement chase and took her to be his wife. [159]

"This lovely doe he shielded from attack of hounds: he let her escape: his eye followed her as she bounded from bush to bush, till she reached Cremlin of the woody thickets.

"There the doe remained till I was born amidst the branches, instead of a kid: by her side I ran like a kid, sucking my mother's milk till I was seven years old: wild in the woods I ran till I was three times seven years old. Boomin, the tuneful foster mother of Fionn, came into the woods to pluck berries: she ran to Fionn and told him that in the thickets she had seen an animal like a red, wild man.

"All the Fenii gathered together to find out the truth of the story which ran from man to man.

"To prevent my escape they placed two hounds in Aughavilla, two in Aughavalla, two in Auchagower, two in Ogoul near the sea, two on the ridge of Lenane, two on the dizzy heights of Achil, two in Cuirrsloova, two swift hounds on the hill of Tarramud, and at the foot of Binna they placed the son of Boovil, with his two swift dogs straining at the leash. The melodious voices of the hounds roused the stately stags of Barraglauna, does, badgers, and boars of the glens stole away. At evening's hour they raised the spear to stop the chase: they rested their hunting spears on their shoulders: they slept in Thauver of much people.

"At sunrise next day Fionn, in his hunting dress, followed his melodious hounds through the woody glens: they started me and the doe my mother: all day they chased us: when the sun went down I was tired: the hound Sheeve came up and caught me by the hair of my head: the doe left me, alone. Then came Shrocco in strong running, and took a sufficient hold of my back: Guntaugh seized me by the left side, and Creautagh by the right: Fuiltaugh held me by the loin, and the hound Verran by the leg. Bran came running up, she was only nine months old and not yet strong in chase: when she came up she began to lick my wounds, she was kind and gentle, she treated me well.

"Caoilte was the first hunter who came to me; after him all the Fenii; they led me by the hand to Fionn. When the son of Cumhal felt the strength of the bones of my arms he said, 'These arms and hands are like those of the children of Baoisgne.'

"Then the Fenii came round in friendship: they brought shears: they sheared me from head to foot: they washed me and put clothing upon me in place of the coarse hair which covered me before. Fionn and all the Fenii taught me to speak. Thus was I born in Gremlin of the shady thickets." [160]

The counsel given by Ossian to his mother, Highland legend expresses thus: [161]

> Mas tu mo mhathair 's gur fiadh thu
> Éirich mu'n éirich a' ghrīan ort.
> = Mother mine, if deer thou be
> Arise ere sun arise on thee.

This counsel was given, according to Miss Tolmie, in order that the deer, i.e. his mother, might break the spell which bound her before Ossian was born.

The name Ossian, Irish Oisín, i.e. little deer or os, is a diminutive from Gadhelic os, deer, cognate with Cymric uch, English ox; not from the Saxon 'Oswine, as Dr. Zimmer imagined, which in Gadhelic would yield a long initial vowel, whereas it is short.

In addition to that of Ossian, which denotes 'little deer,' there are many other names of animal parentage in Gadhelic: Mac Echern, MacLellan, MacKichan, MacMahon, MacCulloch, derive from the names for horse, wolf, bear, boar; Shaw seemingly is from Sithech 'wolf,' as is also M'Keith; the Prince of Teffia, The O'Caharny, had as his official title 'The Wolf.' Malcolm, through the Gaelic Maol-Coluim, derives ultimately from Columba, 'dove.' Adamnán gives the older diminutive form Oisseneus, from Gaelic Oisséne, and there is the female form Ossnat, as well as the tribal name Ossraighe, whence Ossory. Nicknames are still given to persons in the Highlands, and such names as 'the lion,' 'the jackdaw,' 'the little horse,' 'the rat,' 'the eagle' were current a few years ago. Analogy thus strengthens the conception as to the name Ossín being given from his deer parentage.

The Ossraighe have been held to be a pre-Milesian race. Rhys derived os here from Basque otso, 'a wolf.' But compare Gamhanraighe, 'the calf-tribe'; Conraighe, 'the hound tribe'; Soghraighe, the bitch-tribe?' as Mr. MacNeill renders the names in the New Ireland Review. [162]

The same idea occurs in another old tale of the transformation of Tuan mac Cairill, who tells the story to St. Finnian of Moville. "As I was asleep one night I saw myself passing into the shape of a stag (dul i richt oiss allaid). . . . After this, from the time that I was in the shape of a stag, I was the leader of the herds of Ireland, and wherever I went there was a large herd of stags about me (bói alma mór do ossaib alta immum). This Tuan afterwards passes into the shape of a boar, then into that of a. hawk, then into that of a salmon, which on being eaten by Cairell's wife, he was reborn as human. He was of great age when Patrick came to Ireland and was baptized, and he 'alone believed in the king of all things with his elements.' Every pedigree that is in Ireland, 'tis from Tuan, son of Cairell, the origin of that history is. For he had conversed with the ages and was known as Tuan, the son of Starn, the brother of Partholon (whence Mac Pharlane, -Farlane), the first man who came to Ireland. One hundred years was he in man's shape, eighty as a stag, twenty as a boar, a hundred as an eagle, twenty as a salmon, so that three hundred and twenty years elapsed until he was reborn a man."

The Colloquy tells us that Ossian went to the síd of ucht Cleitigh (síd octa Cleitig), where was his mother Blái, daughter of Derc surnamed dianscothach, i.e. 'of the forcible language.' [163] In another part of the Colloquy we read of Ubhalroiscc, from the Síd Ochta Cleitig in the plain of Bregia. [164] This passage enumerates the chiefs and territorial lords of the Tuatha de Danann, and it follows that the deer parentage of Ossian connects him with the Tuatha dé.

Again, in the Highlands we meet with the deer as sacred, as possessing the theriomorphic soul. In the Island of Rum it was thought that if one of the family of Lachlin shot a deer in the mountain of Finchra that he would die suddenly or contract a distemper which would soon prove fatal. Probably the life of the Lachlins was bound up with the deer on Finchra as the life of the Hays was bound up with the mistletoe on Errol's oak. [165] One recollects that the Gauls are referred to as sacrificing to Artemis or Diana (v. Grimm's Teutonic Mythology, iv. 1592).

The deer is thus clearly a phase of the theriomorphic soul, and thus we can account for the survival of stag-ceremonies connected with church worship in Britain. Thus, Camden says as to the site of St. Paul's, London: "Some have imagined that a temple of Diana formerly stood here, and when I was a boy I have seen a stag's head fixed upon a spear (agreeably enough to the sacrifice of Diana) and conveyed about within the church with great solemnity and sound of horns. And I have heard that the stag which the family of Bawd in Essex were bound to pay for certain lands used to be received at the steps of the church by the priests in their sacerdotal robes, and with garlands of flowers on their heads. Certain it is this ceremony savours more of the worship of Diana and of Gentile errours than of the Christian religion." [166] Statues and stone-altars to Diana have been found in the neighbourhood. [167] The 'playing of the stag,' referred to in penitential books and homilies, points in the same direction. Men on New Year's Day clothed themselves in the skin of a stag, with its horns upon their heads, and were accompanied by other men dressed in woman's clothing. In this costume with licentious songs and drinking, they proceeded to the doors of the churches, where they danced and sung with extraordinary antics. Tacitus, in his Germania, tells us of a priest clothed as a woman, and when men first usurped the office of priestess there is little doubt that they clothed as women. Hence the men dressed as women who occur in so many Twelfth Day, May Day and Midsummer Day celebrations are, I think, fossils of the old priestesses, often occurring as fossils of the old sacrificial animal. The 'playing of the stag' at the church door seems to me, therefore, another relic of the old religious rites accompanied by choral dance and licentious song. [168] And I may refer to the stags' horns which I have seen four years ago in the church of Abbots Bromley, Staffs., which are carried by the mummers who annually enact the 'Hobby Horse.'

With the deer-mother of Ossian, one may compare the story of the Deer Park in Benares, where Buddha first caused the wheel of the good to revolve. The story tells of a king who was one of the former incarnations of Bodhisattva Shâkyamuni.

Moved by the entreaty of a mother-doe to save its offspring, the Deer-Bodhisattva approached the king on her behalf. The king said: ". . . I am a deer in man's form. Though you are in appearance a lower animal, you are in heart a human being. . . . If endowed with a loving heart, though a bear in form, one is human. . . ." [169]

(f) Transformation and Incarnation into Bull-form. The Divine Bull (Tarbh) of the Epos and of Legend.—It may seem a strange thing to give a great tale in which the leading incidents turn on the possession of a bull the title of Táin Bó Cúalnge, the Foray (or Driving) of the Kine of Cualnge. But all Tána according to the old Gadhelic categories fall under the title of Táin Bó; and besides, the Bull sought is of super-animal origin; it is the seventh form assumed by the swine-herd of the gods, for the Donn Cualnge had (1) a human form, (2) the form of a raven, (3) that of a seal, sea-dog, (4) that of an eminent warrior, (5) the form of a phantom, (6) that of a worm or moth, (7) that of a bull. It is distinctly stated in the Táin that the Donn of Cúalnge had human reason: 'atchuala Dond Cualngi anní sein acus bae cíall dunetta aice' [170] = 'the Dond of C. heard this, for it had human understanding.' The two bulls were incarnations of rival swine-herds from the Síd. [171] 'The Begetting of the Two Swine-herds ' forms a tale in the Book of Leinster; [172] Friuch and Riucht were their names, "and there was also friendship between them, viz., both possessed the lore of paganism, and used to shape themselves into any shape, as did Mongan the son of Fiachna." They underwent various transformations:

. . . they were two stags. . .

They were two champions wounding each other.

They were two spectres, either of them terrifying the other.

They were two dragons, either of them beating (?) the snow on the land of the other. They dropped down from the air and were two worms. One of them went into the well of Glass Cruind in Cualnge, where a cow of Dáre mac Fiachnai drunk it up; and the other went into the well of Garad in Connaught, where a cow of Medb and Ailill's drank it, so that from them sprang the two bulls, the Whitehorn Ai and the Donn of Cualnge.

I suggest that we have here to do with the Tarbh Boibhre [173] of living Highland tradition. Boibre is given in O'Davoren's glossary and explained as from boabartach abairt amail in mboin, i.e. 'cow-behaviour, behaving like the cow.' It was conceived as a sort of hermaphrodite lusting to graze at a loch side along with cows. From recent tradition I know of the Tarbh Boibhre having been spoken of; the description given pointed to some mythic animal often emerging from deep inland lochs—for instance, Loch Bruiach in Inverness-shire--and capable of assuming the form of a bull or of a cow at pleasure, and of emitting a peculiar cry like to that of powerful birds in the night time. I have come across a fuller description in the Campbell of Islay MSS., which I reproduce. It is entitled The Boobrie, and is thus described in its three-fold manifestations or imaginary emanations.

(a) The Boobrie as Bird.—"This species of animal which within the last century was by no means rare in the districts of Upper Lochaber and Argyll, has for many years been totally extinct, the assigned cause being the extent to which heather burning has been practised in those districts for so many years past. Very long heather was the natural resting place and shelter of the Boobrie. According to the most authentic reports the animal was endowed with the power of assuming at pleasure the forms of three different animals, viz., those of a most enormous and ferocious water-bird (when he was designated the Boobrie), of a water-horse or each-uisg, and of a water-bull or tarbh-uisg. The first of these was the one which he preferred assuming. I intend giving a short description of him in these three various forms—first as the Boobrie from the report of an eye-witness, who not only saw him but waded up to his shoulders into a very large muir loch on a very cold morning in February in the hope of getting a shot at him, but when he had reached within eighty-five yards of him the animal dived, and my informant after waiting for three quarters of an hour where he was, returned on shore to watch for his reappearance, which, though my informant remained in his uncomfortable position for more than five hours and a half on the bank, did not take place. Although this man was not so fortunate as to get a shot at him, he was near enough to have been enabled to furnish me with a most satisfactory account of the animal's appearance and dimensions. In form and colour the Boobrie strongly resembles the Great Northern Diver, with the exception of the white on the neck and breast; the wings of both, bearing about the same proportion to the size of their bodies, appear to have been given them by nature more for the purpose of assisting them in swimming under water, than flying. In size of body he is larger than seventeen of the biggest eagles put together. His neck is two feet eleven inches long, and twenty-three inches in circumference, his bill is about seventeen inches long, black in colour, measuring round the root about eleven inches; for the first twelve inches the bill is straight, but after that assumes the shape of an eagle's, and of proportionate strength. His legs are remarkably short for his size, black in colour, but tremendously powerful, the feet are webbed till within five inches of the toes, which then terminate in immense claws of most destructive nature. The print of his foot on the mud at the east end of the lake (as accurately measured by an authority) covers the space generally contained within the span of a large wide-spreading pair of red deer's horns. The sound he utters resembles that of a large bull in his most angry humours, but much superior in strength. The favourite food of the Boobrie is the flesh of calves; failing them he feeds upon sheep or lambs, as suits him, or seizing his prey he carries it off to the largest neighbouring muir loch, swims out to the deepest part, where he dives, carrying his victim along with him, and there feeds, returning on shore at pleasure. He is also particularly fond of otters, which he swallows in great numbers, and with considerable avidity.

"It is a notorious fact that about sixty years ago a Boobrie frequented a loch named Loch Leathan, anglice 'the Broad Loch,' in the West of Argyllshire, and caused great consternation in the district.

"The clergyman of this parish was a remarkable man, not only for the assiduity with which he followed his calling, but for his talents and accomplishments. Whenever it was known that he was to preach, a large congregation was certain. On one occasion the parson had agreed to preach for a neighbouring clergyman who was absent on duty, and all the neighbouring gentry made a point of attending. As distances were great the heritors ordered dinner. [Here story tells of their chance of falling in with the Boobrie. . . . . the minister and his servant fell over one another in a burn. Each thought the other was the Boobrie. Sandy, the servant, always thought they had been glamoured by the Boobrie!]"

(b) The Boobrie as Water-horse (Each-Uisge)." On the banks of Loch Freisa, a fresh-water loch on the property of Lochadashenaig, in the island of Mull, the tenant was ploughing some land that was so hard and strong that he was compelled to use four horses. Early one day one of the horses cast a shoe, they were nine miles from a smithy, and the nature of the ground prevented any possibility of the horse ploughing without one. 'Here's the best part of our day's work gone,' said the tenant to his son, who was leading the foremost horses. 'I am not sure,' replied the son. 'I see a horse feeding beside the loch, we'll take a lend of him, as we don't know who he belongs to.' The father approved of the proposal. The son went down and fetched up the horse, which appeared to have been quite used to ploughing, drawing first up hill, then down, perfectly steadily until they reached the end of the furrow, close to the loch. On an attempt to turn the horses this borrowed one became rather restive, which brought the whip into use, though lightly; no sooner had the thong touched him than he instantly assumed the form of a most enormous Boobrie, and uttering a shout which appeared to shake the earth, plunged into the loch, carrying with him the three horses and plough. [174] The tenant and his son had both the sense to let go their respective holds. The Boobrie swam out with his victims to the middle of the loch, where he dived, carrying them along with him to the bottom, where he apparently took his pleasure of them. The tenant and his son got a most awful fright (as well may be imagined), but remained hid behind a large stone for seven hours in the earnest hope of perhaps even one of their horses coming ashore. But no."

(c) Boobrie as Tarbh-Uisge.—"In the two preceding anecdotes we have described the Boobrie merely as a rapacious and predatory animal, causing general dismay from his frightful appearance and voracious appetite, but the following anecdote seems to give colour to the now generally received belief that this form in its different shapes was the abode of a spirit, condemned to such penance by way of expiation for the violation of certain ordinances of the superior spirits, and was in many instances friendly, if not beneficent to mankind."

The following abstract will explain the subsequent story:

[Scene in winter on west coast of Argyll, on west Lank of Loch nan Dobhran, where one Eachann suddenly came upon a large black bull which was lying down, apparently dying and groaning piteously: Eachann feeds him. Eachann's sweetheart Phemie had a rejected suitor, Murdoch MacPherson: Scene changes to summer, at the shieling beside Loch nan Dobhran.]

"Once or twice Phemie had been startled by the momentary vision of a shadow on the lake, one which made her shudder, for the fleeting outline reminded her of the rejected suitor.... One evening as she sat at some distance from the shieling and thought of Eachann, the shadow again crossed her, but this time when she looked around Murdoch himself was there. Before she could scream he threw his plaid over her head, bound down her hands.... Help came to her in a most unexpected form. The Tarbh Uisg came tearing along, and rushing at Murdoch, seemed to crush him to the earth before he had any time to make any resistance.... The Tarbh Uisg approached Phemie, and kneeled down, as if to invite her to mount upon his back, which she did. He immediately sped off, and with the quickness of thought she found herself safely deposited at her mother's door. The Tarbh Uisg was gone in a moment, but a voice was heard in the air calling out loudly:

Chaidh comhnadh rium le ògair caomh
S ri òigh rinn mise bàigh;
Deigh tri cheud bliadhna do dhaorsa chruaidh
  Thoir fuasgladh dhomh gun dàil,

which may be thus translated:

I was assisted by a young man
And I aided a maid in distress;
Then after three hundred years of bondage
  Relieve me quickly.

Since then the Tarbh Uisg has not been seen."

The above reveals the persistence in folk-belief of the idea of transformation, the Boobrie being the abode of a spirit, just as the Donn Cualnge had human reason. Sometimes the tarbh boidhbhre has been thought of as asexual, and the phrase has been rendered 'the bull of lust.' Calves with any peculiarities were once upon a time held to be from this stock, and corresponded to the Manx idea of the far-lheiy, which Cregeen's Dictionary defines as "a false conception of a calf, said to be generated between a cow and what is called a tarroo-ushtey." In parts of Inverness-shire it has been defined to me as [175] a serpent-bull, further defined as a great fly, or as a big striped brown gobhlachan or 'ear-wig,' as long as one's little finger, with a crave for sucking horse-blood. It was thought to be very rare, to appear only in great heat in August and September, and to have lots of tentacles or feelers (tha gràinne spògan air). In the same district the water-horse was thought of as at times like unto a man, similar to a carle in ribbons and rags; every one will not see it: to see it is an omen of drowning. [176]

The water-horse (in t-ech usci) is spoken of in the Life of St. Féchin of Fore: "It came to them and was harnessed to the chariot, and it was tamer and gentler than any other horse." [177] Cossar Ewart has lately spoken of the old species of horse of 30,000 years ago, and may be the wild-horse of Scotland is reflected in its folklore. Mr. D. M. Rose drew attention to this in the Scotsman, and as what he says of Sutherland holds further south, I cannot but quote his words:

"In the folklore of the north, extending over a wide area, from Caithness to Aberdeen, there is much concerning horses that at first sight seems fabulous. But a different complexion is put on these tales when it is taken into consideration that wild horses survived in the north until the sixteenth century. Through the progress of time folklore became invested with the supernatural. For instance, in Sutherland there are many legends about the wild horses of the interior, and from these yarns it would appear that later generations (in the absence of the real wild horse) entertained a belief that his Satanic Majesty must have assumed the shape of a horse to beguile wayfarers. A queer thing is that in folklore all these wild horses were lovely yellow coloured animals with bristling manes and long flowing tails. If yellow was the prevailing colour of the wild animal, it is somewhat singular that the yellow dun type of horse is somewhat rare in the north.

"Let me give the story of the golden horse of Loch Lundie. Two men from Culmailie went one Sunday to fish on Loch Lundie, and they saw, pasturing in a meadow, one of the most lovely golden coloured ponies they had ever seen. One of the men determined to seize the animal and bring it home. His companion, in a state of great alarm tried to dissuade him, assuring him that the animal was none other than the devil in disguise. The man, nothing daunted, began to stalk the pony, declaring that if he could get a chance he would mount on the beast, even if it were the Evil One. At length he managed to get within reach, and making a bound he seized the bristling mane, and leaped on the animal's back. In an instant the pony gave one or two snorts that shook the hills, fire flashed from its eyes and nostrils, and tossing its tail into the air, it galloped away with the man to the hills, and he was never again seen by mortal being.

"According to another version, the yellow horse of Loch Lundie was last seen in a meadow near Brora by two boys who broke the Sabbath. They tried to mount the animal, and one of them succeeded in doing so. The other boy, getting alarmed, tried to withdraw, but found to his horror that his finger had stuck in the animal's side. With great presence of mind, he immediately pulled out his knife and cut off his finger. The pony immediately gave an appallingly shrill neigh and galloped madly away with his rider, who was never seen again.

"Of course, in folklore the pony was undoubtedly regarded as Auld Nick, but the truth is that wild horses actually existed in the Sutherland hills until after 1545. This wild herd was claimed by the Bishops of Moray, but Sutherland of Duffus succeeded in making good his right to them. They are described as the herd of 'wild meris, staigs, and folis,' and they could hardly have been of the domesticated species, though possibly later on they were captured and tamed, or died away. In Aberdeenshire the same folklore exists regarding wild horses. There is a story told about a son of Rose of Tullisnaught, who was lost in the neighbouring Forest of Birse. When he and his servant went out hunting one day he suddenly came upon a beautiful yellow pony in a glade of the forest. The servant tried to persuade him that the pony was merely the devil in disguise, but Rose determined to capture and mount the animal. He managed to do this, but in a twinkling horse and rider disappeared and were never seen again. Now, the recently issued Records of the Sheriffdom of Aberdeen (vol. i. pp. 106-7), by the New Spalding Club, clearly establishes the existence of a herd of wild horses in the Forest of Birse in 1507. From the references they do not appear to have been of the domesticated species, though they were being dispersed and apparently broken in."

As regards the Boobrie as bird, this is the bird Forbes gives as bubaire, 'the common bittern.' The upper parts of its body and wings are of a rich brown buff, with cross bars and shaft lines which give it colour-protection among the reeds of the marsh it frequents. The bittern boom, at the breeding season, is a strangely weird sound. Its early arrival was a good omen:

You may knaw there's na mair winter to cum
When the Bull o' Prestwick beats his drum.
              (Northumberland Lore.)

By Tweedside the bird was called the Miredrum; it is known as Botaurus stellaris, starred or speckled bird which bellows like an ox-bull. The French call it butor, or else bœuf du marais, 'ox of the swamp,' or taureau d'étang, 'bull of the pond.' Other English names are butter-bumps, bog-bull. It is its weird hollow cry at evening or at night that has led to its being regarded as an omen of disaster or death. Few retreats are left for it, comparatively, and its irregular visits have caused a good deal of confused belief regarding it. Burns calls it the bluiter, e.g.

The howlet cried from the castle wa',
The bluiter from the bogie.

Scott's description is probably the best in poetry: it suggests the solitary habits and the aloofness of the bird:

Yet the lark's shrill fife may come
  At the daybreak from the fallow;
And the bittern sound his drum
  Booming from the sedgy shallow,
Ruder sounds shall none be near,
Guards nor warders challenge here.

The sound is described as hollow; a booming sound, as that of a drum; a sort of bellow, but not so loud as that of a cow or bull, but suggestive of that sound. Its note during the breeding season is variously described as booming, bumping, bellowing, 'bumbling in the mire,' and Sir Thomas Browne refers to the belief that "a bitter maketh that mugient noyse, or as we term it bumping, by putting its bill into a reed." The Germans call it moosochse, mooskuhe. It is questionable whether the Latin botaurus has not been suggested by some survival of a Celtic *bo-tarvos, issuing in Old English botor, perhaps also in the Gaelic bo'ithre, tarbh eithre, if we put O'Davoren's bo-oibre aside. A bird called a bull, which imitates the lowing of oxen is spoken of by Pliny: "est quae boum mugitus imitetur in Arelatensi agro taurus appellata" (Hist. Nat. x. 42). Its note has typified desolateness and gloom from of old: cf. Isaiah xiv. 23, xxxiv. 11; Zephaniah ii. 14. Though changed in the Revised Version to porcupine (hedge-hog), Principal G. A. Smith, for instance, renders the last passage: "Yea, pelican and bittern shall roost on the capitals,"[178] and points out that the other animals mentioned here are birds, and that it is birds which would naturally roost on capitals. [178] By the Tigris the bittern abounds, as in the marshes of Syria. "No traveller," says Canon Tristram, "who has heard the weird booming of the bittern in the stillness of the night, while encamped near some ruined site, can ever forget it, or mistake any other sound for it. The bird belongs to the heron tribe, but is utterly different in its habits; always solitary, standing still and motionless through the day, with its beak upturned, looking like a tuft of weathered leaves, and only feeding at night." The sound is produced by the bird expelling the air from its throat while it stands with neck outstretched and holding its bill vertically upwards,—so Mr. J. E. Harting, who has observed the bird in the act. It is uncommon now in Scotland. One has been found at Taprain Law, East Lothian, on January 21, 1908. From a description given me over twenty years ago it was heard about Loch Bruiach, Inverness-shire, several years previously, and was known as the tarbh boidhre (bo'eithre, bo-oibhre). I had made most of my investigation of the Boobrie over six years ago when, following on an article on the 'Bull o' the Bog,' by Mr. J. Logie Robertson (Scotsman, March 1, 1910; cf. also that of Feb. 5, 1910, as to its rarity), there appeared this note, which I beg to insert as quite confirmatory of my suggestion:

"The Legend of the Water Bull.—When reading 'J. L. R.'s' interesting notes in The Scotsman of March 1st on the 'Bull o' the Bog,' it occurred to me that possibly in that bird of nocturnal habits we might find a natural explanation of the water bull (sometimes called the water horse) of Celtic legend. The main facts, viz., that the bittern haunts damp and reedy quarters such as are quite common round so many of our Highland lakes, that its booming notes are not unlike the guttural bellowing of a bull, and more particularly that its voice is usually heard after night-fall, all seem to suggest that it may have been the natural source of the various mythological tales in which the water bull figures. Some twenty years ago I came across an old Highlander in the north-west of Argyllshire who thoroughly believed in the existence of the water bull (the Tarbh-uisge). He told me a long tale about it. It dwelt in a loch not far from his dwelling. It only appeared at night. He had heard its roaring more than once. It was the reputed sire of one of the calves in the next farm, and that particular calf had, on being sent out with the others, gone straight to the loch, and plunged into its waters, and disappeared—a sure proof of its paternity. At the time, knowing that old Donald's hut was on the edge of a deer forest, I came to the conclusion that he had attached a mythical significance to the sound of the stag's roaring in the rutting season—a weird melancholy sound when heard towards the gloaming, full of pathos, and most appealing to the imagination. Now, however, after reading 'J. L. R.'s' article on the bittern and its ways, I wonder if that nocturnal bird—presuming it frequented the Highlands of old—may not be responsible for some at least of the myths associated with the water bull.—B. B."

I may add that the long claw of a bittern's hind toe was once used as an amulet. Its boom is reserved for the pairing or breeding season, and less than a century ago it caused strange misgivings and mingled feelings to whole communities.

References to the divine bull of the Celts can be carried very far back. In the Banquet of the Sophists by Athenaeus, Ulpien, one of the interlocutors, speaking of the tiger, cites a verse from one of the lost comedies of Philemon, who, at the age of 99, died in 262 B.C.:

ὥσπερ Σέλευκος δεῦρ᾽ ἔπεμψε τὴν τίγριν
ἣν ἴδομεν ἡμεῖς τῷ Σελεύκῳ πάλιν ἔδει
ἡμᾶς τι παρ᾽ ἡμῶν ἀντιπέμψαι θηρίον
τρυγέρανον· οὐ γὰρ γίγνεται τοῦτ᾽ αὐτόθι.
Athenaeus, xiii. 57, p. 590 A.

I.e. as Seleucus has brought hither the tiger which we have seen, we ought to send him back some animal in exchange, a trugeranos; there are none there. This, as Monsieur J. Vendryes has pointed out, is simply the Gaulish Trigaranos, an epithet of the divine Tarvos, à trois grues, which figures on the altar of Notre Dame at Paris and on the bas-relief of Treves (Revue Celtique, 28, 124). The king referred to is Seleucus Nicator, one of the successors of Alexander the Great; having visited the confines of India he met the famous prince, Chandragupta, and brought back, in addition to some five hundred elephants, some exotic animals such as tigers, to which he fell a prey in the city of Athens. The Gauls about this time were invading Macedonia and Thrace; they were checked at Delphi in 279. The fear of the Gauls,—ὁ ἀπὸ Γαλατῶν φόβος,—was become proverbial; a decree of the year 278 B.C., discovered in the ruins of the Asklepeion at Cos, expresses the joy caused in the island by the tidings of the Gaulish defeat, and prescribes a festival in honour of Apollo, of Zeus Soter and of Nikē in celebration of the event.

The Celts had made three different expeditions in the Orient, and in the age of Alexander some of them were in contact with Greek civilisation; the Greeks recovered some booty from their enemy, and it would have been an easy matter probably to have seen in the Celtic camp some such symbolic representations as are to be met with on the altar of Notre Dame at Paris, or on the bas-relief of Treves,—figured emblems of the Celtic Tarvos Trigaranos. A creature so bizarre was bound to excite curiosity among a people who noted that a Gaulish word for horse was marca (cf. Gaelic marcach, rider'), and whose Pausanias describes the τριμαρκισία or group of three cavaliers fighting in unison.

That reverence was paid to the bull among the Celts is indicated by the frequency of river-names signifying 'bull'; for instance, the river Tarf, whence Abertarff, Gaelic Obair-thairbh, in Stratherrick, Inverness-shire; while Tarf is a stream name in the shires of Perth, Forfar, Kirkcudbright, Wigton. These Tarf names go back to Pictish times. Rivers of old were held in holy reverence: witness names like Boyne, *bo-vinda, 'white-cow,' appearing in legend as a personal female name; Dee; Aberdeen, G. Obair-dhea'on, 'the mouth or inver of the Devona,' a goddess-name; Affric, a river name, older Aithbhrecc, a female name Affrica, and suitable as a nymph name, which is also the case with Ness, from Pictish; [179] Lōchy, the 'nigra dea,' or black goddess of Adamnan's Life of Columba. The early human attitude may be inferred from what is told regarding the Kaffirs asking permission of a river ere profaning it by crossing it. The Roman bridge-builder or pontifex was the intermediary between the divinity and man, hence our pontiff; cf. Virgil's pontem indignatus Araxes. The old Celt Viridomaros thought himself descended from the Rhine.

One meets also with the name Rhenogenos, 'born of the Rhine' god. Certain of the Gaulish inhabitants plunged their newly-born infants into its waters; if they survived the ordeal it was a token of their being protected by the common ancestor. Gaulish inscriptions likewise testify that rivers were the objects of a cult: e.g. DEÆ SEQVAÆ (the Seine), DEÆ ICAUNI (the Yonne). [180] In Scotland, too, the river names are mostly pre-Christian and testify to their having been looked on with more than sacred awe. Almost all of them have legends such as Hugh Miller tells of the water-wraith of the Conon River in his Schools and Schoolmasters, and Dr. Walter Gregor, of the water-spirit of Donside. Scott in his Journal (23rd Nov., 1827) tells of an attempt to bait the water-cow, while Mr. Dixon in his Gairloch (p. 162) tells a very similar story. A plaid has several times been made an offering to the water-spirit of the Dee, Aberdeenshire, which levied a heavy toll on human life, if we believe the rhyme:

Blood-thirsty Dee
Each year needs three,
But bonny Don
She needs non.

There are traces of a custom of throwing salt over the water and the nets to propitiate the Fairies of the Tweed. In Scott's Pirate we find the belief that whoever rescues a drowning man incurs the monster's wrath by cheating him of his victim: perhaps from this idea we may infer the belief, prevalent in the Highlands, in the unluck sure to come to the family of the man who is the first to find a victim of drowning: the unluck follows from robbing the spirit of the waters of its victim. The legends of water-horses in Loch Ness and in the Beauly River, indeed in all considerable streams, point to the spirit of the raging flood as an external soul in the waters. [181] Indeed, other river names, such as Ness, Don, Nevis, Annan, go back to early Celtic nomenclature, which reveals them to be names of nymphs, especially divine water-nymphs.

One of the altars discovered at Paris in 1710, under the apsis of the Church of Notre Dame, has four interesting carvings, which represent:

1. Jupiter, in standing posture, holding a sceptre in his left hand, which is raised, the left side being covered with a tunic, which leaves the right shoulder exposed. To the right of the god, on the ground, is placed an eagle. The frame-work above the figure bears the inscription IOVIS.

2. Vulcan, in upright posture, clothed in working tunic, leaving the right side exposed, as also the lower left arm. The left hand holds or grips a tongs. The figure is inscribed VOLCANUS.

3. A woodcutter, clad in a tunic similar to Vulcan's, is shown as holding in his right hand, which is raised, an axe with which he is to give a blow to

some stems on the gnarled trunk, while in his left hand he holds one of the branches. Inscribed above is ESVS.

4. A bull carrying on his back a dorsal covering above which is a tree, the foliage of which is the same as that on the tree in figure 3—in fact, the foliage of the tree seems to be portrayed here as in continuation of the preceding scene. On the bull's head is placed a crane, while two other cranes are portrayed back to back on the animal's croup. Above is the inscription TARVOS TRIGARANVS.

In December, 1895, there was discovered on the left bank of the Moselle, above Trèves, on the road leading to Luxembourg and to Metz, another interesting sculpture, the first publication of which is due to Lehner in the Korrespondenzblatt der Westdeutschen Zeitschrift for 1896. It appeared next in the issue for 1897 of the Bonner Jahrbücher, and was carefully discussed by the celebrated savant, M. Salomon Reinach, in the Revue Celtique for that year. Though in very bad preservation, the monument seems to have been an altar-piece. One face of this sculpture portrays the Mercury and Rosmerta of the Gauls, according to Reinach. Beneath it is. inscribed:

NDVS MEDIOM ·
MERCVRIO V · VS

which Lehner has restored thus: Indus Mediomatricus Mercurio votum libens merito (?) solvit. The face to the right is well preserved and shows, but on a much smaller scale than that on the principal face, a figure of a man, probably beardless, clothed in a short tunic; he holds in his hands the handle of a long implement which he is about to drive into a tree. This tree, the denticulated leaves of which call to mind the foliage on the altar found at Paris, supports a bull's head on the left; and three great birds, [182] with long beak, are on the right thereof. We are in the presence of a representation of the same scene as is depicted on the altar of Notre Dame—it shows us the woodcutter, the tree, the bull, and the three cranes—with the sole difference that Esus and the Tarvos Trigaranos are depicted on one piece instead of on two, as in the other case. This tree, the foliage of which recalls that of the willow, is an essential element in the representation. The more one considers the bas-relief of Trèves, the more readily does one agree with Monsieur Reinach's conclusion that there exists a relation between the tree and the woodman, and the bull with the three cranes;

that instead of four isolated figures, Vulcan, Jupiter, Esus, and Tarvos Trigaranos, of the altar at Paris, there are only three figures symbolised,— Esus and Tarvos Trigaranos being elements of one scene though shown in juxtaposition.

Reinach points out that the bull often personifies the forces of the sun and of the waters, and thinks that the god-bull prepared for sacrifice (Notre Dame) and shown as slaughtered at Trèves, may be the Gaulish Belenos, the Celtic Apollo-Hélios (Cultes, iii. 177).

The bull on the Trèves bas-relief is seemingly but an attribute in the scene of which the tree is the central and basic symbol. The bull represents some divinity conceived as inhabiting a tree: we have, in a word, a primitive representation of the tree-soul animating a tree which is about to be felled by some semi-divine hero known in legend surviving among, though not necessarily original to, the Celts. Or if among a Celtic people, it may have formed part of legendary belief among the forerunners of the Gauls, to wit, the Ligurians, whose speech has been called Celtican by Rhŷs, [183] who has essayed recently to show it as most closely allied to Gadhelic. The Highland survival of the Boobrie has much that may be traced to a common origin with the root idea symbolised in bas-relief at Paris and at Trèves, and I see no reason why one might not expect to find among Gadhelic survivals some close parallels to the idea at the root of the tree-cutter portrayed on these reliefs. Hirschfield has agreed that certain Pyrenean gods of a non-Iberian type are to be attributed to the Ligurian predecessors of the Celts, or, as I should prefer to say, of the Gauls: he instances the oak-god (Fagus deus, the translation of the name of a local god), the gods Sexarbor, Sexarbores, and the nameless god on some coniferous tree represented on an altar found at Toulouse. [184] Esus, on the Paris altar, may have been the local name in that district, and not at all Pan-Celtic. D'Arbois has tried to make out a close parallel for Cuchulainn. The primary creation of the root ideas in this myth may be due to precursors of the Celts alike in Gaul and Ireland, but they point to early tree-worship, and to survivals of dendrolatry among the Celts. May we not infer with Reinach the idea of a cosmic tree and of a cosmic bull? Maximus of Tyre relates that the Celts worshipped Zeus under the image of an oak—δρῦς ἄγαλμα Δίος—and Claudian in his praise of Stilicho says of Celtdom: robora Numinis instar barbarici. M. Reinach recalls the ideas associated with the Scandinavian Yggdrasil or world-ash, in the branches of which, as it covered the universe, sat an eagle cognisant of all things, while a serpent gnawed at the root. The parallel to the semi-divine wood-cutter is met with in the Kalevala and in the legends of Esthonia, in which a dwarf becomes transformed into a giant and fells the tree that obscured the light of sun and moon, shaking at its fall the whole heavens and earth. The bull appears in Gaulish art of the Hallstatt and Là Tène periods, and symbolises a religious idea at the stage when religious expression is at one with the myth. The legend, which associates a semi-divine hero with the cutting down of the tree which supports a bull with three cranes, must be of great antiquity among the Celts, and in some way emblemises, how rudely soever, the presence which pervades all thought and things. Certain of the Greeks expressed this when they conceived Dionysos, not only as tutelary divinity of the tree, but as in the tree, ἔνδενδρος, παρὰ Ῥοδίοις Ζεὺς καὶ Δίονυσος ἐν Βοιωτίᾳ—a gloss of Hesychius. As to a connection between death or transformation and eating the flesh of cranes, compare the obscure formula in West Highland Tales (i. 240); to cause the death of one who has lived too long it suffices to call thrice through the keyhole: "Wish you to go or wish you to stay, or wish you to eat the flesh of cranes?"

Nor need the fact of the divine bull being prominent in Celtic belief surprise us. Elsewhere the bull, as the source of all wealth among a people of shepherds and hunters, became the object of religious veneration. "In the eyes of such a people the capture of a wild bull was an achievement so highly fraught with honour as to be apparently no derogation even for a god." Thus the bull-slaying Mithra, dragged along on the horns of the infuriated animal, was transformed until his painful journey became the symbol of human sufferings. "But the bull, it would appear, succeeded in making its escape from its prison, and roamed again at large over the mountain pastures." The sun then sent the raven, his messenger, to carry to his ally the command to slay the fugitive. Mithra received this cruel mission much against his will, but submitting to the decree of heaven he pursued the truant beast with his agile dog, succeeded in overtaking it just at the moment when it was taking refuge in the cave which it had quitted. and seizing it by the nostrils with one hand, with the other he plunged deep into its flank his 'hunting knife.' [185] In the Mithraic religion, as Justin tells us, there was a 'baptism for the remission of sins': the bull being the recognised emblem of life, its blood constituted the recognised laver of regeneration. In the rite known as Blood-Baptism or Taurobolia, the person to be initiated, being stripped of all clothing, went into a pit covered with planks pierced full of holes, whereupon the hot blood of a newly-slaughtered bull was allowed down through the apertures, as in a shower bath, upon the person to be regenerated. To judge from the statement of Lampridius that the priest-emperor Heliogabalus submitted to it, the rite must have been an important one, and a pit for the purpose has been discovered within the precincts of the temple at Eleusis in Greece.

The Celtic personal name, Donno-taurus, 'noble-bull' (lord-bull), mentioned by Caesar, may contain a word cognate with Irish donn, explained in O'Davoren's Glossary by 'noble, judge, king,' and may come, according to Stokes, from *domno-s, and be cognate with L. dominus, 'lord, master.' [186] This is most probably the same word that meets us in Donn, the name of the divine bull located in the Irish epic at Cualnge (Cooley). In course of time it easily got confused with an entirely different word, donn, 'dun.' In referring to this latter, de Jubainville seems to have forgotten the former word. [187]

To the Donn Cualnge one perhaps might compare the Minotaure, which also had a divine origin, its father having been a bull given by Poseidon to Minos, and its mother Pasiphae, daughter of the sun. During the Athenian war Minos exacted as a condition of peace that each year there should be sent to Crete seven youths and seven young maidens to be devoured by the Minotaure. The Minotaure was killed by Theseus, as we learn from Pherecydes. It has been suggested [188] that the legend of Pasiphae and the Minotaure contains a reminiscence of a marriage ceremony in which the King and Queen of Cnossos figured in the disguise of a bull and cow respectively. Marrying a queen to a bull-god was portrayed by marrying her to a man disguised as a bull. The vine-god Dionysos was annually married to a queen at a building on the N.E. slope of the Acropolis at Athens, named the Cattle-Stall, whence Miss Harrison [189] conjectured that Dionysos may have been represented as a bull at the marriage. "In that case the part of the bridegroom might be played by a man wearing a bull's head, just as in Egypt in similar rites the sacred animals were represented by men and women wearing the masks of cows, hawks, crocodiles, and so forth." [190]

I recall the wake orgy in Ireland mentioned by Lady Wilde, in which a bull is married to a cow; compare Calluinn a' Bhuilg ceremonies in the Highlands, wherein a hide figures. Add for Britain perhaps the Hobby Horse at Padstow.

Minos is suspected of having been murdered every nine years; his death was a secret. His going into the Labyrinth is equivalent to going into the

Bull god's cave. [191] On Gadhelic ground, when the Donn or Brown Bull of Cualnge triumphed over its rival the Find Bennach, it soon after died itself of its wounds, but paralleling the cruelty of the Minotaure it killed one hundred infants, or two-thirds of the one hundred and fifty children that came in groups of fifty to enjoy themselves after mid-day on its great and glossy back. [192]

M. D'Arbois de Jubainville regards the Tarvos Trigaronos, now in the museum at Cluny, as identical with the Donn Cualnge, and further, the personage called Esus, who is about to apply his axe to the tree, appears to him identical with the hero Cuchulainn, who is portrayed as felling trees to arrest the march of the forces of Queen Medb: [193] "At one blow Cuchulainn cut the chief stem of an oak, root and branch."

Again, Cuchulainn's divine father was Lug of the Long Hand, already referred to, and well remembered in Celtic myth. The name appears often in Gaul, for instance in the place-name Lugudunum, now Lyons, also in Leyden. His cult was widely diffused, to judge from the name being met with in the plural Lugoues, Lugouibus, on inscriptions, one from Switzerland, another from Spain. He was the Gaulish Mercury in Caesar's time who speaks of him as the inventor of all the arts. The Irish Lug, according to the account in the 'Second Battle of Moytura,' [194] was skilful as poet, warrior, physician, sorcerer, harpist, poet, and to him is given the epithet of 'master of all the arts.' Balor of the evil eye received his death at the hand of Lug, who thereupon is accorded the sovereignty of the Tuatha dé Danann on the death of Nuada their king. [195] In the effort at filling up pre-Christian history, the Annalists of course make him figure as king in Ireland. I agree with M. D'Arbois in regarding Lug, in his continental aspects, as having been chief among the gods of Gaul, the god whom Caesar identified with Mercury: Deum maxime Mercurium colunt. [196] The Mercury of the menhir of Kervadel, now preserved at Kernuz, D'Arbois identifies with Lug, while he recalls the exploit of Cuchulainn's youth when, on having slain the hound of Culann the Smith, he offered reparation by taking guard himself, on which account his name was changed from the Setanta (older form *Setantios?) of his boyhood to Cú-chulainn, Hound of Culann. The name Setanta is not Gadhelic: it existed probably among the Picts of Ulidia, and was an ethnic name in Britain,—the Setantii were a tribe near the River Mersey in Ptolemy's day. Among the near Gaulish kinsmen of the British tribes the god may have been simply designated by a personal epithet or title such as Esus, 'master, lord,' the name of the god on the altar-piece of

Notre Dame now in the Museum of Cluny. Cuchulainn alone was exempted from the malady which befell the Ultonian heroes during the war of the Tāin, but at last there came a moment when, weary and fatigued with wounds, he felt unable to endure any longer. His hero's call was answered by the appearance of a wondrous warrior whom the Book of the Dun depicts as saying: "I come to succour thee, I am thy father come from the abode of the gods, I am Lug the son of Ethniu." If we examine the menhir of Kervadel in the light of comparative Celtic myth, it is most probable that it depicts the Gaulish Mercury and his avatar or son, in other words Lug (Lugos) and Esus. M. D'Arbois would go even further, and suggests that the myth of Cuchulainn and the story now worked up into the Tāin may have been brought from Britain by the Druids, who were there taught the existing lore at a time when as yet the story had not been entirely localised in Erin. But I cannot think that we are justified in assuming an entire absence of at least parallel tales in Gaul itself. The P-group of similar speaking tribes would have much in common, including what they may have imbibed from their predecessors of the Q-group, the Gadhelic Celts. For we must pre-suppose a time when both groups were not as yet, in their continental home, foreign to one another.

THE WANDERINGS OF PSYCHE (PART 3)

(g) The Water-horse (cf. the Boobrie as water-horse in a preceding section).—After the bull one thinks next of the water-horse, which is not, at least in all its phases, to be classified under the theriomorphic-soul. For in part it goes back on nature-myth, and is perhaps a personification of the destroying waters. A portion of this phase belongs to the Celtic Dragon-Myth, which is a water-myth in so far as some aspects of the monster met with is concerned. It would be difficult to say what lochs in the Highlands were formerly not associated with the water-horse. A linne na badhbh is met with in many places. The Black Glen river in Morvern was once the resort of a water-horse. A recent writer says:

"In Arisaig there is a loch, which, according to tradition, there lived at one time a sea-horse. Boswell, in his Journal of Johnson's Tour to the Hebrides, informs us that an old man told the following fabulous story of one of the lochs of Raasay:

"There was once a wild beast in it, a sea-horse, which came and devoured a man's daughter, upon which the man lighted a great fire and had a sow roasted in it, the smell of which attracted the monster. In the fire was put a spit. The man lay concealed behind a low wall of loose stones. The monster came, and the man with the red hot spit destroyed it.

"It is reported that a horse used to frequent the road near Loch Ness, till a stout, brave Highlander, meeting the monster one night, drew his sword in the name of the Trinity, and finished the supposed kelpie forever. Hugh Miller relates some very weird stories about the uncanny doings of a sea-horse or water-wraith that frequented the waters of the River Conon, Ross-shire. The Black Glen kelpie very early one morning was seen near the source of the river, making very unusual sounds. After a little while it left the waters of the river altogether; and at last, with fearful bellowings, it ran in the direction of Loch Uisge and Kingair-loch, and has neither been seen nor heard of any more to this day.

"This glen also used to be much frequented by wild boars and wolves. Owing to its evil reputation in this respect, people were afraid to pass through the glen."

For the water-bull in the Isle of Man, see Moore's Folk-Lore of the Isle of Man (p. 59). And for Scotland, the Rev. J. G. Campbell's Superstitions.

In many districts we are told of "the lurking place of the water-horse, which, under the form of a handsome youth, won and kept a maiden's heart until, by chance, she found him asleep on the hillock where they were wont to meet, and on bending over him noticed a bunch of rushes in his hair. Then she knew with what she had to deal, and fled in terror to her father's house, reaching it just in time to bar the door in the kelpie's face, whose voice she heard crying:

Ann an là 's bliadhna,
Mo bhean òg, thig mi dh' iarraidh.

In a day and a year,
I'll come seeking my dear.

So she was warned never to go near the hillock again; her parents found her a more eligible suitor; and all went well till her wedding day, when on leaving the church after the ceremony was over, a big black horse came suddenly upon them, seized the bridle and galloped off with her. Since that time no one has ever seen the horse or its burden, unless, indeed, at the fall of night, some passer-by catches a glimpse of a white face rising out of the water, and hears a low sweet voice croon the love song she was singing when first she saw her kelpie lover."

I give two accounts which I have from the late Rev. Allan Macdonald of Eriskay. They indicate how universal this folk-belief was in the Highlands:

"Water-horse.—There was a young woman in Barra who met a handsome looking man on the hill. They chatted together, and at last he laid his head on her lap. She noticed when he slept that his hair was mixed with 'rafagach an locha,' a weed that grows in lakes, and she became suspicious that her friend was the water-horse in disguise. She cut off the part of her clothes on which his head rested, and slipped away without wakening him. A considerable time after, on a Sunday after Mass, a number of people were sitting on the hill and she along with them. She noticed the stranger whom she had met on the hill approaching, and she got up to go home so as to avoid him. He made up to her, notwithstanding, and caught her, and hurried off and plunged with her into the lake, and not a trace of her was ever found but a little bit of one of her lungs on the shore of the lake.—Anne M'Intyre."

"In the island of Mingulay a young woman had a similar adventure, only in her case the stranger appeared often to her, and they became at last so fond of each other that they agreed to marry at the end of a year and a day, and till then the stranger was not to be seen by her. The girl went home, and as the year was drawing to an end, she was observed to be fast sinking in health and losing her good colour, yet she would not say what it was that made her fall away so. Her father at last extorted an unwilling confession of the truth from her, and word was given to the islanders as to what was causing the girl such trouble. She was very beautiful and a great favourite, and when the people heard what was to happen to her, they made up their minds that they would allow no harm befall her. When the day came all the men of the place were armed with clubs, and the young woman was put sitting on the wall of the house,—the young men forming a guard round the house. All were in a state of expectancy when the stranger was seen appearing above the great cliff of Mingulay and coming down swiftly towards the village. One of the islanders stepped forward to meet the stranger and asked him his errand. 'Such as it is,' said the stranger, 'you are not the man to stand in my way, strong though you be, and you may as well not detain me.' He went forward and reached the guard round the house, and, in the twinkling of an eye, seized the young woman by the hand, and, before the guard had made up their minds to pursue him and rescue the girl, he had so far retraced his way with his prize. The islanders started in pursuit, but in vain. They saw him and the woman disappear at a certain well, and when they reached this the well was full of blood and of shreds of her garments. The well is still called 'Tobar na Fala' = the well of blood.—Calum Dhomhnuill, 1895."

(h) The Soul in Serpent-form.—I will illustrate by a story: A man and wife in Ardnamurchan went out to the hill for heather. When tired pulling it the wife lay down and slept. The husband sat down, and when his eyes were about to close, on looking towards his wife he saw a serpent disappearing down her mouth. He wakened her and they went home, but he did not tell her what he had seen. On getting home he went to the doctor, who advised him to feed his wife well and to give her plenty flesh meat, so that the serpent, getting sufficient food in this way, might not begin to gnaw herself. The woman was surprised at the change in her fare, and she ate well. In due course she was delivered of a child, and round the child's neck was coiled the serpent.

The true members of the Clan Iver, says Principal Mac Iver-Campbell in his Memoir of Clan Iver, were supposed to be invulnerable to serpents: he quotes a rhyme supposed to have been uttered by a serpent or adder:

Mhionnaich mise do Chlann Imheair
S mhionnaich Clann Imheair dhomh,
Nach beanainn-se do Chlann Imheair
'S nach beanadh Clann Imheair dhomh,

i.e., 'I have sworn to Clan Iver and Clan Iver have sworn to me, that I would not injure Clan Iver and that Clan Iver would not injure me.' As another explanation, Principal MacIver-Campbell thought the lines commemorated an alliance between Clan Iver and some race symbolised by the serpent with "every probability that the alliance referred to is that which is known to have existed between the MacIvers in Perthshire and the Clan Donnachaidh or Robertsons, one of whose cognisances was the serpent which still appears as one of the supporters in the arms of their chief, Robertson of Strowan." Another form of the rhyme he gives thus:

Latha an Fhéille-Bríde
Their an nathair as an tom:
Cha bhi mise ri Nic Imheair,
'S cha mho bhios Nic Imheair rium,

i.e. 'On St. Brigit's Day the serpent will say from off the knoll: I will not injure Nic Imheair, neither will Nic Imheair injure me.' In Skye at least I have heard of these lines having been repeated on St. Brigit's Day, the woman doing so having placed a burning peat in one of her stockings, and pounding at it the while on the threshold of the outer door (a specially sacred place) as a precaution against the entrance of evil spirits. The Clan Iver are of Norse origin, [197] but whatever the origin of this belief I am satisfied it is a phase of manism in the wide sense. MacIver-Campbell was in his day Principal of Aberdeen University, and related to Campbell, the poet of The Pleasures of Hope and of Hohenlinden. At a time when totemism was not as yet much thought about, he notes as one interested in family origins and crests that certain animals were symbolical of particular clans: the magpie as friendly to the Campbells (for its wearing argent and sable, the old Campbell colours?), the horse a symbol or friend of the MacIvers of Glassary. Further, there were certain nick-names, e.g.:

Crodh maol Chnapadail,
Eich chlòimheach Ghlasairigh,
Fithich dhubh Chraiginnis,
Is Coilich Airigh Sceodnis,

i.e., 'The polled oxen of Cnapdale, the shaggy horses of Glassary, the black ravens of Craignish, the cocks of Airigh Sceodnish, meaning the folk of these parts.'

It is proper to add, however, that another variant of the serpent rhyme typifies the serpent as queen: Là fhéille Brìghde thig an rìghinn as an tom, i.e. 'On St. Bride's (Brigit's) Day the queen will come from the knoll,' and its association with the act of pounding a burning peat on the threshold [198] involuntarily reminds one of the Siberian 'Fiery Snake' or zagovor (invoked for kindling amorous longing), with which has been compared the folk-belief that with the beginning of every January—i.e. at the end of the festival in honour of the return of the sun towards summer—the Fiery Snake begins to fly, enters into the izbá through the chimney, turns into a brave youth and steals by magic the hearts of fair maidens. In a Servian song a girl who has been carried off by a 'fiery-snake' calls herself his 'true love,' and it is thought that in mythical language the 'Fiery Snake' is one of the forms of the lightning. "The blooming earth, fructified by the rains poured forth during the first spring storms, is turned in the myth into the bride of the Fiery Snake. But the wedder of nature became looked upon at a later period as the patron of weddings among the children of men, and so the inducing of love-pangs naturally became ascribed to the Fiery Snake." [199] This explanation is founded upon nature-myth, but on Celtic ground I incline to postulate ancestor worship, if not by the Celts, on the part of pre-Celtic tribes in Britain. There is a serpent mound in Glenelg, on the way to Scalasaig Farm; also in Lorne; there are serpents figured on some stones; and a folk-cure for serpent bite is to wash the parts with water in which a serpent's head has been boiled. On a Gaulish altar of the first century of our era there is sculptured a serpent with a ram's head. We may perhaps infer a serpent-totem among the Gauls. [200] Greek vase-paintings portray the occupants of graves in the form of snakes. [201] In Virgil we meet Aeneas pouring libations on his father's tomb, when a gorgeous serpent appeared, either the genius of the place or an attendant on his father in the other world:

Silent, amazed stood Aeneas; but the serpent its long length trailing
Glided among the cups and the polished vessels of service,
Tasted the viands and back to the depths of the tomb receded,
Mindless of harm and left the tasted food and the altars.
Aeneid, v. 90-93.

One parallel from the lower cults will show that the belief in the serpent-soul may be very real:

"In S. Africa the dead may re-appear in the form of animals, but only for pure mischief. Widows are often held in bondage and terror by their lords returning in the guise of a serpent. This brute will enter the house, hide in the thatch, and look at its victim from between the rafters. It will coil itself by the fire and steal into the beds; it will glide over articles of food and explore the interior of cooking utensils. For this persistent persecution there is but one remedy, and that is to kill the serpent, when there is nothing left but 'pure spirit,' which cannot appear in material form any more." [202]

(i) The Soul in Wolf-form.—The existence of this belief in animal parentage is seen from the Leabhar Breathnach. Here we read: "The descendants of the wolf are in Ossory (síl in Faelchon i n-Osraigib). There are certain people in Eri, viz. the race of Laighne Faelaidh, in Ossory; they pass into the form of wolves whenever they please, and kill cattle according to the custom of wolves, and they quit their own bodies; when they go forth in the wolf-forms they charge their friends not to remove their bodies, for if they are moved they will not be able to come again into them (their bodies); and if they are wounded while abroad, the same wounds will be on their bodies in their houses; and the raw flesh devoured while abroad will be in their teeth." [203] This belief was current in the days of Fynes Moryson, who mentions the report that in Upper Ossory and Ormond men are yearly turned. into wolves. And long before then Gerald, the Welsh-man, had heard a story of two wolves who had been a man and woman of the Ossorians. They were transformed into wolves every seven years through a curse imposed by St. Naal or Natalis, abbot of Kilmanagh,

Kilkenny, in the sixth century. They were banished to Meath, where they met a priest in a wood, shortly ere Earl John came to Ireland in the days of Henry II. They retained the use of language and were fabled with having foretold the invasion of the foreigner. The Latin legend declares the substance of what the wolf said to the priest: "A certain sept of the men of Ossory are we; every seventh year through the curse of St. Natalis the Abbot, we two, man and woman, are compelled to leave our shape and our bounds." Then having been divested of human form, animal form is assumed. Having completed their seven years, should they survive so long, if two other Ossorians be substituted instead of these, the former return to their pristine form and fatherland.

In personal and tribal names the wolf meets us, e.g. Cinel Loairn, whence modern Lorne in Argyll, after which is named the marquisate in the ducal family, from Gadhelic Loarn, 'wolf.' In Ireland it is told of Laignech Fáelad that he was the man "that used to shift into wolf-shapes. He and his offspring after him used to go whenever they pleased, into the shapes of the wolves, and, after the custom of wolves, kill the herds. Wherefore he was called Laignech Fáelad, for he was the first of them to go into a wolf-shape." [204]

The Celtic god Dis Pater, from whom, according to Caesar's account, the Gauls were descended, is represented as clad in wolf-skin, and holding a vessel, also a mallet with a long shaft, which, Monsieur Reinach thinks, recalls the image of the Etruscan Charon. "A low-relief at Sarrebourg, in Lorraine," says this eminent authority, "proves that one of the epithets of this Gaulish god was Sucellus, signifying 'one who strikes well.'" The wolf skin leads to the presumption that the god was originally a wolf, roving and ravaging during the night time. This god has been identified with the Latin Silvanus, the woodman or forester who gave chase to the wolves—of old a wolf himself. On this view, which M. Reinach favours, at least a section of the Gauls had a national legend identical with that of the Romans: like Romulus they were the children of the wolf, and M. Reinach suggests that perhaps it was on this account that the Arverni called themselves brethren of the Latins. [205] If so, we have a close parallel to Gadhelic tradition.

Spenser says that "some of the Irish doe use to make the wolf their gossip"; and Camden adds that they term them "Chari Christi, praying for them, and wishing them well, and having contracted this intimacy, professed to have no fear from their four-footed allies." Fynes Moryson expressly mentions the popular dislike to killing wolves. Aubrey adds that "in Ireland they value the fang-tooth of an wolfe, which they set in silver and gold as we doe ye Coralls." [206]

At Claddagh there is a local saint, Mac Dara, whose real name according to folk-belief was Sinach, 'a fox,' [207] a probably non-Aryan name. The Irish onchú, 'leopard,' also 'standard,' whence G. onnchon, 'standard,' from French onceau, once, 'a species of jaguar,' seems preserved in Wester Ross with the change of n to r, as o'r chu, written odhar chu, in the sense of 'wolf': the howl of the creature thus named inspired the natives of old with a fear and awe which had their origin in days when the wolf prowled of evenings among the flocks.

(j) The Soul in Dog-form.—The dog is taboo in almost the whole of Europe: it was a totem animal; and to eat tabooed food brings down the anger of the spirits. The occurrence of dog-names among the Celts, such as Cu-roi, Cu-chulainn would lead one to include this phase likewise among the transformations of the soul. Eating of dog flesh was forbidden Cuchulainn, and the breaking of the taboo brought him death. The West Mayo tradition quoted above, under section (e), states that Oisin was half-brother to Bran, Fionn's Hound; that Bran was the daughter of Fionn by a lady who came to him as an enchanted hound. There are names of animal origin to be met with among Highland surnames, e.g. Matheson is MacMhathain, older Macmaghan, 'son of the bear'; Mac-Culloch is Mac-Culloch, 'son of the boar.' Though wild stories of supernatural dogs, such as the Black Dog of Kinlochbervie and the wild black dog with fiery eyes that came from the river at Eskadale may be now ascribed in folk-lore to demonic influence, yet the demon at an earlier stage is an aspect of the theriomorphic soul. Cuilean, 'whelp,' is used in the Highlands as a form of endearment. The black dog (Manx: Moddey Doo, Manthe Doo) that was seen at Peel Castle, Isle of Man, was believed to be an evil spirit, which only waited permission to do the soldiers hurt, and for that reason they forbore swearing and all profane discourse while in its company. [208] None of them liked to be left alone with such a companion. Now as the Manthe Doog used to come out and return by the passage through the church, by which one of the men had to go to deliver the keys every night to the captain on duty, the men used to do the duty in couples, and never would a man do it alone. One of the soldiers, however, on a certain night, having taken more drink than was good for him, insisted on going with the keys alone, although it was not his turn. His comrades in vain tried to dissuade him from what they felt to be a dangerous and foolhardy freak. Some time afterwards a great noise disturbed the men in the guard-house, and, while they were sitting wondering and awe-stricken, the adventurous soldier broke in upon them. He was inarticulate with horror and fright. He could not even make signs to convey to his comrades what had happened to him. The man was distracted, mentally paralysed, and in an hour or two he died, with his features distorted, obviously in mental agony. After this no one would go through the passage, which was soon closed up. The apparition was never seen again!

(k) The Soul in Seal-form.—For an account of this phase the reader is referred to my Norse Influence on Celtic Scotland. It is unlucky to kill the seal: it is a human being under spells.

(l) Boar-form.--The association of Diarmad's death with his act of measuring the poisonous boar against the bristle leads to an inference that the hero's life was bound up with that of the boar. Yet here there might be another explanation. But the fact that swine's blood is held to be a sovereign cure for warts by laving the parts therein, along with the great aversion to eating pork in any form which I have met with in old Highlanders, seems to point to swine as sacred. The Gauls had a god Succellos, from *sukku, 'a pig.' In Campbell's West Highland Tales there is an obsolete phrase an t-sreath chuileanach, left untranslated: it should read 'an treith chuileanach s a dà chuilean deug,' i.e. 'the mother sow with her litter of twelve.' See Cormac's Glossary, sub Orc treth. Ultimately the word seems the same as triath, 'lord, chief,' from *treitos, which Stokes compared with L. tritavos, an ancestor in the sixth degree. The Turc Trwyth of Welsh romance and emblems on the so-called Boar-stones are probably in origin to be derived from a belief in kinship with the boar.

A story is told of a he-goat having been seen very often in a certain part of the islands and of people who met with violence and sometimes with death when they came to the spot frequented by him. There was a suspicion that the goat was only a form assumed by a weaver (breabadair) in the place. A man called at the weaver's one day on his way through the country. The weaver asked where he was going to. The man told him. The weaver asked if he were not afraid of passing the spot where the goat was seen,—a spot fatal to many. The man replied that he was not, that he bore his help on his hip ('tha cobhair chruachainn agam'). When he came to the spot the goat stood above him and began to attack him. The man was being worsted when the goat said: 'Cà 'eil do chobhair air chruachainn a nisd?' 'Where is the help on your hip now?' The man replied as he drew forth a dagger he had on his hip: "'S ann air a chuimhne bha'n diùlanas,' 'It was thy memory that had the fortitude.' He killed the goat, and when he returned to the weaver's house the blood of the weaver had frozen ('bha fuil a' bhreabadair air reothadh').—Hugh M'Lennan, Dec. 7, 1895.

(m) The Soul in Semi-theriomorphic Form.—Here the transition is made to the half-human aspect of the soul in god-form. Creatures of the imagination which have their basis in nature-myth, e.g. the glaistig, the Bodach Glas, Peallaidh, perhaps the Gruagach, and such as the Ūruisg, are not to be included here. In point are the demons which were said to haunt particular families as their good or evil genius. The family of Rothiemurchus was said to have been haunted by Bodach an Dūin, the Goblin or Ghost of the Dūne; the Baron of Kinchardine's family by Red Hand (Lāmh Dhearg), or a 'ghost,' one of whose hands was bloody red; Gartinbeg by Bodach-Gartin; Glenlochie by Brownie, as was also Belladrum House; Tullochgorm by Māg Molach, i.e. Hairy Hand or 'one with the left hand all over hairy,' as Lachlan Shaw's History of the Province of Moray put it. "I find," says Shaw, "in the Synod Records of Moray, frequent orders to the Presbyteries of Aberlaure and Abernethie, to enquire into the truth of Maag Moulach's appearing. But they could make no discovery, only that one or two men declared they once saw in the evening a young girl whose left hand was all hairy, and who instantly disappeared." [209] This famous apparition is referred to also in the Laird of Macfarlane's Geographical Collections. Hairy Hand was supposed to come down the chimney and to take children away. The nearest parallel I find in the Russian Domovy, an hirsute creature the whole of whose body save the eyes and nose is covered with hair. The tracks of his shaggy feet may be seen in winter time in the snow; his hairy hand is felt by night gliding over the faces of sleepers. [210] The Domovy is the house-spirit, and specially haunts the stove; the cultus was connected with the burning fire on the domestic hearth. In the Highlands too the hearth-fire is held in awe, as witness the fact that it is forbidden to pass between an epileptic and the fire; to do so was to draw upon one's self the disease.

The names given to some appearances show us gods in the making, as when in Inverness-shire the small-pox is called The Good Wife (A' Bhean Mhath), and the Devil is elsewhere euphemistically spoken of as Caomhan, 'the dear one, darling.' Among Greeks and Slays small-pox is personified as a female; the Servians call her bogine or goddess. The conception of the

Hairy Hand of the Highlands is met with to a fuller extent in the Fynnodderee of the Isle of Man; the word 'satyr' of Isaiah xxxiv. 14 is rendered in the Manx Bible as yn Phynnodderree; the name signifies 'the hairy-dun one,' and this satyr is conceived as "something between a man and a beast, being covered with black shaggy hair and having fiery eyes"; he is prodigiously strong, is credited with giving aid in lifting heavy stones for mansion-buildings, and with help in mowing the meadow grass; some think of him as a fairy expelled the Fairy Bower for having loved a nymph as she sat beneath a tree in Glen Aldyn; "the scythe he had was cutting everything, skinning the meadow to the sods, and if a leaf were left standing he stamped it down with his heels." [211]

His was the wizard hand that toiled
At midnight's witching hour;
That gathered the sheep from the coming storm
Ere the shepherd saw it lower.
Yet asked no fee save a scattered sheaf
From the peasants' garnered hoard,
Or cream-bowl kissed by a virgin lip
To be left on the household board.

From the thought of the nymph beneath the tree in dalliance with the Phynnodderree (there has not been a merry world since he lost his ground, the old Manxman said) I pass now to the spirit of the tree or tree-soul.

(n) The Tree-Soul.—The Strathspey story given above in illustration of the tree-soul tells also of a tree as taken to witness, which points to a belief in the tree-soul. The soul of the dead was believed to pass into the tree. Herbs and flowers were fabled to grow from the blood of the dead and so to re-embody his spirit. Such metempsychosis is connected with solemn sayings.

How a man's word of truth, if not his soul, may be thus linked with a tree is shown from the belief current in my boyhood as to a tree which grew from the spot on which was the pulpit of Mr. Lachlan Mackenzie, the gifted and eminent minister of Lochcarron. Some said it was out of his grave that the tree grew, and that Mr. Lachlan's solemn words to his people were that they were not to believe a word of what he preached unless after his death a certain tree should grow on the spot on which he stood or would be buried in. I have seen slips cut from that tree at Lochcarron taken several days' journey in memory of one regarded as a prophet. And I may quote the following from a successor of his:

"A large and beautiful red elder-berry tree,—after the roof was taken off the church,—grew out of the stone foundation of Mr. Lachlan's pulpit. After the tree grew it was reported that Mr. Lachlan had stated that when a tree, growing out of the spot where he stood, grew to the height of the church walls, popery would be in the ascendant in the district. That was how I heard it reported when the Duke of Leeds, whose Duchess was a keen Roman Catholic, owned the property.

"It was thought there was not another tree of the kind in the world. My father, however, had one in front of the manse close by, and I have now more than one here, grown from slips cut off Mr. Lachlan's the year I left Lochcarron." [212] Folk-belief ever reflects the shadows of its own fears and fancies, and likewise of its hopes. Iseult, in Cornish legend, after the loss of her lover, died broken-hearted and was buried in the same church with Tristram. Ivy, or else a rose and vine, sprang from either grave until it met its fellow at the crown of the vault roof.

Under this heading one might place a good deal of the folk-lore of the rowan tree. Everywhere in Celtdom it is semi-sacred. In Wales "it was considered lucky to have a mountain ash growing near your premises. The berries brought into the house were followed by prosperity and success. A bunch of the berries worn in girdle or bodice kept women from being bewitched." [213] In the Highlands crosses of rowan twigs are placed under the milk-pans, and one has sometimes seen them tied with red thread to a cow's tail. Pieces of rowan wood are stuck in the turf from the inside above the byre door, with the intent of keeping the cattle and their milk from being bewitched. And it is thought lucky to have a rowan tree growing near the house. In the Highland version of the legend of Fraoch, given in the Dean of Lismore's book, the rowan tree is a sort of tree of Life; it bears fruit every month and every quarter, and the virtue of its red berries when tasted was such as to stave off hunger for long.

Its berries' juice and fruit when red
For a year would life prolong.
From dread disease it gave relief
If what is told be our belief.
Yet though it proved a means of life

Peril lay closely nigh;
Coiled by its root a dragon lay
Forbidding passage by.

And Queen Mève feigned sickness and said:

That ne'er would she be whole
Till her soft palm were full
Of berries from the island on the lake— [214]

And of old, in the case of the oak, when stripped of its leaves, its spirit was held to have gone into the mistletoe, and thus became a means of blessing and of fertility.

The Teutons and the Celts, and other peoples, seem, with regard to the tree-soul, to think alike. When the innocent are put to death, white lilies grow out of the graves, three lilies on that of a maiden, [215] which no one but her lover may pluck. From the mounds of buried lovers flowering shrubs spring up, whose branches intertwine,—a belief illustrated in the Barra version of the story of Deirdire: "The wicked king ordered her body to be lifted out of the grave and to be buried on the other side of the loch. It was done as the king commanded, and the grave was closed. Then a young pine branch grew from the grave of Deirdire, and a young pine branch from the grave of Naoise, and the two branches twined together over the lake. Then the king commanded that the two young pine branches should be cut down, and this was done twice, till the wife whom the king married made him to cease from the bad work and his persecution of the way of the dead! [216] With this I would compare the lilies and limes said to grow out of graves in Swedish songs; also Percy's ballad of Fair Margaret and Sweet William:

Out of her breast there sprang a rose
And out of his a briar:
'They grew till they grew unto the church top,
And there they tied in a true lover's knot.

There originally underlay this the idea of the instantaneous passage of the soul into a flower, a bush, a tree, just as Daphne and Syrinx, when they cannot elude the pursuit of Apollo or Pan, change themselves into a laurel or a reed.

Virgil makes the cornel and myrtle which grew on the grave of Polydorus at once bleed and speak when torn up by the hand of Aeneas. [217] And Ovid speaks of an ancient oak, itself a grove, with votive tablets hung and grateful gifts for vows accomplished. [218] Underneath its shade the dryads wove their festal dance. Theocritus tells how at the consecration of Helen's plane tree at Sparta the choir of maidens hung consecrated wreaths of lotus flowers upon the tree, with costly spikenard anointed it, and attached to it the dedicatory placard: [219] "Honour me all ye that pass by for I am Helen's tree."

We may compare the fortune of the Hays of Errol, bound up with an immemorial oak:

While the mistletoe bats on Errol's aik,
  And the aik stands fast,
The Hays shall flourish, and their good grey hawk
  Shall nocht flinch before the blast.

But when the root of the aik decays,
  And the mistletoe dwines on its withered breast,
The grass shall grow on Errol's hearth-stane
  And the corbie roup in the falcon's nest.
            Thomas the Rhymer.

At Glasgow it seems probable that Christianity was grafted on pre-Christian faith. The oak, the salmon, and the red-breast on the arms of the city of Glasgow allow of this interpretation. Upon a tree in the forest clearing, St. Kentigern is said to have hung his bell. The pet red-breast of Servanus, his teacher at Culross, he restored to life; the signet ring of Queen Langweneth he found in the belly of a salmon. Kentigern's oak had a sanctity of its own, apart from its use as a Christian belfry. Compare the oaks of Brigit and of Colum Cille. [220]

Let me give in few words an instance of tree-lore from living tradition, not far from the capital of old Pictland. Pīreig, it says, was a woman who was murdered, and a tree planted in remembrance of her grew near Conon-bank, in the parish of Kirkhill, Inverness-shire. It was an uncanny place. A grey beast used at times to be seen there; it was cat-like in appearance, and thought by some to be a tannasg or tāsg, 'apparition, ghost.' [221] Such a creature followed in the track of a cart which was going to town at an early hour. My informants said it followed them until dawn, when, on coming to a bridge, it gave an unearthly yell, it being a property of the ghost or apparition to give a loud cry as it passes over running water.[222] An intelligent correspondent, whose memory goes back to the first quarter of the nineteenth century, writes me: "Your enquiry about Craobh Pīreig put me in mind of old times. I knew the tree well. It was considered an unlucky place to be about that tree before the ground round about was brought into cultivation. I used to be frightened if passing there at night; fairies, ghosts, and robbers were said to be dwellers in the locality, but all this is changed now. The railway whistle and the plough have chased all the bogies away. In my younger days the road passing Craobh Pīreig was a desolate place, surrounded by trees and bushes of all kinds, but this is now all under cultivation and clear of all romance. I may say Craobh Pīreig was what I may call a geen (cherry) tree of good average size, growing at the road side between Beauly and Inverness, and hardly used by the boys on their way to Kirkhill parish school, as long as a single Been could be found on it. It was in my younger days a lonely tree on a lonely muir about five miles from Beauly. There was no sign of any stone circle about it. The country people did not like to be in the locality after sunset."

The name of the ancient sacred tree was Bile, wrongly translated in Lord Archibald Campbell's Records of Argyll (p. 123). The tradition there narrated clearly points to a sacred tree, near the well called Tobar Bhile na Beinne. Any one who drank its water left some equivalent to the fairy who was supposed to guard it. "Beside it was a very old elm tree with a hole in the side and a hollow in the middle, and into this hole was thrown anything given; and in my young days I remember it being full of all sorts of things—coins, pins, buttons, beads, of which it has all been emptied long ago. There is also beside it a little unenclosed graveyard, where none were put but infants who died before being baptized; and to this day the little graves are seen lying thick and close in their resting-place."

Another Tobar na Bile is between Torran and Inverliver, by the road side two miles or so from Ford. Its water had some connection with the owner's life. For legend tells us that when some Inverliver chieftain was abroad, that the family jester one day noticed the water beginning to sink and by-and-by disappearing. But one happy morning he found the well again full of water, and ran to the house crying out that his master was in Scotland, which afterwards proved to be the case. In the cemetery near hand there 'fell from the sky' a bone that cured madness, Barbreck's bone, now in the Antiquarian Museum, Edinburgh.

Manx billey-glas, 'a growing or green tree,' occurs in the Manx Bible (Jer. xi. 16). In Scotland it is met with at Benderloch in Tobar bhile nam miann, 'the well of the wishing tree.' There were formerly some stones near the place, as if a little graveyard had been there at one time (cf. The Oban Times, 4th and 18th March, 1907). I believe it is the word in Balavil, near Kingussie; there is an exceedingly old elm tree at the house, and also a well quite near it. The sacred associations are there absent, but they are met with in Cladh Bhile, Kintyre.

There is an ancient burying ground termed Cladh Bhile, near Ellary, Loch Caolisport, Knapdale, "situated about mid-way down the western side of Loch Caolisport, at the height of over 200 ft. above the sea-level, and nearly in the centre of the steep hill slopes immediately abutting upon this portion of the loch, between Eilean-na-Bruachain at Ellary, and Rudha-an-Tubhaidh." [223] There is an absence of recumbent stones, everything upon the ground that can in any way be ranked as memorials of the dead being exclusively pillar-stones, intended not to be flat but to be set upright upon the grave. The burying ground is of ancient date. Here we meet with the old Gaelic word Bile, 'a tree.' "The word was generally applied," says Joyce, "to a large tree which, for any reason, was held in veneration by the people; for instance, one under which their chiefs used to be inaugurated, or periodical games celebrated. Trees of this kind were regarded with intense reverence and affection; one of the greatest triumphs that a tribe could achieve over their enemies, was to cut down their inauguration tree, and no outrage was more keenly resented, or, when possible, visited with sharper retribution. . . . These trees were pretty common in past times; some of them remain to this day, and are often called Bell trees, or Bellow trees, an echo of the old word bile. In most cases, however, they have long since disappeared, but their names remain on many places to attest their former existence." [224] Magh-Bile, modernised Movile, is 'the plain of the [sacred] tree,' where St. Finian founded his monastery in Co. Down, in the sixth century; Domnach-Bile, on the banks of Loch Foyle, where was a monastery said to have been founded by Patrick (Archdall's Monasticon Hib. p. 103); Bile-Chuais, now Ballyhoos, Clonfert, Galway; Clochán-Bile-teine, now Cloghaunnatinny, Kilmurry, Clare, is interpreted by Joyce, 'the stepping stones of the fire-tree,' from a large tree which grew near the crossing, under which May fires used to be lighted; Bile-teineadh, 'the old tree of the fire,' identified by O'Donovan as near Moynalty, in Meath, and now called Coill-a'-bhile, the wood of the bile or old tree, anglicised Billywood; alt-a'-bile, now Altavilla, in Limerick and Queen's County; Rinn-bhile, now Ringville; Tobar-Bile, 'the well of the ancient tree,' "some wells taking their names from the picturesque old trees that overshadowed them, and which are preserved by the people with great veneration," as at Tobervilly, Antrim, and at Tobervilla, Westmeath; Garran-a'-bhile, Garnavilla, Tipperary; Rathbile, now Rathvilly, Carlow.

Mr. Galloway, in a note, adds that it was under these trees that the Lia Fāil or Stone of Destiny, pertaining to the tribe, was placed,—to break it up or carry it away being a necessary complement to the destruction of the tree. Dr. Stuart suggests that Edward I. may have been actuated by analogous motives in carrying off the Scottish Stone of Destiny from Scone. [225]

There was another tree that I know of which was regarded with awe, viz. an old ash tree (A' Chraobh Uinnsinn), now no longer standing, on the Eskadale estate in Kiltarlity; a light seen therein from time to time was looked on as a foreboding of death. As the Norse influence extended to this district, clearly evident in the name Eskadale, i.e. 'Ash-dale,' from the Norse, the ash-tree associations may not be quite native. Old Icelandic legend tells that at Mödhrufell there stood a mountain-ash which sprang from the blood of two innocent persons who had been executed there. Every Christmas eve the tree was to be seen covered with lights, which the strongest gale could not extinguish.

From St. Rodan's tree, called Tylia, there dropped a fluid on which his monks lived. And, again, one recollects the celebrated tree of Glastonbury, said to have been sprung from Joseph of Arimathea's staff. King James I. and his Queen gave large sums for cuttings from this variety of hawthorn—the crataegus oxyacantha praecox, a winter flower.

    the winter thorn
Which blossoms at Xmas, mindful of our Lord.

In Ireland there were specially celebrated trees such as the oak of Mugna, the ash of Usnech, the ash of Tortu, mentioned as having fallen in the days of Aed Slane. [226]

An unpublished Gadhelic tale, Cailleach Na Riobaig, which is the same story as that of the witch in the Lady of the Lake, shows the tree-soul associated with the element of water. [227]

"The Bile Tortan stood in Magh Tortan in Meath, near Ardbreacan, and was blown down in the reign of the sons of Aedh Slaine, about the middle of the seventh century. This tree was one of the three wonderful trees of Eirinn, and had stood at the time of the Milesian conquest, more than a thousand years." [228] "Bile Tortan, Eo Rossa, Craebh Mughna, Craebh Dathi, Bile Uisnigh were five ancient trees which sprang up in Erin in the reign of Conaing Begeglach (Anno Mundi 4388). Conaing held a certain assembly at Tara . . . and they saw coming towards them from the west a man of wonderful size, carrying in his hand a branch of a tree bearing apples, nuts, acorns, and berries. . . . He told them he had come from the place of the sun's rising in the east to the place of its going down in the west, to know why it had stood still for a day, and having obtained the cause of this irregularity that he was now on his return again to the east. He shook the produce of this branch on the ground; and these being taken up by various persons and planted in various localities, produced these wonderful trees which were all blown down in the seventh century. The Bile Tortan near Ardbreacan, in the Co. Meath, was ash. The Eo Rossa near Leith-Ghleann (Leithlin) was a yew tree, and became the property of St. Molaise of Leith-Ghlenn, from which St. Moling obtained as much of it as made shingles for his Duirthech or Oratory, at Tech Moling, now St. Mullin's, on the river Barrow in Co. Carlow, and which was built for him by . . . Goban Saor. According to an Irish life of St. Moling . . . the Craebh Mughna was oak, and stood near Bealach Mughna in Magh Ailbhe, in the southern part of Co. Kildare. The Craebh Dathi was ash, and stood in the district of Fir Bile (now Ferbil), to which it gave name, in Co. Westmeath. The Craebh Uisnigh was ash, and stood on the hill of Uisnech, in Co. Westmeath." [229]

In passing one may query whether the Sanskrit bilva in uru-bilva, the wide-spreading Bel- or wood-apple tree, be cognate with G. bile. Indian legend says that at the moment of Buddha's birth his future wife was born, and also the sacred Bo-tree, under which he was destined to attain Buddhahood,—a form of the Life-tree.

"King Conchobair had three houses, namely, the Craebh Ruaidh, and the Téte Brec, and the Craebh Derg [that is, the 'Royal Branch' or Court, and the Speckled Branch, and the Red Branch]. In the Red Court were kept the skulls [of the enemies], and their spoils and trophies. In the Royal Court sat the kings; that is, it was Ruadh [or royal] because of the kings. [230] In the Speckled Court were kept the spears and the shields and the swords; that is, it was speckled from the hilts of golden-hilted swords, and from the glistening of the green spears, with their rings or collars and their bands of gold and silver; and the scales and borders of the shields, composed of gold and of silver; and from the lustre of the vessels and [drinking] horns, and the flagons." Now Ruad ro-fhessa, which has been rendered 'Lord of great knowledge,' is another name for the Dagdha in Cormac's Glossary, so that the suggestion strikes one that here we have to do with a tree sacred to the Dagdha, or to some one of the name Ruad. Are we to think of a blood or life-tree, much as in Scotland a tree is associated with the 'luck' of the Hays of Errol, and as one wishes 'freshness to the hawthorn tree of Cawdor,' now about five hundred years old? O'Clery has ruad .i. trén, 'strong,' which may be but a secondary sense. For meaning one might compare the Sanskrit raudh, 'blood'; but consider Church Slavonic rodu, 'birth,' and the Russian rod, 'clan.' A satisfactory solution would be found in the life of the king being united to the life of the tree, an incarnation of the Dagda or Oll-athair. Certain it is that a sacred tree figures in Irish legend, e.g. 'the apple tree of Emain.' When Bran, the son of Febal, awoke from his entranced sleep, he saw beside him a branch of silver with white blossoms; thereafter the woman in strange raiment sang and said: [231]

A branch of the apple-tree from Emain
I bring, like those one knows;
Twigs of white silver are on it,
Crystal brows with blossoms

. . . . .

An ancient tree (bile) there is with blossoms
On which birds call to the Hours.

The passage occurs in a context which undoubtedly describes a vision of the Happy Land. Again, in the Sickbed of Cuchulainn, [232] three trees of bright purple (tri bile do chorcoir glain) are described as a feature in the Other-World landscape.

Near that house to the westward
  Where sunlight sinks down,
Stand grey steeds with manes dappled
  And steeds purple-brown.

On its east side are standing
  Three bright purple trees,
Whence the birds' songs oft ringing
  The king's children please.

From a tree in the fore-court
  Sweet harmony streams,
It stands silver yet sunlit
  With gold's glitter gleams.

The silver bough [233] is a feature of Gadhelic legend, as the golden bough is of Italic. Just as Jupiter was originally worshipped in the form of a lofty oak tree which grew on the Capitol, and as Dodona was the haunt of deity among the Greeks, so the Celts, as Maxim of Tyre tells us, worshipped Zeus under the image of an oak. Only rare fragments survive now to remind us of the god-tree, as when on the first of May the pilgrim to St. Mary Well, near Culloden, has not fulfilled his duty until he has bound some rag on the adjoining tree, even if he has no coin to put into the holy well. To leave something on the tree or bush near by the well was an essential; this bound one's offering to the habitation of the deity of the spring; it took the tree-spirit to witness. And in my own recollection, when a death occurred among the cattle in spring, the earchall or misfortune was put away by conveying, in secrecy and in silence, the hooves of the animal and other portions preferably across a water-boundary to a neighbouring estate or to a wood, where they were buried under the roots of some great tree not likely to be soon moved.

In the Tristran saga the tree whispers the secret told it, viz. that King Mark had horse's ears,—another instance of the tree-soul; and some reflex of the tree-spirit survives in the branch of laurel given to a bride at Carnac, in Brittany, with which one may compare the decorated pine-bough brought to the house of a bride in parts of Russia. The tree is a thing of life; the wind in the leaves, from the mystic whisper to the roaring blast, seems to come from some mind or spirit. The Australians took these for the voices of the spirits communing with one another, and some of their tribes held that it was through understanding these voices that their medicine-men got supernatural knowledge by communicating with the world of spirits. [234] Similarly, the Greeks spoke of the oracular oak of Zeus and the Semites of a tree of knowledge. And sundry Persian families traced their descent from a tree. Primitive man, it has been said, was arboreal. A hollow tree was his home, its branches his place of refuge, its fruit his sustenance. Naturally, the tree became associated with his earliest religious thoughts. It represented his protecting deity. He would not willingly injure it. When the Mandans cut a pole for their tents, they swathe it in bandages so that its pain may be allayed. The Hidatsas would not cut down a large cotton-wood tree because it guarded their tribe. The Algonquins decked an old oak with offerings suspended to its branches, for the same reason. Trees, from their dripping foliage, and because their shade was associated with the grey of a cloudy day, were believed to make the rains, and thus to refresh the fields and to fertilise the seeds of the vegetable world. The step was easily taken to extend this to all germs, animal as well as vegetable. Thus the tree came to symbolise the source of life. [235]

Tacitus describes the Germans as building no temples, but worshipping their mysterious divinity, secretum illud, in the gloom of the forest.

Not otherwise would it have been with the Celts. The same root as in τέμενος, 'a sacred precinct,' seems to occur in the word Temair, of which there are many instances in Ireland, e.g. Temhair Luachra, a celebrated royal residence in Munster, and others cited by Hennessy in a footnote to his edition of the Mesca Ulad. Temair Erand was the burial place of the Clanna Dedad, who occupied a great part of Cork and Kerry. Most readers have heard of the Temair in Meath, the celebrated Tara of the Kings. The word is thus explained:

"Temair, then, every place from which there is a remarkable prospect, both in plain and house," temair na tuaithe, the temair of the country, i.e. 'a hill,' temair in tige, the temair of a house, i.e. 'an upper room.' It is still the name of several conspicuous hills in Ireland; it is defined in the Dinnsenchas: "omnis locus conspicuus et eminens sive in campo sive in domu, sive in quocumque loco sit, hoc vocabulo quod dicitur Temair nominari potest." [236] Dr. Joyce observes that every Temhair in Ireland is conspicuously situated; the great Tara in Meath is a most characteristic example. It is the genitive form, teamhrach, that is the origin of the name Tara. The other names given to the great Tara by the Firbolg, viz. Druim-Caein [Drumkeen], 'beautiful ridge,' and also Liathdruim (Leitrim), may point to a time when it was not used for temple purposes, or may at least indicate that the chosen temple sites were places that invariably commanded a good view. The instinct which led the Christian priests and monks to select beautiful sites for their churches, we may pre-suppose as active in those who chose the positions of the pre-Christian temples. Yet the idea at the root was not 'good view'—a secondary though accompanying thought—but a precinct, a sacred enclosure cut off, perhaps for purposes of royal burial at first, as is allowable to infer from Senchus nan Relec.

I will conclude by mentioning the legend Keating narrates of Labhraidh Loingseach, who had ears like those of a horse. He had his hair cropped yearly, and thereafter killed whosoever chanced to cut it. It was necessary to cast lots to determine who should perform this office. On one occasion the lot fell on a widow's son, and the king granted him life if he promised to keep the secret till his death. But having cropped the king, the youth was obliged to lie on a bed of sickness, and no medicine availed him. A druid found that the cause was the burden of a secret, and that he would not be well till he revealed his secret to something; and he directed him, since he was bound not to tell his secret to a person, to go to where four roads met, and to turn to his right and to address the first tree he met, and to tell his secret to it. He did so, and the pain left him. It was a willow tree; and it chanced soon after that Craiftine's harp got broken, and he went to seek the material for a harp. He came upon this very willow, and when the harp was made of it, as often as it was played its burden of song was: 'Two horse's ears on Labhraidh Lorc.' The king then repented of having put so many people to death, showed his ears ever afterwards openly. It is clearly an instance of the tree-soul. [237]

I may add that parallels to the idea of the tree-soul are abundant. In the Malay Peninsula the name of every child is taken "from some tree which stands near the prospective birth-place of the child; as soon as the child is born, this name is shouted aloud by the wise woman in attendance, who then hands over the child to another woman, and buries the after-birth underneath the birth-tree or name-tree of the child; as soon as this has been done, the father cuts a series of notches in the tree, starting from the ground and terminating at the height of the breast." [238]

This tree, or any of its species, the child must not in after life injure or eat the fruit of. This points to an early theory of conception, from which Dr. Frazer would explain Totemism. For human souls grow upon a soul-tree in the Other World: the birds which fetch them from thence are killed and eaten by the expectant mother. The consistency of this belief is seen in the fancy that if the mother does not eat the soul-bird during her lying-in, the child will be still-born or die shortly after being born. Such ideas should be remembered when one reads of the flock of birds into which Dechtere and her maidens are transformed in the Cuchulainn Saga. [239]

In Greece, where Zeus and Dionysos are conceived as dwelling in trees—ἔνδενδροι—the transition was made from the tree to the tree-column or pillar as the depository of divine life, and rites of invocation took place at the shrines. In Gaul inscriptions [240] such as SEX ARBORIBUS ET FATIS DERVONIBUS, dedicated to the genii of the oaks, point to tree worship: DEA ABNOBA and DEA ARDVINNA, the Black Forest and the Ardennes respectively, confirm this, and are parallel to the nigra dea, 'black goddess,' which Adamnan gave as a rendering for Lōchy, the river and loch of the name in Lochaber.

(o) The Soul in Stones or the God-stone.—Stones were formerly believed to have a soul, and certain large ones not readily moved were held to be in intimate connection with spirits. In the Highlands it is regarded as a source of danger to make use of pillared stones (clachan carraghan) in building human or other dwellings. Ill-luck or death follows any one who meddles with such 'druidical' stones as are found in the numerous stone circles in Inverness-shire. After ceremonies for averting the evil eye' (G. cronach-duinn, Gr. ἀποτροπή), what remains of the water ritually used is poured over a block of stone that is either immovable or not likely to be interfered with; when cracks make their appearance in such stones the explanation given is that envy will split the rocks (sgoiltidh farmad a chlach). When one is narrating some untoward disaster, or even making mention thereof, a Highland woman of the old school will add under her breath, 'telling it to the stones' (ga innseadh dha na clachan), and proceed with her narrative with much dignity and solemnity. The use of this phrase is supposed to avert any harm arising either to the speaker or the listener.

For Ireland I find that Keating [241] mentions the striking of the head against a stone as a ceremony boding success. Stones such as the Līa Fāil, known as 'the stone of destiny,' possibly 'the stone of light' if Welsh gwawl be cognate, would know their rightful owner. This involves animistic belief, which would explain the late form of the tradition in Keating [242] that on the Līa Fāil 'were enchantments, for it used to roar under the person who had the best right to obtain the sovereignty of Ireland.' Among the four jewels of the Tuatha De Danann a certain poem [243] mentions the Līa Fāil, 'which used to roar under a king of Ireland.' The stone is said to have come from the island of Foal to abide for ever in the land of Tailtiu.

In Scottish records it is mentioned in 1249 at the coronation of Alexander III. at Scone; in 1296 it was carried off by Edward I. and placed in the chair of the celebrant priest in St. Edward's Chapel in Westminster Abbey. It is a stone of magic in origin, and the prophecies associated with it were thought to have been in part at least fulfilled when James VI. of Scotland acceded to the English Crown. Stones were often ascribed prophetical and healing virtues among the Celts. It was owing to the crystal stone which the Brahan Seer possessed that he had the gift of prophecy: such was also the case with his Irish parallel, Red Brian O'Cearbhan, who owned a precious jewel (āilleagan). Magic stones were associated with healing and were known to be in the possession of wizards: dipped in water they were held potent to avert the evil eye, to my own knowledge. In a book which appeared a few years ago by the late Rev. Mr. Macdonald, for long a clergyman in West Ross-shire, he writes: "The stitch-stone was a charm supposed to give relief in cases of severe pain from sciatica up to acute pleurisy. It was common property, and always kept by the person who used it last till required by another. The last specimen of which I heard about 30 years ago was in Erradale, parish of Gairloch. Mr. Matheson, F.C. minister, got hold of it and took it to the pulpit one day. At the close of the service he held it up before the congregation, remarking that the god of Erradale was the smallest god of which he had ever heard or read. It was a small piece of flint stone, 3 or 4 in. long, found on the shore and highly polished by the action of the waves. . . . Mr. Matheson broke it in their presence, and yet no dire results followed." [244]

Pennant mentions the belief as current in the Highlands of the eighteenth century. He writes:

"Elf-shots, i.e. the stone arrow-heads of the old inhabitants of this island, are supposed to be weapons shot by Fairies at cattle, to which are attributed any disorders they have: in order to effect a cure, the cow is to be touched by an elf-shot, or made to drink the water in which one has been- dipped. The same virtue is said to be found in the crystal gems, and in the adder-stone, our Glein Naidr; and it is also believed that good fortune must attend the owner; so, for that reason, the first is called Clach bhuaidh, or the powerful stone (recte, stone of virtues). Captain Archibald Campbell showed me one, a spheroid set in silver, which people came for the use of above a hundred miles, and brought the water it was to be dipt in with them; for without that, in human cases, it was believed to have no effect.

"These have been supposed to be magical stones or gems used by the Druids to be inspected by a chaste boy, who was to see in them an apparition informing him of future events. This imposture, as we are told by Dr. Woodward, was revived in the last century by the famous Dr. Dee, who called it his shew stone or holy stone, and pretended, by its means, to foretell events. I find in Montfaucon that it was customary in early times to deposit balls of this kind in urns or sepulchres; thus twenty were found at Rome in an alabastrine urn, and one was discovered in 1653, in the tomb of Childeric at Tournai; he was king of France, and died A.D. 480."

Further illustration of stones in ritual I will give later on. Suffice it to add that such magic use presupposes that the stone was believed to have a soul. It is an idea not confined to uncivilised man. Bertholet remarks that in ancient Athens, with its famous culture, if a man was killed by a falling stone, a special court was held to pass sentence upon the offending object, which was condemned and transported beyond the frontier!

All over the Celtic area the stone-cult is met with. In parts of France newly-born children are placed on or passed over certain stones in the vicinity of or in certain churches. I need only refer to the innumerable instances given by M. Salomon Reinach [245] of the respect and awe inspired still by menhirs, dolmens and other sacred stones from which we may form some idea of the reverence in which they were held of old in Gaul. In parts of Brittany it is believed that certain stones go once a year, or once in every century, to be laved in the sea or in a river, and speedily return. Sacred stones when removed are held to come back of themselves in the night. The number of stones in the dolmen at Essé are held to change continually, to have the gift of going and coming like the Roman Penates which, according to Varro, were transported from Lavinium to Alba, but returned of their own accord to their ancient domicile. When sacred stones are credited with soul, i.e. with life and motion, they may be inferred to possess the gift of going and coming,—or as it is put regarding the stones of Callernish, Lewis, they cannot be counted, for they are never the same.

'Telling it to the stones' then is a phrase implying that certain sacred stones have souls. Elsewhere a stone may represent the image of earth as the common Great Mother: such, by the testimony of Arnobius, [246] was the image brought from Phrygia to Rome, merely a small black stone rough and unhewn. Some races (the Mexicans, the Indians of Colomba) think that all men were once stones; in Guatamela they placed polished stones in the mouth of the dying to supply a permanent abode for the soul; in New South Wales the blacks gave each novitiate at manhood ceremonials a white stone or quartz crystal [247] as an accompaniment to his new name, the women being forbidden to look at it on pain of death (Angas's Savage Life, ii. 21). In many quarters of the globe the decrees of fate are held to be revealed to the seer gazing into his crystal; higher races have in their past had their stone of Bethel and holy Kaaba. Tomb-stones erected for the dead chief gave further impetus to belief in the god-stone; decked with flowers and garlands, to the accompaniment of invocations and of dancing, the way was paved for the ceremonial cult of the idol (G. arracht), which among the Irish Celts we meet with on the Plain of Adoration (Mag Slecht) around Crom Cruach, to whom they used to offer the firstlings of every issue, and the chief scions of every clan. The name Crom may be cognate with the Teutonic hrúm, 'soot,' and if so Crom Cruach may mean 'the black one of the pile (heap or stack).' As the central idol was surrounded by twelve smaller ones in a circle, I take it that Crom himself was on an elevated heap in the centre. I shall return to him in treating of sacrifice, premising here that the modern name is Crom Dubh, i.e. Black Crom, and that the epithet 'black' (dubh) was only added by the moderns to make the archaic name Crom, which I infer to have signified 'black,' intelligible to a later age. Crom in folk tradition is said to have been accompanied by a leannan-sídhe or fairy sweetheart, who imparted him of her wiles as he required. He was as fleet as the wind and as nimble as the March hare, and he is depicted along with his two sons and their two mastiffs as careering the country to levy tribute; Crom came in the rear as a sort of chariot into which he stowed away the levies. So far he reminds one of the Wild Huntsman of Odin. But in Irish folklore the god-idol Crom Cruach or Crom Dubh has been humanised. In Mayo story he appears as a ruler, who had his own will in everything: "and that was the bad will, for he was an evil disposed man, venomous, fierce and morose." He is credited with two sons, Téideach and Clonnach, the former a folk-invention from a place named Poll a' t-Séididh, 'the blowing hole,' the latter from clonn, 'a pillar, a chimney piece' (as it is given in O'Reilly). Crom, it is said, levied tribute on his people according to their means: any one who refused was brought into his presence as he sat at the fireside to pass judgement, and thereafter the recusant was cast into the fire. [248] This seems a reminiscence of the sacrifices and holocausts offered formerly to the god-idol. At his death, says legend, he was devoured by gnats and worms, and multitudes of people congregated in honour of St. Patrick's achievement over Crom, and were baptised at a well near hand, at Kilcummin, at the western end of Killala Bay (Benwee), where on Garland Sunday the anniversary is still kept up. The name not long ago survived in Lochaber, and is met with in the lines

Di-Domhnaich Slat-Pailm 's ann ris tha mo stoirm,
Di-Domhnaich Crom-Dubh, plaoisgidh mi'n t-ubh,

which Nicolson [249] renders: 'On Palm Sunday is my stir; on crooked black Sunday I'll peel the egg.' He writes the word with the u vowel, Crum-dubh, "apparently for 'Crom-dubh,' and is known in Ireland as the title of the first Sunday of August, but in Lochaber it is applied to Easter." The u-form is due to the genitive Cruim-duibh. But there is no authority for taking the word to be the same as G. crom, 'crooked, bent.' From the account we get in the Tripartite Life of St. Patrick it was to all appearance a stone-idol, and falls thus to be included under the god-soul in stone, as to conception. As to the rites more anon. It would not do to destroy the old worship-stones (clachan aoraidh), said a Perthshire man to the Rev. Mr. Mackenzie, Kenmore. There had been one near his own door which was very much in the way, but he had with great labour dug a hole into which he had let it drop and covered it up, for it would never do to incur the anger of the spiritual beings by breaking it up. This was more than 30 years ago. [250]

THE EARTHLY JOURNEY

VERY journey has its stages, and for the purposes of these pages account is to be taken of the following:

1. Lustration, or lustral rites, whether by fire, by water, by milk or by blood.

2. Illumination, under which come premonitions, omens, divination, inclusive of second-sight. Here mysticism is recognised from the outset: it is so far a testimony to the fact that all human knowledge is in part.

3. Healing, passing in spiritual religion to salvation, wherein all healing culminates. It has its preshadowings in

(a) The rites that unite. Here fall the ceremonies relating to espousals and marriage, and some forms of pagan eucharists.

(b) The rites that avert. Here account is taken of the evil workings of envy; the effects of the evil eye; the belief that an issue of blood may be magically stopped; some phases of magic and of sacrifice.

(c) Faith-healing under psychic suggestion.

This is a constant element in human life, but it assumes lower and higher forms. Account is here taken of old elementary rites only, such as that at Loch Mo Nāir; those at Holy Wells, such as Holywell; a special instance is the pilgrimage to Lough Derg (St. Patrick's Purgatory).

(d) Folk-medicine.

We treat in order:

1. Lustration—the rites appertaining to the progress of the pilgrim range from the cradle to the grave.—In folk-practice probably only a few of the more significant have survived until within recent memory. Midwives, according to Pennant's account (18th cent.) gave new-born babes a small

spoonful of earth and whisky as the first-food. In the Isle of Man salt was put in the baby's mouth as soon as possible after birth. If the child had once partaken of any food it could not be exposed. [251] Among the old midwives it was a sacred practice to roast the omphalos after it fell off, about the ninth day, and give it to the child to drink, powdered and mixed with water (Inverness-shire). This was, as it were, the child's first eucharist. In Man, from the birth of a child until after it was baptised, it was customary to keep in the room a peck or wooden hoop covered with sheep's skin, which was filled with oaten cakes and cheese for visitors, and small pieces of cheese and bread called blithe meat were scattered in and about the house for the fairies. [252] In the Highlands fire-lustration was resorted to, as Martin testifies; and Pennant, who was a diligent inquirer, says, "It has happened that, after baptism, the father has placed a basket, filled with bread and cheese, on the pothook that impended over the fire in the middle of the room, which the company sit around; and the child is thrice handed across the fire, with the design to frustrate all attempts of evil spirits or evil eyes. This originally seems to have been designed as a purification. . . ." This is parallel with the old Scottish practice of whirling a fir-candle three times round the bed on which the mother and newly-born child lay. [253] The Bible was put under the mother's pillow, with a piece of silk from her marriage dress, and fire or light was carried thrice round the bed after a birth; this was done at Loch Eck 40 years ago as a protection against the Fairies. Martin in his Western Isles records that fire was also carried morning and evening round the mother till she was churched, and round the child till it was christened. May one here compare the Persian practice of lighting a fire on the roof of a house where any one is ill? The purpose is to ward off any further evil, not as Mr. Frazer thinks when he suggests 'the intention possibly being to interpose a barrier of fire to prevent the escape of the soul.' [254] In the Highlands there existed the rite of the Leigheas Cuairte, passing children through a hoop of fire, described by the late Rev. Dr. A. Stewart, Nether Lochaber, in Proceedings of the Society of Antiquaries of Scotland. [255]

In the account of the Leigheas Cuairte five women were seen: "Two of them were standing opposite each other, were holding a hoop vertically between them, and the hoop all around, except where they held it in the middle, was wrapped in something that was burning briskly, emitting small jets of flame and a good deal of smoke. Opposite each other, on either side of the opening of the hoop, stood other two engaged in handing backwards and forwards to each other, through the centre of the hoop of fire, a child, whose age, as I afterwards learned, was eighteen months. The fifth woman, who was the mother of the child, stood a little aside, earnestly looking on. They did not notice me, and I stood quietly viewing the scene until the child, having been several times passed and returned again through the fiery circle, was handed to its mother; and then the burning hoop was carried by the two women that held it to a pool of the burn, into which it was thrown.... The child was a weakling, constantly clamouring for food, which it ate voraciously, and yet it did not thrive ... the child was under the influence of an evil eye of great power; and nothing but that it should be subjected to the rite I had witnessed (called in Gaelic Beannachd Na Cuairte, 'the Blessing of the Round or of the Circle') could avail to counteract the evil influence ... an old woman's evil eye had put the wasting into the child (a chuir an t-seacadh san leanabh), at the same time put the hunger into it (a chuir an t-acras ann).... The child's mother and four of the neighbouring women having been duly initiated into the mysteries of the Beannachd Chuairte, an iron hoop that had once encircled the rim of a big washing-tub was got hold of, and a straw rope (siaman) wound round it. Here and there along the windings of the siaman a little oil was dropped to make it burn the brighter when it should be set on fire." The child had to be passed and repassed eighteen times, once for each of the eighteen moons that represented the child's age. A bunch of bog-myrtle was put above its bed, and not touched nor taken down until the next crescent moon ('nuair thainig a cheud fhàs soluis mu'n cuairt') (Proceed. Soc. Antiq. Scot. March 10, 1890).

A parallel rite is testified to from Wigtownshire, while the late Rev. Dr. Scott of St. George's, Edinburgh, testifies to his remembrance of new-born children having been passed through the fire in Lanarkshire. Another correspondent quotes a Gaelic verse:

Mo nighean bhōidheach an fhuilt réidh
Gur spéiseil leam a ghluaiseas tu;
Ged a robh mi tinn gu bàs
Do ghràdh bu leigheas cuairt' dhomh e.

Beautiful maiden of smoothest hair,
Delightful to me thine every movement;
Even if I were sick unto death,
Thy love would be as the healing of the circle to me.

One of the commonest sayings in the Highlands still is: cha tig olc a teine, i.e. 'no evil comes from fire.' It is believed that getting the hearth-fire enables a witch to spirit away all family blessing. It is taboo to go between an epileptic and the hearth-fire on pain of the spirit of epilepsy getting hold of one; by violating this prohibition one easily caught the disease. The rite of smooring the fire ere going to bed was reverently performed and accompanied with prayer full of Christian associations: "I am smooring the fire, O God, as the Son of Mary would smoor it." Swellings and sprains were alleviated by making the sign of the cross in soot by aid of the chimney-pot chain, or by soot taken from the chimney 'hanging-stick, maidecrochaidh, or 'cross-beam.' Embers of smouldering fire (āine theine) were put into a pot and carried in circuit sun-wise around the house at bed-time to ward off evil. Ortha nam Buadh [256] speaks of the laving of the palms in lustral low or fire (ann an liù nan lasair). The sacredness of fire is evidenced in the perpetual fires kept formerly at the monasteries of Seirkieran, Kilmainham, Inishmurray. [257] Brigit was a fire-goddess whose festival may have been the precursor of that of the Christian St. Brigit on the day before Candlemas. She was a goddess of the crops as well as of fire. [258] Perpetual fires were kept up at Kildare (Cill-dara), 'the church of the oak.' The holy fires of the Aryans were commonly kindled and fed with oak wood, with some exceptions. [259] Flint was in all likelihood used in kindling the 'paschal' fires which were formerly lit about Eastertide. But the purifying fire known as teine éiginn, usually construed as 'fire of necessity,' through a mistaken fancy that need in 'need-fire' means 'necessity,' whereas it properly means 'friction,' hence 'friction-fire,' was properly produced by friction from oak beams. As the Gadhelic teine-éignn is a name unknown apparently in Ireland, I am led to think that it may be founded on the Norse eikinn, 'oaken,' eik being of old the 'oak,' though now in Icelandic it has come to mean 'tree of any kind.'

The need-fire was made in Mull by turning an oaken wheel over nine oaken spindles from east to west. [260] In houses between the two nearest running streams all other fires had to be extinguished. Ramsay of Ochtertyre's account of the Teine Éiginn is one of the oldest and the best: "The night before, all the fires in the country were carefully extinguished, and next morning the materials for exciting the sacred fires were prepared. The most primitive method seems to be that which was used in the islands of Skye, Mull and Tiree. A well-seasoned plank of oak was procured, in the midst of which a hole was bored. A wimble of the same timber was then applied, the end of which they fitted to the hole. But in some parts of the mainland the machinery was different. They used a frame of greenwood of a square form, in the centre of which was an axle-tree. In some places three times three persons, in others three times nine, were required for turning round by turns the axle-tree or wimble. If any of them had been guilty of murder, adultery, theft or other atrocious crime, it was imagined either that the fire would not kindle, or that it would be devoid of its usual virtue. So soon as any sparks were emitted by means of violent friction, they applied a species of agaric which grows on birch trees, and is very combustible. This fire had the appearance of being immediately derived from heaven, and manifold were the virtues ascribed to it. They esteemed it a preservative against witchcraft and a sovereign remedy against malignant diseases, both in the human species and in cattle; and by it the strongest poisons were supposed to have their nature changed."

Fire-lustration is a very ancient rite. According to Caesar the Druids held that fire and water would in the end prevail. In the Book of Armagh a name for the day of judgement is erdáthe: "usque ad diem erdathe apud magos, id est, iudicii diem domini," [261] and it may possibly reflect a similar belief. Parallel rites occur elsewhere; for illustration I adduce a Greek rite, the Ἀμφιδρόμια; "A ritual at which the new-born child was solemnly carried round the hearth-fire and named in the presence of the kinsmen. . . . Charondas speaks of certain δαίμονες ἑστιοῦχοι, powers of the sacred hearth. Sometimes a hero or daimon might protect the gateway of the house or city or the city-walls or the entrance to the temple, as we hear of a ἥρως πρὸ πυλῶν in Thrace, of an ἐπιτέγιος ἥρως and τειχοφύλαξ at Athens, the guardian of roof and wall of κλαϊκοφόρος, the 'holder of the temple keys,' at Epidauros." [262]

Parallel conceptions may be traced in the following: "In Sonnenberg a light must be kept constantly burning after the birth or the witches will carry off the child. Amongst the Albanians a fire is kept constantly burning in the room for forty days after the birth; the mother is not allowed to leave the house all this time, and at night she may not leave the room; and any one during this time who enters the house by night is obliged to leap over a burning brand. In the Cyclades no one is allowed to enter the house after sunset for many days after a birth, and in modern Greece generally the woman may not enter the church for forty days after the birth, just as in ancient Greece she might not enter a temple during the same period." [263]

"The mother never sets about any work till she has been kirked. In the Church of Scotland there is no ceremony on the occasion; but the woman, attended by some of her neighbours, goes into the church, sometimes in service time, but oftener when it is empty; goes out again, surrounds it, refreshes herself at some public-house, and then returns home. Before this ceremony she is looked on as unclean, never is permitted to eat with the family; nor will any one eat of the victuals she has dressed" (Pennant's Tour). Within my own recollection the idea of 'uncleanness' before the 'kirking' was retained.

The Manx term for the churching of women, lostey-chainley, lit. 'candle-burning,' points to the old custom of keeping a consecrated candle burning in the room where a birth took place, and 'candle-burning' in religious rites of later times has its roots in primitive fire-lustration.

Next comes lustration by water or baptism. Some might be inclined to think that Irish baithis, 'baptism,' is a native word; or would hold by a verb baitsim, 'I sprinkle.' But even if Gaelic baist, 'baptise,' be taken as through Latin baptiso, 'I baptise,' the lustral rite itself, there can be no question, was known in pre-Christian times. The Cogadh Gaedhel re Gallaibh refers to the 'pagan baptism' as well as other Gadhelic texts. It occurs to me in passing that the rite (with which I have been long familiar as practised by the old 'knee-women' or midwives) of roasting the imleag or omphalos and, when ground to a powder, giving it mixed with water to the infant to drink about the eighth or ninth day, was a concomitant of a form of pagan baptismal rites. Maurer, who has written on the old heathen baptism of the Teutons, suggests that baptism was a recognition of the child on the part of the father whereby the infant was made an heir; he shows that on the eighth day, or within the ninth day, the rite was to be performed, from evidence in the old laws of the Visi-Goths and Anglo-Saxons; the Romans, too, named a female infant on the eighth and a male on the ninth day; the Greeks celebrated the seventh day after birth with rites of cleansing, gifts, sacrifices and feasts. [264]

Most of the old rites have left few traces. In Pennant's time he was able to state that after baptism the first meat that the company tastes is crowdie, a mixture of meal and water, or meal and ale thoroughly mixed. 'Of this every person takes three spoonfuls.' In many parts still it is a rule to have at least partial baptism administered, it being held to be unlucky for the child to pass unchristened; when the infant can be brought to church the rite is further proceeded with by the priest. In the early nineteenth century it was customary to carry the bread or bairn's piece in the procession on the way to church, and custom prescribed that the 'piece' was to be offered to the first person, whether high or low, who met the child, and it was considered unlucky 'to decline the present.' [265] One who was not a cleric could 'sprinkle' the child.

At Rome baptism was restricted to the period of Easter, the vigil of Eastertide to Pentecost, while in Africa and in Ireland Epiphany was a baptismal festival. [266] A relic of this still exists in those parts of the Highlands, e.g. Strathglass, where the Epiphany is called Féille Fairc, the latter word having dialectally r for l in this word, hence Féille Failc, 'festival of laving.' The importance of water-lustration is clear from Gadhelic having a special word, taran, for 'the ghost of an unbaptised infant,' which was thought of as going about wailing in distress, though in some districts unbaptised infants were thought of as being dipped in water at the feet of Christ in the world unseen,—a thought charitable and sweet. The importance of water itself is strongly evident in the Isle of Gigha belief: "Here is a strange superstition for you. A parishioner told me that he was in a house in the island after the children had gone to bed; one of the children was restless in his sleep and often sitting up, as if startled. The father ordered the boy to be quiet, with graphic maledictions, and added: 'After all, I should not speak like that to the boy, but reserve my bad language for the minister, who put far too little water on the boy at baptism.' He assured this parishioner—an Ileach (Islay-man)—that this was always the result of using little water." [267]

In the Proceedings of the Synod of Cashel, A. D. 1172, Benedict of Peterborough mentions for Ireland the following curious facts, which show that the father, in accordance with old custom, could immerse the child thrice in water immediately after birth, or, in the case of a rich man's child, thrice in milk. Thus we could perhaps speak of a rite of milk-baptism: "In illo autem concilio statuerunt, et auctoritate summi pontificis praeceperunt, pueros in ecclesia baptizari, In nomine Patris et Filii et Spiritus Sancti, et hoc a sacerdotibus fieri praeceperunt. Mos enim prius erat per diversa loca Hiberniae, quod statim cum puer nasceretur, pater ipsius vel quilibet alius eum ter mergeret in aqua. Et si divitis filius esset, ter mergeret in lacte." [268]

The mention of the milk reminds of the rite after Christian baptism at Rome on Easter eve in the ninth century: "For the newly-baptised the chalice is filled, not with wine but with milk and honey, that they may understand . . . that they have entered already upon the promised land. And there was one more symbolical rite in that early Easter Sacrament, the mention of which is often suppressed,—a lamb was offered on the altar, afterwards cakes in the shape of a lamb. It was simply the ritual which we have seen in the mysteries." [269]

Of ceremonies connected with weaning, the following is of interest. At Carrickfergus it was formerly the custom for mothers, when giving their child the breast for the last time, to put an egg in its hand and sit on the threshold of the altar door with a leg on each side; this ceremony was usually done on Sunday.

In the Highlands (Uist) it is held that no person should sleep in a house without water in it, and least of all should a house where there is a little child be without water. In a house of this kind the slender one of the green coat was seen washing the child in a basin of milk. [270] And water is efficacious against the fairies. In a folk-tale the fairies are pictured as calling at the door on a 'cake' to come out to them: the inmates threw water on the cake, and it replied: 'I can't go, I am undone.' [271] In Tiree, Gregorson Campbell says [272] it was customary in many places to place a drink of water beside the corpse previous to the funeral, in case the dead should return.

Baptism is one of the most universal forms of lustration: 'the pagan baptism,' referred to in the eleventh century text of the Wars of the Gaedhil and the Gall, need not surprise us.

Blood forms the transition between water-lustration and sacrifice. Its use in the cure of epilepsy may suffice here. I take it from the Rev. K. Macdonald's Social and Religious Life in the Highlands (pp. 29 ff.): "If an epileptic patient had been so fortunate as to be observed the first time he had a fit, he might be cured by the sacrifice of a black cock. This mode of healing is still resorted to. The cock is to be caught at once and split down in the middle. Then it is wrapped in its warm blood on the patient's head. When it cools it is removed and buried, and the affliction is supposed to be buried along with it. In the case of herpes or skin diseases of that class, the blood of a black cock without a white feather, or a white cock without a black feather, is recommended as a remedy. The blood of a black cat is used to check erysipelas." In Ireland also the blood of a black cat is used as a cure for the same complaint (teine-dhiadh). [273] In Nest Ross the blood of a black cock or of a black cat, or the blood of a male Munro, is a recognised cure for teine-Dé, St. Anthony's Fire or 'shingles.' [274] Blood taken from the patient's own leg and given him to drink was a part of the cure quite recently in Lewis. [275]

2. Illumination.—It embraces every form of vision and of magic knowledge. From being adepts in the magic arts, the wise man of old received the name of Druid, i.e. *dru-vid, 'very knowing, very wise.' [276] This species of attempted knowledge ranges from the premonition (meanmuin) to various kinds of omens (manadh, tuar, glaim) and the arts of divination (fiosachid, fàistneachd, tairngireachd, fàth-fìth). The terms fàth-fìth or fìth-fàth was "applied to the occult power which rendered a person invisible to mortal eyes and which transformed one object into another." [277] Dr. Joyce [278] has equated this with the fáed-fíada associated with St. Patrick when he and his companions were transformed into deer on their way to Tara.

Vision in folk-belief may embrace the seeing of the semblance or form (riochd) of the departed by one who cannot recognise them, not having known them when alive. One of the instances in point is connected with the old manse of Lairg. That this house was haunted was long believed by the people in the parish to my own knowledge; nor is the belief yet dead. The Rev. Thomas Mackay, minister of Lairg, died in 1803. A son of a successor, the late Rev. A. G. MacGillivray, a most excellent man whom I warmly remember, tells the story in a lecture appended to William Mackay's Narrative of the Shipwreck of the 'Juno,' [279] of which Byron says it is one of the narratives in which poetry must be content to yield the palm to prose. MacGillivray, with whose father's [280] family the incident is connected, writes ". . . it was firmly believed in our parish that Mr. Thomas Mackay was once seen, twenty-three years after his death, in the old manse. Of course the story must have some satisfactory explanation, but it was not explained in my time. On a fine summer day, in 1826, two young girls were sitting in the manse dining-room; they heard a step advancing to the door, the door opened, and there stood a thin venerable old man, dressed in black, with knee breeches and buckles, black silk stockings, and shoes with buckles. He looked closely all round the room, at them, and then walked out. One of the girls ran upstairs and told the minister then in the manse that a very old minister had come in and was looking for him. The minister hurried down and looked for his visitor, but in vain; he could nowhere be found. The manse is so placed that every object can be seen for a quarter of a mile around, but not a trace of the visitor was visible. The old people who heard the girls describe the old man they had seen, declared that they recognised Mr. Thomas Mackay from their description. Ten or twelve years thereafter granddaughters of Mr. Mackay came to reside in the parish. One of the young girls, by that time grown a woman, said to one of these ladies, 'Oh! how like you are to your grandfather'; to which the other replied, 'So the old people tell me, but how can you know that, for he died before you were born?' The other coloured and got confused, and could give no reply. She had recognised the lady's resemblance to the old minister who had appeared to her in the manse.

I cannot say how the truth may be,
I say the tale as 'twas told to me."

When it is the evil eye that has fallen on a creature, the person who makes the snàithlean, or magic 'thread,' for its cure is seized with a fit of yawning. It is by the frìth that those who cure the evil eye tell whether it be the eye of a male or female that has done the harm [281] (Benbecula). The longer the evil eye has lain on a creature unobserved, the longer it takes to be cured, and the sicker the person, becomes who makes the snàithlein.

In making the frìth some enjoin the reciting of the formula through the hand loosely closed. A formula used in Benbecula is:

Mise dol a mach orra (= air do) shlighe-sa, Dhé! Dia romham, Dia 'm dheaghaidh 's Dia 'm luirg! An t-eolas rinn Moire dha 'mac, shéid Brighd 'romh bǎs (glaic). Fios firinne gun fhios bréige; mar a fhuair ise gum faic mise samlaladh air an rud a tha mi fhéin ag ìarraidh, i.e. 'I am going out on thy path, O God! God be before me, God be behind me, God be in my footsteps. The charm which Mary (the Virgin) made for her Son, Brigit blew through her palms,—knowledge of truth and no lie. As she found, may I see the likeness of what I myself am seeking.' The use of the frìth or horoscope is not at all extinct, as declared by a young woman who was present, and who actually asked the frìth to be made so that information might be got as to the state of health of a person at some distance who was ill. The woman who made the frìth said after making it that she would rather say the woman was dead. The woman was actually dead at the time, so my authority was informed.

It is not right for a woman to try and kindle the fire by fanning it with the skirt of her dress. The reason is that when Our Lord was going to be nailed to the Cross, and the nails were being got ready, that the smith's bellows refused to work, and the smith's daughter fanned the fire with her skirt.

The Omen (Manadh) forms the transition to what it is felt proper to do, and is thus the initial and rudimentary stage of illumination. It is a subjective sort of oracle. Early Irish mama, 'omen,' is cognate with Latin moneo, Old English manian, 'warn.' Examples are: "When one hears piping in the ears it is recommended to say a prayer for the dead." Others say: "May it be well for us and our friends; if thou it be who didst hear it, it will not be thou who wilt weep."[282] For this piping is a sign of somebody dying at the time.

It was an omen of ill-luck to hear the cuckoo on its first return without having broken one's fast, [283] or to see a lamb with its back towards one if it were seen for the first time for the season.

If a cat mewed for flesh meat it was an omen of the death of a cow, and to avert the prediction one said: "With your wanting (the meat of an animal), misfortune take thee! May it be thine own hide that will be the first hide to go on the roof-spar."[284]

In the rite of 'averting,' water is taken from a boundary stream, and put into a vessel in which is a silver coin. The water is thrown over the beast. If the coin adheres to the bottom of the vessel it is taken as an omen that the evil eye was at work.

Another word for omen is tuar, used in that sense by Keating, and surviving in the Highland proverb: Cha do chuir gual chuige nach do chuir tuar thairis, i.e. none ever set shoulder to that did not overcome foreboding. It is thus specially something foreboding of evil. Among such may be put the cry of a cuckoo heard from a house-top or chimney, as a presage of death to one of the inmates within the year. Mr. Forbes notes for some district in Ireland that a cuckoo always appears to a certain family before a death in that family. He quotes the late Rev. Dr. Stewart of Nether Lochaber as to a euphemistic way of speaking of the cuckoo as the 'grey bird of May-tide' (ian glas a Chéitein), it being discreet not to speak of it by its proper name. "In the popular imagination so connected with fairyland was the cuckoo that the very name was in a sense taboo." [285] The howling of the house dog at night is usually held to be an omen of a funeral that will soon pass by. In Breadalbane a moving ball of fire or a moving light (gealbhan) is a precursor of a funeral. [286]

This corresponds to the dreag, driug of other parts. In Lochbroom a cat washing its face is an omen of its soon getting either fish or flesh: as there is a danger of its fulfilment being brought about through the death by mishap of cattle or sheep, the cat is given a cuff to stop it and avert the evil. [287] To be suddenly seized by peculiar sensations of horror at certain places may be an omen of one having drowned one's self there. [288] A white bird flapping its wings towards a burying ground is a precursor of a corpse and an omen of death. [289] An omen of calamity is known as glaim, [290] a peculiar sound in the ear, a howling; it has been taken as cognate with the German klagen, 'weep, complain' the root idea is 'make moan.'

If a particle of food get into the wind-pipe it is polite to say: Deiseal, i.e. 'sun-ways or right! it is not grudging it that I am to thee.' [291]

When going from home with a mare at early morning it is a good omen if one put the right foot over and around the beast's head in name of the Father, and then make the sign of the Cross on one's self, which ensures that no witch or evil spirit can come nigh. It was said of a country carrier who did so: R. M. never went from home without putting his left foot over his mare's head in the name of the Father, and making the sign of the Cross of Christ on himself, and then no wizard nor any evil spirit could come nigh him. [292]

Prognostications were made from the 'first-foot': [293] to meet a woman with red hair was unlucky; a beast, man or thing unexpectedly encountered on stepping out of doors or on setting out on a journey betokened weal or woe. On entering a new abode it was unlucky to find a dead crow before one on the hearthstone. Out of ill-will it has been known to have been put in the pulpit of a vacant parish.

Some stones or crystals have associations with curative magical agencies: such are the Ardvoirlich Charm, Barbreck's Stone, the Loch Mo Nàir Stone, and the varieties of 'witch' stones one has known of; others are associated with clairvoyance and divination, such as Cinneach Odhar's Stone; a few may be specially remarkable as having been omens of success: the merits imputed to such have influenced human lives, and their story belongs to local history. An instance of a stone of good omen is that of Clach Na Brataich, i.e. the Banner Stone of the Clan Robertson. Its story as told by Mr. D. Robertson [294] is as follows:

"In joining the muster of St. Ninians under King Robert Bruce, previous to the Battle of Bannockburn, Donnachadh Reamhar encamped with his men on their march to the rendezvous. On pulling up the standard pole out of the ground one morning before marching off, the chief observed something glittering in a clod of earth which adhered to the end of the staff. He immediately plucked it out, and there being something apparently fateful in such an incident occurring under such circumstances, he retained it in his own possession after holding it up to his followers, as a happy omen of success in the fortunes of their expedition.

"It became associated with the glorious victory of Bannockburn, and thenceforth was accepted by the clan as its Stone of Destiny or Palladium. It has always been carried by the chief on his person when the clan mustered for war or foray, and its various changes of hue were consulted as to the result of the coming strife.

"It was carried by 'The Tutor' when in command of Clan Donnachaidh under the great Montrose, and the Poet Chief carried it gallantly at the head of 500 of his men at Sheriffmuir. On this occasion he, as his ancestors had done before him, consulted the oracle, and observed for the first time an extensive flaw or crack in it. This was accepted as an adverse omen, inasmuch as the Stuart cause was for the time crushed, and from this time, it has been held, dates the decline of the power and influence of the clan.

"But besides being regarded merely as a warlike emblem, the 'Clach na Brataich' was also employed as a charm-stone against sickness. It was, after a short preliminary prayer, dipped in water by the chief, who then with his own hands distributed the water thus qualified to the applicants for it. In this connection it was used by the grandfather of the present chief, in whose possession it now of course remains. For a time it was deposited by him in the museum of the Society of Antiquaries of Scotland for the inspection of the public, but serious warnings were addressed to him as to the fatality which might result.

"In form it is a ball of clear rock crystal, in appearance like glass, two inches in diameter, and has been supposed to be a Druidical beryl. It may, however, quite as probably be one of those crystal balls which have from time to time been unearthed from ancient graves in the country, and which are said to be the abodes of good or evil spirits, or amulets against sickness or the sword. These symbols were usually carried on the person of the chief, attached to his girdle or suspended from his helmet."

The ancient rite of divination by dream was once regarded as in the last resort a reasonable and proper method of ascertaining the person appropriate to be king. We read in the Sick-Bed of Cuchulainn of a 'bull-feast' being made the occasion of superinducing such a dream. "It is thus that the bull-feast was wont to be made, viz., a white bull was killed and a man partook to his full of its flesh and juice, and slept under that satiety while a spell of truth was chaunted over him by four druids, and in vision there would be divined by him the semblance of the man who would be made king there from his form and description and the manner of work which was performed. The man woke up from his sleep and related his vision. . . ." [295] Lugaidh of the Red Stripes, the pupil of Cuchulainn, who was then lying ill, was so recognised and proclaimed monarch of Ireland.

In the Sack of Da Derga's Hostel [296] we read that Conaire was thus elected. Though really begotten by a supernatural bird-man, he was regarded as the son of his predecessor Eterscéle. But this does not seem to have given him any title to succeed. A bull-feast was accordingly given; and the bull-feaster in his sleep at the end of the night beheld a man stark-naked passing along the road of Tara with a stone in his sling. Warned and counselled by his bird relatives, Conaire fulfilled these requirements. He found three kings (doubtless from among the under-kings of Ireland) awaiting him with royal raiment to clothe his nakedness, and a chariot to convey him to Tara. It was a disappointment to the folk of Tara to find that their bull-feast and their spell of truth chanted over the feaster had resulted in the selection of a beardless lad. But he convinced them that he was the true successor, and was admitted to the kingship.

Divination in later times takes various forms, chief of which of old was (slinneineachd) the reading of omens in shoulder-blades. About 40 years ago the shoulder-blade of a bear (math-ghamhuin) took in belief a foremost place, but as this could not be got, that of a fox or sheep might be used. X. Y., the wife of L. C. Z., who was credited with the gift of stopping blood by a spell, lost one of her young boys. He was missed, and though searched for, he could not be found. G. P., a man notable in the line of finding any dead bodies, failed. She then betook her to a wise man who could divine by reading the omens on the shoulder-blades of a bear. [297] He divined and told her to walk to a certain part of the hill which stretched away from her house; he described certain stones near to which the body was to be found. She went thither; found her boy as a heap of bones; she carried them home and had them buried. This falls under the scapulimantia of Grimm, [298] and is met with among many races. A kindred rite survives in the reading of one's fate as to marriage in the 'merry thought' or breast-bone of a fowl. One's vision of the future was widened by prognostications of all sorts by the seeing of wraiths and the barking of dogs before funerals, by the phenomena of second-sight and of phantom-funerals and death-lights. Special honour was accorded to any traces of the presence of St. Brigit on Candlemas Eve. This belief was until recently held in Arisaig. It existed, as we learn from Moore, in the Isle of Man, and Martin [299] writes: "The mistress and servants of each family take a sheaf of oats and dress it up in woman's apparel, put it in a large basket and lay a wooden club by it, and this they call Briid's bed, and then the mistress and servants cry three times: 'Briid is come, Briid is welcome.' This they do just before going to bed, and when they rise in the morning, they look among the ashes expecting to see the impression of Briid's club there, which if they do they reckon it a true presage of a good crop and a prosperous year, and the contrary they take as an ill omen."

Gregorson Campbell has a section dealing with Premonitions and Divination (Fiosachd): for his instances suffice it to refer to his book. [300] He gives prophecies attributed to the Lady of Lawers and to Coinneach Odhar, 'whose name is hardly known in Argyllshire.' Consequently he only devotes a page to him, in which we learn that Kenneth acquired his prophetic gift from a stone found in a raven's nest. The variants of Kenneth's legend are instructive.

The Inverness-shire tradition of Coinneach Odhar takes us back to the birth of the seer. Here we have a story with so strong a resemblance to that of Brian as to show that the tale belongs to a remote period. If I take the Skye tradition there is evidence of interest. "We in Bracadale, Duirinish, never heard that Coinneach Odhar was a Mackenzie, or that his death took place at so recent a date as the seventeenth century, That could not have been. We never heard of the manner of his death. The historian Mackenzie mixed the legend of the original Coinneach with the true fact as to the cruel death of a certain Kenneth who was possessed of clairvoyant faculties and who was buried below the town of Fortrose." So states Miss Fanny Tolmie, a lady of rare talent and exceptional knowledge of Skye and its traditions. Miss Tolmie's account is as follows:

"On a Hallowe'en the people of Boisdale in South Uist were assembling, according to long-established. custom, to spend some hours together in mirth and dance. There was a cattle-fold in the neighbourhood which was always watched by night, and on this occasion the duty of guarding it devolved on two young women, who were vexed that they should thus be excluded from participating in the general enjoyment. Casting in their minds how they might find a substitute, they bethought them of an elderly maid who lived in a cottage at no distance from the fold, which in the remote past had been a burying-ground, and probably was of pre-Christian date. The woman acceded kindly to their request, and repaired to her watching station with her distaff in her hand, where she sat beside a fire for a while,—spinning peacefully. There were some graves close to where she was sitting, and about midnight she was astonished and awe-stricken to see them moving and heaving and forms emerging from them and passing out of sight in all directions, north, south, east and west. Venturing to approach one of these open graves which seemed larger than the rest, she laid her distaff across the opening, waiting to see the result of this action. Before long the spectres began to return one by one, and every one lay down in his own place while the sod became firm and green over the grave as it had been before.

"Last of all arrived the occupant of the largest grave, who seemed to have had a longer way to go, and who, seeing the distaff, exclaimed to the woman: 'Why dost thou hinder me from lying down in peace?' 'First tell me,' she replied, 'who thou art, where thou hast been, and what is to be my fate, and then I will allow thee return once more to thy resting-place.' He answered: 'I was a warrior from Lochlinn and, after having been wrecked and drowned, my body was washed ashore in Boisdale. The corpse of one of my companions, whose name was Til, was found on the west coast of Skye, at a place which has been named after him, Poll' til. It is permitted to us on Hallowe'en to visit our native lands, and I have just been to Lochlinn for an hour. This is what in the fulness of time shall happen to thee: though no longer young, thou shalt bear a son who will be a prophet.' Then raising the distaff, the warrior lay down, and the grave closed over him. When the elderly woman gave birth to a son, there was great wonder in the land. She named him Coinneach, in addition to which name, because of his sallow complexion, he received the surname of Odhar. Coinneach Odhar's name is still well known all over the Highlands and Hebridean Isles, and several districts claim to have given him birth. He received the blue stone of prophecy from the Maighdeann Shīdhe or Banshee, with the injunction that he was never to give it to any one. H e was once pursued by a wicked person, who wished to wrest from him the precious stone, as he was walking near Loch Ness. Fearful of being overcome, he flung the stone into the lake, crying that a pike (geadas) would swallow it, and that in after times it would be found again by a man who would have four and twenty fingers and toes, and two navels,—who would also with it receive the prophetic power.

"Some prophecies attributed to him in Skye are:

"Tribesmen will cross over linns and will leave this isle a black isle of foreigners.

"The folks of the white coats, and those of the red-coats in Rome will meet in Baileshear.

"Six oarsmen will bring every Macleod in the country around Gob-an-t-snoid, beyond Dunvegan Head.

"In the battle the ravens will drink their fill from the stone of Ard Ūige, and from a stone in Glendale.

"St. Columba's stone in Snizort churchyard will turn right about."

In Ireland, Brian of the saga appears in Red Brian Carabine's Prophecy, which gives the title to a collection of much merit we owe to Mr. Michael O Tiománaidhe. [301] He is there pictured as having had his abode at Fál Ruadh, a village in Erris, by the seaside; a decent man who at first did not possess the prophetic gift which was bestowed on him about 1648. At a rent collection he had gone surety for a poor widow and paid on her behalf, whereby he received the divine favour,—the woman having taken God to witness that she would pay on such and such a day. "I like to have another (to give surety) in company with God," said the lord of the land. Crossing a hill on his way home, what should happen but that Brian fell asleep for he knew not how long. He had a dream, and it was told him in vision that what he would find in the right sleeve of his coat he was to carefully put by, without letting wife nor child nor any one have a sight of it save himself alone. It was a sparkling jewel, which clearly revealed to him the future, both good and evil; a magic stone of prophecy which shone with resplendent lustre. Numerous are the prophecies ascribed him; they are of a nature parallel to those of the Highland Coinneach Odhar, Dun Kenneth. At last his wife's curiosity was aroused, and one day, as she saw him gazing at the magic stone, she came behind him, and what portion of the crystal her eye fell on became black as coal and shone no more. He has the faculty of foreseeing the approach of death in his own case and in that of others. One day, while dictating his visions to his son, a poor woman entered, and she was scornfully rebuked by the busy scribe. "List to her," quoth Brian, "for some of thine own bodily members will perish seven years before thyself." And true this proved to be, for the son lost a finger which was buried in earth. But when this fore-warning was foretold to Brian's son, he angrily cast the prophetic record into the fire. The first portion, had already been thrown into a pool, and thus the written prophecies of Brian perished. Naturally, what survives has come down by word of mouth, and forms the subject of fireside entertainments in West Ireland, in the discourses of William Fleming in Leth-ardan; of Seamus Mac Enri, Inish Bigil; of Seaghan O Conway, Dubh-Thuma; all of which is duly recorded in Michael Timony's narrative. The story of the loss of the written prophecy is similar to a tale told me at Loch Arkaig of how Ossian's works and the history of the Féinne have for the most part perished, having been cast into the fire in his anger by St. Patrick. He found them to be mostly lies; but his daughter rescued some!

The legend of Brian the wizard-hermit much resembles in essentials what is told in Highland legend of Coinneach Odhar (Sallow or Dun Kenneth), whose legend does not all fit in with so modern a date as that of the Kenneth on whom Lady Seaforth wreaked her vengeance for his prophecies. It seems to have been taken as fact that a certain unfortunate crystal gazer, possessed of what were held to be clairvoyant faculties, suffered at the hands of the Lady Mackenzie of Seaforth, who is associated with the sad fate of Coinneach Odhar, the Brahan seer, whose prophecies were published in a second edition at Inverness in 1878 by the late Mr. Alexander Mackenzie, and re-printed some years ago with a preface by Mr. Andrew Lang. The material, however, was collected by the late Mr. A. B. MacLennan [302] and forwarded to the editor of the Celtic Magazine for insertion. This gives the Ross-shire version. When the old legend got mixed up with a later personality on the Mackenzie of Seaforth's estates, it was natural that his birth should be located at Baile-na-Cille, Uig, Lewis. While his mother one evening was tending cattle in a summer shieling on a ridge called Cnoc-eothail, overlooking the burying ground of Baile-na-Cille (i.e.

Kirk-ton), she saw, says the legend, about the still hour of midnight, the whole of the graves in the churchyard opening and a vast multitude of people of every age, from the newly-born babe to the gray-haired sage, rising from their graves, and going away in every conceivable direction. In an hour they began to return, and were all soon after back in their graves, which closed upon them as before. But, on scanning the burying-ground more closely, Kenneth's mother observed one grave, near the side, still open. Being a courageous woman, she determined to ascertain the cause of this singular circumstance, so hastening to the grave, and placing her cuigeal or 'distaff' athwart its mouth (for she had heard it said that the spirit could not enter the grave again while that instrument was upon it), she watched the result. She had not to wait long, for in a minute or two she noticed a fair lady coming in the direction of the churchyard, rushing through the air from the north. On her arrival, the fair one addressed her thus—"Lift thy distaff from off my grave, and let me enter my dwelling of the dead." "I shall do so," answered the other, "when you explain to me what detained you so long after your neighbours." "That you shall soon hear," the ghost replied; "my journey was much longer than theirs—I had to go all the way to Norway." She then addressed her: "I am a daughter of the King of Norway, I was drowned while bathing in that country; my body was found on the beach close to where we now stand, and I was interred in this grave. In remembrance of me, and as a small reward for your intrepidity and courage, I shall possess you of a valuable secret—go and find in yonder lake a small round blue stone, which give to your son, Kenneth, who by it shall reveal future events." She did as requested, found the stone, and gave it to her son, Kenneth. No sooner had he thus received the gift of divination than his fame spread far and wide. Being born on the lands of Seaforth, he was more associated with that family than with any other in the country, and he latterly removed to the neighbourhood of Loch Ussie, on the Brahan estate. [303]

Tradition associated this Loch with his death. For having at a gathering at Brahan Castle, legend says, given expression to some remarks displeasing to Lady Seaforth and others, his punishment was determined on. Having no way of escape, he applied his magic white stone to his eye, uttered the well-known prophetic curse: "I see into the far future, and I read the doom of the race of my oppressor. The long descended line of Seaforth will, ere many generations have passed, end in extinction and in sorrow. I see a chief, the last of his house, both deaf and dumb. He will be the father of four fair sons, all of whom he will follow to the tomb. He will live care-worn and die mourning, knowing that the honours of his line are to be extinguished for ever, and that no future chief of the Mackenzies shall bear rule at Brahan or in Kintail. After lamenting over the last and most promising of his sons, he himself shall sink into the grave, and the remnant of his possessions shall be inherited by a white-coifed (or white-hooded) lassie from the East, and she is to kill her sister. And as a sign by which it may be known that these things are coming to pass, there shall be four great lairds in the days of the last deaf and dumb Seaforth—Gairloch, Chisholm, Grant, and Raasay,—of whom one shall be bucktoothed, another hair-lipped, another half-witted, and the fourth a stammerer. Chiefs distinguished by these personal marks shall be the allies and neighbours of the last Seaforth; and when he looks round and sees them, he may know that his sons are doomed to death, that his broad lands shall pass away to the stranger, and that his race shall come to an end."

The prediction ended, he threw the white stone into the loch, declaring that the finder thereof would be similarly gifted. Another version has it that he then threw the stone into a cow's foot-mark, which was full of water, declaring that a child would be born with two navels, or, as some say, with four thumbs and six toes, who would in course of time discover it inside a pike, and who would then be gifted with the seer's power. "As it was the purpose of his pursuers to obtain possession of this wonderful stone, as well as of the prophet's person, search was eagerly made for it in the muddy waters in the footprint, when, to! it was found that more water was copiously oozing from the boggy ground around, and rapidly forming a considerable lake, that effectually concealed the much-coveted stone. The waters steadily increased, and the result, as the story goes, was the formation of Loch Ussie. The poor prophet was then taken to Chanonry Point, where the stern arm of ecclesiastical authority, with unrelenting severity, burnt him to death in a tar-barrel for witchcraft." [304]

His attainment of the seer's gift is invariably connected with this stone. He got it, says one version, as he was out on the hill cutting peats. His mistress, a farmer's wife, greatly annoyed at his seeing-gift, determined to poison the food which was to be sent to him. It was somewhat late in arriving, and, exhausted, it is said that "he lay down on the heath and fell into a heavy slumber. In this position he was suddenly awakened by feeling something cold in his breast, which on examination he found to be a small white stone, with a hole through the centre. He looked through it, when a vision appeared to him, which revealed the treachery and diabolical intention of his mistress. To test the truth of the vision, he gave the dinner intended for himself to his faithful collie; the poor brute writhed and died soon after in the greatest agony." [305]

Another variant is that, resting his head upon a little knoll, he waited the arrival of his wife with his dinner, whereupon he fell asleep. On awaking he felt something hard under his head, and, examining the cause of the uneasiness, discovered a small round stone with a hole through the middle. He picked it up, and looking through it he saw, by the aid of this prophetic stone, that his wife was coming to him with a dinner consisting of sowans and milk, polluted though, unknown to her, in a manner which, as well as several other particulars connected with it, we forbear to mention. But Coinneach found that, though this stone was the means by which a supernatural power had been conferred upon him, it had, as its very first application, deprived him of the sight of that eye with which he looked through it, and he continued ever afterwards cam, or blind of an eye. [306] Kenneth's prophecies vary in different parts of the Highlands; some of them may have touches in common with those credited to Thomas the Rhymer, whose legend, however, has elements that go back on native folk belief of the pre-mediaeval age. This finds confirmation in that the death of the Kenneth said to have been burnt at Chanonry is placed under the third Earl of Seaforth, who was born in 1635. But Mr. W. M. Mackenzie has found in a Commission against witchcraft, issued in Ross-shire in 1577, a reference to Coinneach Odhar as the head of a school of witchcraft even then.

Coinneach's legend is essentially the sane as the Irish one of Red Brian Carabine, but it is in continuous development. In a modern Lewis poem of seventy quatrains, which is in Mr. J. N. Macleod's still unpublished collection, there is a different version of the getting of the stone. Coinneach is depicted as on the strand, when a lady appears in the form of a light, and tells her story. After the light turns into a maiden, she declares herself as Gràdhag, daughter of King Swaran of the North. Arna, priest of Odin, was a keen seer, and possessed of a Stone of Virtues, prepared by Odin himself. The king having ordered the priest to be shot with an arrow, the maiden Gràdhag (Dear One) intervened, and saved the priest's life, for which she got the prophetic stone. Then she is pictured as having seen Diarmuid and the Fianna in vision, and seized by a desire to come to Alba, whereupon Swaran determines on invading Eire and on conquering Finn. The lady was shipwrecked on the way, and the stone hidden in the sand at a spot which her wraith points out. Whereupon she changes her human form to a gleam of light, which twinkled thrice, and then vanished. Kenneth dug at the spot and found the jewel, which gold could not buy; such were its virtues.

But Illumination has its widest popular development apart from Stones of Virtue, and under the category of second-sight (an dà shealladh, i.e. the two sights), which has a literature of its own. [307] Under peculiar psychic conditions the reproductive imagination, working upon memory images, transforms what might remain as 'conjecture' into vision. It takes on the aspect of 'first sight' proper, as when one has a vision of a person absolutely strange to one, and with such vividness that one recognises what answers to all the foreseen details in actual life afterwards. Parallel to this is the case of the coming of strangers being interpreted from a premonition or warning (tàrmachduinn), such as sounds from the opening of presses, or other articles; as also the seeing of forms, which one recognises afterwards on the arrival of strangers whose 'doubles,' it is thought, must have manifested themselves beforehand. This is the so-called phenomenon of apparent double presence. The following incident, of which the scene is in Sutherland, will suffice to illustrate this phantasy or vision proper:

"One evening a crofter was sitting outside his cottage door, when he saw a stranger coming along the high road towards the house. He watched the man for some minutes till, leaving the main road, the traveller took a branch path leading to the crofter's door. The crofter then stepped inside for a moment to inform his wife of the approach of a visitor. On going out again he was more than puzzled to find that the stranger had in the brief interval completely vanished. The house stood, and still stands, on a slight eminence from which an unobstructed view can be had of the immediate neighbourhood. But though the astonished crofter looked on all sides, he could see nothing further of the stranger. None of the villagers whose houses he must have passed had observed him. It is important to note that the crofter there and then gave a full description of the man to his wife and to a brother. In a short time the incident, uncanny though it was, was forgotten. Some months later a child of the same crofter was suddenly taken ill. The doctor, a young practitioner who had but recently come into the district, was sent for, and in the course of the day the father was standing at the door of his cottage waiting impatiently for the doctor's arrival, when, at a bend of the road, appeared the mysterious stranger of several months before. He turned out to be the expected doctor; but in features, dress, and appearance generally he was the exact counterpart of the individual who had formerly presented himself. On inquiry it was ascertained that the doctor had never before been in the neighbourhood, and on the particular day in question had been in the south of Scotland. The crofter, his wife, and brother, most respectable and estimable people, are still hale and hearty, and fond of describing this remarkable incident" (Chambers's Journal).

Yet man in his essence is one. Hence Healing embraces the means that are moments in realising his unity; and such moments include the rites that unite

(α) the human with the human,
(β) the human with the divine.

The former has its physical correspondence: on its psychical side it embraces Love alike towards the human and the divine. Man on one side may be seen as, to a certain extent, finding realisation through such things as nuptial rites, covenants and betrothal (réite, i.e. 'concord'). Here may be found the 'agreement-whisky' (uisge-beatha na réite), known as 'the knitting or covenant-cup'[308] elsewhere. The Highland betrothal was sometimes spoken of as 'the booking or contracting' (an leabhrachduinn), and in some places there was in vogue the ceremony of the feet-washing, which may fitly form the transition to the marriage ritual. I know this existed in Inverness-shire, where Oidhche Ghlanadh nan Cas, 'the night of the feet-washing,' was a preliminary of importance, and afforded the friends of both contracting parties the opportunity of using at times an abundance of soot along with the water. As connected with the hearth and with the fire, soot had a magical influence. It seemed, too, to have been the correct etiquette in that district for the Highland women to wash the feet of friends and acquaintances travelling from the neighbouring parts. It may now have passed away, but it reminds of the old church rite referred to by Duchesne: Ego tibi lavo pedes, sicut dominus noster Jesus Christus fecit discipulis suis, ut tu facias hospitibus et peregrinis, ut habeas vitam aeternam—As Christ washed the feet of His disciples, so others were to do the same towards guests and strangers, in order to inheriting eternal life. The ceremony of the feet-washing was observed in Ireland,[309] in Southern Gaul and in Northern Italy. The ecclesiastical rite may have influenced folk-practice. On the eve of marriage, however, the lustration of the feet was to neutralise the mutual dangers of contact; compare the custom in the South

Celebes, where before the wedding the bridegroom bathes in holy water. The soul, in short, was thought to be in danger of flying away, although after all it may not be unconnected with a speculation put in the words of Plato: human nature was originally one, and the desire and pursuit of the whole is called Love. And Aristophanes seems to preserve a folk-belief when he says earliest man was a bisexual hermaphrodite, to humble him he was cut in two by Zeus. At any rate, the wedding-bath as a solemn pre-nuptial ablution was part of the preparation for wedlock in Greece, where it also formed part of the Mysteries. [310]

A curious side-light upon nuptial covenants is reflected from a folk-saying current alike in parts of the Highlands and in Ireland: "If you wish to be blamed, marry; if you wish to be praised, die."[311] One of the preliminaries to marriage was the faoighdhe, [312] a sort of genteel asking of aid to set up house, or as token of good-will. It was the part of the bride's duty to seek for these gifts, which were also supplemented by the presents [313] forwarded by those attending the wedding. Such wedding-presents were a matter of course, for the festivities formerly lasted over a week. It was held proper for a woman to be married in a dress borrowed from a married woman: this was a token of luck, as were likewise the shots fired as the wedding-party set out. Persons met with casually on the way were offered a dram, and the 'healths' proper to the occasion were honoured. One of the most significant archaic customs, found surviving at Little Lochbroom, West Ross, has been regarded by the Rev. C. Robertson as pointing to the primitive institution of marriage by capture. Owing to distance, a trysting place is arranged, where the bride's party meets the clerical celebrant. "The bridegroom's house is a little further away than the bride's home from the trysting place. While the bride's party is at breakfast on the morning of the wedding day, a scout is sent out every few minutes to see what is doing at the bridegroom's house, and to guard against surprise by him and his party. The bridegroom's party in the same way are watching the bride's home. When the bride and her party set out, there immediately arises an appearance of great stir and bustle about the bridegroom's house. Presently he and his party are seen to come out, and, as though they were in hot haste to overtake the bride's party, they take a straight line through fields and over streams and fences. They do not overtake the party in front, however, but keep about two hundred yards behind. When the bride's party sits down to partake of a refreshment by the way, the pursuers still keep at the same respectful distance, and sit down to take their refreshments by themselves. While waiting for the minister at the trysting place, the two parties keep at a distance the one from the other, and even when they are obliged to approach for the performance of the ceremony, they still keep distinct. Immediately on the conclusion of the ceremony by which bride and bridegroom are made one, the two parties mingle together and are associated throughout the remainder of the day's proceedings." [314]

The late Dr. Wilde [315] records that at the Midsummer Eve bonfires many of the old people circumambulated the fire, repeating certain prayers: "If a man was about to perform a long journey, he leaped backwards and forwards three times through the fire, to give him success in his undertaking. If about to wed, he did it to purify himself for the marriage state." Lady Wilde likewise alludes to the feigning of force in carrying off a bride, who was placed on a swift horse before the bridegroom, while all her kindred started in pursuit with shouts and cries. [316]

An eighteenth century visitor [317] to the North recorded: "Soon after the wedding-day, the new-married woman sets herself about spinning her winding sheet, and a husband that should sell or pawn it is esteemed among all men, one the most profligate." The editor of Burt, viz. R. Jamieson, notes that when a woman of the lower class in Scotland, however poor, and whether married or single, commences housekeeping, her first care, after what is absolutely necessary for the time, is to provide death-linen for herself, and those who look to her for that office. [318] And I have heard of cases where the new wedding-dress was set aside awaiting the time of decease, when a matron donned it as her best now that she hourly expected to join her predeceased spouse. Mrs. Macdonald of Kingsburgh was wrapped at death in the sheets wherein Prince Charlie slept. Sympathy was thus expressed by contact with an object: this idea leads to substitution, and that very readily to identity. New cradles were not esteemed; every endeavour was made to preserve the old family cradle, which was especially lucky if a boy had been nursed therein before. To part with the old cradle was to give away the family luck.

The Marriage Customs in Pennant's account are of interest here: "The courtship of the Highlander has these remarkable circumstances attending it: after privately obtaining the consent of the Fair, he formally demands her of the father. The Lover and his friends assemble on a hill allotted for that purpose in every parish, and one of them is dispatched to obtain permission to wait on the daughter; if he is successful, he is again sent to invite the father and his friends to ascend the hill and partake of a whisky cask, which is never forgot: the Lover advances, takes his future Father-in-law by the hand, and then plights his troth, and the Fair-one is surrendered up to him. During the marriage ceremony, great care is taken that dogs do not pass between them, and particular attention is paid to the leaving the Bridegroom's left shoe without buckle or latchet, to prevent witches [319] from depriving him, on the nuptial night, of the power of loosening the virgin zone. As a test, not many years ago, a singular custom prevailed in the Western Highlands the morning after a wedding: a Basket was fastened with a cord round the neck of the Bridegroom by the female part of the company, who immediately filled it with stones, till the poor man was in great danger of being strangled, if his Bride did not take compassion on him, and cut the cord with a knife given her to use at discretion. But such was the tenderness of the Caledonian spouses, that never was an instance of their neglecting an immediate relief of their good man." [320]

At Logierait, 18 miles from Kenmore, as recently as 1811, the custom was: "After arriving at the church, and just immediately before the celebration of the marriage ceremony, every knot about the dress of both bride and bridegroom, such as garters, shoe-strings, strings of petticoats, etc., was carefully loosened. After leaving the church the whole company walk round it, keeping the church wall always on the right hand. The bridegroom first, however, turned aside with a friend to tie the strings of his dress, while the bride retired with her friends to adjust the disorder of hers." [321] Pennant observes thereanent that "the precaution of loosening every knot about the newly-joined pair is strictly observed, for fear of the penalty denounced in the former volumes. It must be remarked that the custom is observed even in France, nouer l'aiguillette being a common phrase for disappointments of this nature. Matrimony is avoided in the month of January, which is called in Erse the cold month, but what is more singular, the ceremony is avoided even in the enlivening month of May."

The Rev. L. Shaw, Historian of Moray, adds in Pennant's Tour that "at marriages and baptisms they make a procession around the church, Deasoil, i.e. sunways, because the sun was the immediate object of the Druids' worship."

I have myself seen the wedding-bannock (bonnach bainnse), baked by a wise matron, broken by her upon the head of the bride as she entered the house on the return from church, in the year 1875. It is parallel to the confarreatio of the Romans in some ways.

And the same rite is met with in Ireland: Lady Wilde [322] states: "On arriving at her future home, the bride was met on the threshold by the bridegroom's mother, who broke an oaten cake over her head as a good augury of plenty in the future."

After marriage the snood of the maid was exchanged for the kerch (bréid) of the spouse, a custom referred to in a marriage ode beginning: "a thousand blessings to thee in thy kerch." [323]

THE EARTHLY JOURNEY (PART 2)

THE rites that unite the human with the divine embrace all forms of partaking in thankfulness in common with the divine as it is recognised; the giving to get; the giving to appease. Here account has to be taken of commensality, or, in other words, of primitive pagan eucharists. To my mind, the earliest thought is that of partaking of food in common with the divine. A very careful person I have known would never have food served to others or partaken of without adding: "May God have as much of his own." [324] And just as it was held highly unlucky for a boy to sweep the floor after a death, some would not have the floor swept after food was cooked or partaken of. The fragments that fell on the floor belonged to the household spirit or sìthich, i.e. the 'fairy.' Close upon the thought to be inferred therefrom is that embraced by all forms of libation. Of old it was common enough to pour a milk libation on the fairy-knoll. [325] In the eighteenth century the Rev. Donald MacQueen, minister of Kilmuir, Skye, contributed some account of the Gruagach to Pennant's Tour. After some references to the classics, he adds that "the superstition or warm imagination of ignorant people introduced him as a sportive salutary guest into several families, in which he played many entertaining tricks, and then disappeared. It is a little more than a century ago since he hath been supposed to have got an honest man's daughter with child, at Shulista, near to Duntulme, the seat of the family of Macdonald: though it is more probable that one of the great man's retinue did that business for him. But though the Gruagach offers himself to every one's fancy as a handsome man, with fair tresses, his emblems, which are in almost every village, are no other than rude unpolished stones of different figures just as they seemed cast up to the hand of the Druid who consecrated them. Carving was not introduced into the Hebrides; and though it had, such of the unformed images as were preserved would for their antiquity be reve-renced, in presence of any attempts in the modern arts.

"The Gruagach Stones, as far as tradition can inform us, were only honoured with libations of milk, from the hands of the dairy maid, which were offered to Gruagach upon the Sunday, for the preservation of the cattle on the ensuing week. From this custom Apollo seems to have derived the epithet Galaxius. This was one of the sober offerings that well became a poor or frugal people, who had neither wine nor oil to bestow; by which they recommended their only stock and subsistence to their favourite Divinity, whom they had always in their eye and whose blessings they enjoyed every day. . . . The idol stones that remain with us are oblong square altars of rough stone, that lie within the Druids' Houses, as we call them. Observe also, that the worship of the sun seems to have continued in England until King Canute's time, by a law of his, which prohibits that, with other idolatrous practices." Martin corroborates this of the island of Valay, where "there is a flat thick stone call'd Brownie's Stone, upon which the ancient inhabitants offered a cow's milk every Sunday, but this custom is now quite abolish'd."

The old custom of libation is clearly seen in the following: "Clanranald used to have a summer shieling on one of the islets off Benbecula. He had a herd and a milkmaid there. They were both of them Catholics, and at the time of changing residence were in the habit of spilling a coggie of milk on the fairy-knoll. The dairy maid left Clanranald's service, and in her stead he engaged a Protestant. On the day of changing from the shieling the herd requested that milk might be left on the knoll. She replied: 'No! I don't heed Popish incantations.' That same night the best cow in the fold was dead, and on the morrow it was blood and not milk that the cows gave. Clanranald sent away the new dairy maid, and he took back the maid who had formerly left his service to take her place. They never heard any further mishap." This on the authority of an old shepherd, whose grandfather, he said, was the herd in question.

The sea-god Shony, according to Martin,[326] "had libations offered him in Lewis at Hallowtide: they gathered to the Church of St. Mulvay, Lewis: each family furnished a peck of malt, and this was brew'd into ale: one of their number was picked out to wade into the sea up to the middle, and carrying a cup of ale in his hand, standing still in that posture, cry'd out with a loud voice, saying: Shony, I give you this cup of ale, hoping that you'll be so kind as to send us plenty of sea-ware, for enriching our ground the ensuing year, and so threw the cup of ale into the sea. This was performed in the night time. At his return to land they all went to church; there was a candle burning upon the altar; and then, standing silent for a little time, one of them gave a signal at which the candle was put out, and immediately all of them went to the fields, where they fell a-drinking their ale, and spent the remainder of the night in dancing and singing."

Of immemorial antiquity is another rite referred to by Martin: "They have a general cavalcade on All Saints' Day, and then they bake St. Michael's Cake at night, and the family and strangers eat it at supper" [327] (South Uist). For Barra he says: "Every family, as soon as the solemnity (the cavalcade) is ended, is accustomed to bake St. Michael's Cake, as above described; and all strangers, together with those of the family, must eat the bread that night." [328] It is met with likewise in Ross-shire: "Perhaps one of the quaintest of old-world customs which still survives in some out-of-the-way places is the preparation of the Struan Michael, or cakes sacred to the celebration of Michaelmas Day. It is more peculiarly a Hebridean custom, and, though fast dying out, it is not unknown, and last autumn I tasted some. Michaelmas Day was always observed in the Celtic Calendar, and Struan Michaels and Beltane Bannocks entered as much into the calculations of the Highland housewife as do Shrove-tide cakes and hot-cross-buns elsewhere. They were prepared somewhat after this fashion. The first sheaves of the harvest were taken, dried and ground into meal with the quern. Then the housewife took some eggs, butter and treacle, mixed them up, and into the mixture put the new meal, making a dough. On the stone slab forming her hearth-stone she put some red-hot peats, and when sufficiently heated, swept it clean. On this the dough was placed to cook with an inverted pot over it. During the process of cooking, it was often basted with beaten eggs, forming a custard-like covering. Finally, after the cake was cooked, a small piece was broken off and cast into the fire. Why? you will ask. Well, as an offering to the Donas, or old Hornie, or whatever may be the correct designation of that presiding genius whom we are led to believe inhabits the fiery regions. The housewife did this in order to safeguard herself and her household against the Evil One. After reserving some of the Struan for the use of the household, she went round the neighbours in triumph and gave them a bit each, there being usually a great rivalry as to who should be the first to grind the new meal and get the Struan ready. The first to do so was generally understood to have the best crops through the corning year." [329]

Offerings to Michael are clearly referred to in the Isle of Eriskay rite, that when a person is paring his nails and having his hair cut, he should say: "My hair and my nails be with Nigh' Mhìcheil for my soul's welfare" (m'fhalt is m'iongnan aig Nigh' Mhìcheil, air rath m'anmanna). The Rev. Allan Macdonald, priest of the island, had the phrase from the late Duncan M'Innes, Ru Bàn, Eriskay, and distinctly noticed "that the pronunciation was not Naomh Mìcheil, 'St. Michael,' but 'nigh Mhicheil' (i.e. daughter of

Michael?), whosoever she may have been." But I have little doubt but the pronunciation with the i was a variant well-known elsewhere for the high-back vowel ao.

The idea of offering clearly appears in the action of fishermen, who, when they thought they saw a mermaid, threw overboard any fish that they might have in order to propitiate her, inasmuch as her appearance was held to portend foul weather. A parallel idea comes out in the old custom once observed on entering a new house for the first time of throwing something into the house before one, saying slàn treabhaidh an so, equivalent to invoking a blessing on the abode. I well remember old people who on no account would enter a house, particularly when the family were at meal, without exclaiming: "Blessing be before me!" [330] A practice the opposite of this was the putting of a dead creature, such as a crow, on the hearth of a house to which another family was flitting. This I have seen in the Highlands, as well as the new tenant go round his fields with 'blessed' water, sprinkling alike boundaries and cattle in a manner that reminded of customs met with in old Italian rites. [331] Offerings also were the coins thrown into wells, as also the twigs of heather cast into them or near them. This leads to the idea, of propitiation. The idea of do ut abeas, 'I give that thou mayest be gone,' is manifest in the Uist ritual of the St. Michael's Cake. [332] A bit of dough is taken from off the baking-board and placed on the embers, where it is burnt. It is called the Devil's Tithe, the Evil One's portion, and such names. The bit of dough, when burnt, is thrown over the left shoulder, the operant saying: "Here to thee, thou rascal [Devil], and stay behind me, stay from my kine!" The cake may be baked for the prosperity (air sealbhaich) of the house, of the household, or of any individual member.

Keating [333] inserts a story which tells how St. Patrick restored Lughaidh, son of King Laoghaire, to life. Michael the Archangel, in form of a bird, put his bill into the lad's throat, and took out the morsel which choked the king's son. "When the queen heard that it was Michael the Archangel who brought back her son to life, she bound herself to give a sheep out of every flock she possessed each year, and a portion of every meal she should take during her life, to the poor of God, in honour of Michael the Archangel; and, moreover, she enjoined this as a custom throughout Ireland on all who received baptism and the faith from Patrick, whence is the custom of the Michaelmas sheep and the Michael's portion (míre Míchil) in Ireland ever since." Gratitude is here the foundation of the sacrificial meal; the converse of this is the thought: when the deity gets what is due, the offerer expects to be granted what is right in return. Not that sacrifice is but a bargain; it is a highly complex act.

The Michaelmas Sheep of Keating's account is doubtless the Michaelmas Lamb which in the Hebrides is slain at the season when the Michael Cake is made. Dr. Carmichael's account [334] tells how, after the cake is cut into sections, the father of the family "cuts up the lamb into small pieces. He takes the board with the bread and the flesh on the centre of the table. Then the family, standing round, and holding a bit of struan (cake) in the left hand and a piece of lamb in the right, raise the 'Iolach Mìcheil,' triumphal song of Michael, in praise of Michael, who guards and guides them, and in praise of God, who gives them food and clothing, health and blessing withal. The man and his wife put struan into one beehive basket (ciosan) and lamb into another, and go out to distribute them among the poor of the neighbourhood who have no flocks nor fruits themselves."

I believe that in a district where, too, the population is not of the Roman persuasion, the Michaelmas Lamb has been killed not so long ago. The whole ceremony has its parallel in the Lithuanian Sabarios, i.e. 'the mixing or throwing together,' at the eating of the new corn. Just as the Michaelmas Cake was made from grain newly ripened in the field and fresh ground in the quern, the grain for the Sabarios was the first thrashed and winnowed, and then baked into little loaves, one for each of the household. From a portion beer was brewed, and a jugful poured on the bung of the barrel, the Lithuanian farmer saying: "O fruitful earth, make rye and barley and all kinds of corn to flourish!" Then a black or white or speckled cock and hen were taken and killed by blows from a wooden spoon, all holding up their hands, saying: "O God, and thou, O earth, we give you this cock and hen as a free-will offering!" The Lithuanian rite, which Dr. Frazer interprets as the body of the corn-spirit, partaken of sacramentally, took place at the beginning of December. [335]

Another cake was made at Beltane on May-Day. This cake had a large hole in the middle, through which each of the cows in the field was milked. In Tiree it was of a triangular form.

Parallel in respect of its pointing to an offering is the Beltane custom at Callander, described by M r. James Robertson, minister of the parish: [336] "The people of this district have two customs, which are fast wearing out, not only here, but all over the Highlands, and therefore ought to be taken notice of while they remain. Upon the first day of May, which is called Beltan, or Bal-tein day, all the boys in a township or hamlet meet in the moors. They cut a table in the green sod, of a round figure, by casting a trench in the ground, of such circumference as to hold the whole company. They kindle a fire, and dress a repast of eggs and milk in the consistence of a custard. They knead a cake of oatmeal, which is toasted at the embers against a stone. After the custard is eaten up, they divide the cake into so many portions, as similar as possible to one another in size and shape, as there are persons in the company. They daub one of these portions all over with charcoal, until it be perfectly black. They put all the bits of cake in a bonnet. Every one, blindfold, draws out a portion. He who holds the bonnet is entitled to the last bit. Whoever draws the black bit is the devoted person who is to be sacrificed to Baal, whose favour they mean to implore in rendering the year productive of the sustenance of man and beast. There is little doubt of these inhuman sacrifices having been once offered in this country, as well as in the east, although they now pass from the act of sacrificing, and only compel the devoted person to leap three times through the flames; with which the ceremonies of this festival are closed. The other custom is, that on All-Saints' Even they set up bonfires in every village. When the bonfire is consumed, the ashes are carefully collected in the form of a circle. There is a stone put in, near the circumference, for every person of the several families interested in the bonfire; and whatever stone is moved out of its place, or injured before next morning, the person represented by that stone is devoted, or fey, and is supposed not to live twelve months from that day. The people received the consecrated fire from the Druid priests next morning, the virtues of which were supposed to continue for a year."

In the parish of Kirkmichael, [337] adjoining Logierait, there was baked a consecrated cake for the first of May. The cake, with knobs, was used, we may infer, formerly for determining who was to be the victim of the flames. The cakes baked at that period at Logierait had small lumps in the form of nipples raised all over the surface.

Thomas Pennant, who travelled in Perthshire in the year 1769, tells us that "on the 1st of May the herdmen of every village hold their Beltein, a rural sacrifice. They cut a square trench on the ground, leaving the turf in the middle; on that they make a fire of wood, on which they dress a large caudle of eggs, butter, oatmeal and milk; and bring besides the ingredients of the caudle, plenty of beer and whisky; for each of the company must contribute something. The rites began with spilling some of the caudle on the ground, by way of libation: on that, every one takes a cake of oatmeal, upon which are raised nine square knobs, each dedicated to some particular being, the supposed preserver of their flocks and herds, and to some particular animal, the real destroyer of them. Each person then turns his face to the fire, breaks off a knob, and flinging it over his shoulders, says, 'This I give to thee, preserve thou my horses; this to thee, preserve thou my sheep; and so on.' After that they use the same ceremony to the noxious animals: 'This I give to thee, O fox, spare thou my lambs; this to thee, O hooded crow! this to thee, O eagle!' When the ceremony is over, they dine on the caudle; and after the feast is finished, what is left is hid by two persons deputed for that purpose, but on the next Sunday they reassemble and finish the reliques of the first entertainment."

The idea of offerings is at times closely associated with purification. It is met with in the rites connected with the caisean-uchd, i.e. the strip of skin from the breast of a sheep killed at Christmas, New Year and other sacred festivals. "The strip is oval, and no knife must be used in removing it from the flesh. It is carried by the carollers when they visit the houses of the townland, and when lit by the head of the house it is given to each person in turn to smell, going sunwise. Should it go out, it is a bad omen for the person in whose hand it becomes extinguished. The inhaling of the fumes of the burning skin and wool is a talisman to safeguard the family from fairies, witches, demons and other uncanny creatures during the year." [338] Macleod and Dewar's Gaelic Dictionary defines it as "the breast-strip of a sheep killed at Christmas or New Year's Eve, and singed and smelled by each member of the family as a charm against fairies and spirits." The word caisean means 'anything curled,' particularly the dew-lap which hangs from the breast of animals. To judge by M'Alpine's phrase, 'never for the sake of fairies,' the rite in Islay was in vogue as a preservative at any time and was not connected with the fairy-world. The practice is referred to in a quite recent account from South Uist, which I may translate: "Now I must conclude. The observers of New Year's Eve (Christmas Eve, old style) are approaching me with the loud shouting proper to the season, and according to old custom they will go sunwise round the house, bringing the Callaig (the Hogmanay) gift with them. At the door the Callaig rhyme is to be said on entering: This is to bless the dwelling; may God bless this house and its inmates all! Going sunwise round the fire, the Hogmanay Breast-strip (Caisein Callaig) is to be set-on-fire or lighted, that is, the breast-skin of a wedder; each person in the house is to seize hold of it as it burns, making the sign of the cross, if he be a Catholic, in the name of the Father, and of the Son and of the Holy Spirit. That burning strip is to be put thrice sunwise about their heads. If the burning skin be extinguished in the process, it is a bad omen for the New Year's happiness. Then they will get their Hogmanay portion, each one according to his opportunity; with good will they then disperse with the words: The blessing of God and of the Hogmanay be with you all; if well to-night, seven times better may ye be a year to-night!"

J. G. Campbell, in his Witchcraft and Second Sight (p. 233), gives a full form of the rhyme with the following lines:

The Calluinn Breast-strip is in my pocket,
    A goodly mist comes from it;
The goodman will get it first,
And shove its nose into the fire upon the hearth.
It will go sunwise round the children,
And particularly the wife will get it.

Mr. Campbell specifies as to the procession that the hide of the mart cow, killed for winter use, was wrapped round the head of one of the men, and he made off, followed by the rest, belabouring the hide, which made a noise like a drum, with switches. One of the participators, that is, had to be clothed in hide. [339] I am reminded of the Roman Luperci who, on 15th February, girt themselves with the skins of slaughtered goats and struck all the women who came near them with strips of skin from the hides of the goat-victims, such strips being among the objects called by the priests februa. The purposes of such rites were purification and fructification; the victim was sacro-sanct, and an effort was thus made towards symbolising by participation the physical unity of all life. The old custom of throwing bones or burnt pieces of animals into the flames is testified to by the name 'bonefire.' Dr. Fowler has noted that the Highland 'man in cowhide' is singularly like the Roman rite as Lydus describes it; the skin-clad man, the old Mars, was beaten with long rods and driven out of Rome on the day preceding the full moon of the old Roman year, which began on March 1. The month of March was dedicated to him as the deity of the sprouting vegetation. Though now we have the Highland rite but in a shadow, we may infer that the intent was to communicate new life by the burnt strip of skin, and that originally there was slaughter of an animal: the man girt with the hide of the sacro-sanct victim became one with the victim; he entered into the nature of the life-giving blood shed. Just as washing the hands in pig's blood is held to be a cure for warts in the Highlands still, of old the virtue of blood was greater. May we not presumably infer that blood purified? Elsewhere the murderer's hands were purified by smearing them with the blood of a young pig (Apollonius Rhodius, 4, 478).

Blood makes the transition to animal sacrifice. Here, making allowance for cross-division in so complex a subject, we arrive at:

(b) The rites that avert.

I give an instance from Ross-shire: "Here is another curious practice in connection with epilepsy which I saw carried out many years ago, and which is, I suppose, a survival of old pagan sacrificial rites. A child, belonging to a family whom I know well, was suddenly seized with convulsions, and its relatives would have it that the child had epilepsy. Accordingly, emissaries were sent through the parish to procure a black cock, without a single white feather, and without blemish of any kind. This latter is important; the finer the animal, the more readily does the spell work. Well, then, a cock was found which suited the requirements; the stone floor in the room where the child was first seized was opened up at the exact spot where the seizure took place. The unfortunate animal was sealed down and buried alive, after which an incantation was muttered over it by a 'wise woman.'" [340] The child was afterwards bathed.

A correspondent from Lewis is quoted. He writes: "The cure for epileptic fits is more barbarous, and to my knowledge was used not three months ago in Barvas (4½ miles from here). A black cock (the barn-door variety), without a light-coloured feather, is buried alive on the spot where the patient experienced his or her first fit; that is all and the cure is effected by [inducing] the evil spirit causing epilepsy to leave the patient and enter into the body of the cock." [341]

A special form of sacrifice is connected with the cat. The ulterior purpose is to invoke the Evil One, according to modern folk-belief, and while the rite is named 'invocation' (taghairm) [342] the means used partake of something of the nature of sacrifice mingled with compelling magic. The account I give is from an authentic source in the London Literary Gazelle, March, 1824. [343] "The last time the Taughairm (sic) was performed in the Highlands was in the island of Mull, in the beginning of the seventeenth century, and the place is still well known to the inhabitants. Allan Maclean, commonly styled Allan mac Echain (son of Hector) was the projector of these horrid rites; and he was joined by Lachlan Maclean, otherwise denominated Lachunn Odhar (Lachlann the Dun). They were of resolute and determined character, and both young and unmarried.

"The institution was no doubt of pagan origin, and was a sacrifice offered to the Evil Spirit, in return for which the votaries were entitled to demand two boons. The idea entertained of it at the time must have been dreadful, and it is still often quoted for the purpose of terrifying the young and credulous. The sacrifice consisted of living cats roasted on a spit while life remained, and when the animal expired another was put on in its place. This operation was continued for four days and nights without tasting food. The Taughairm commenced at midnight between Friday and Saturday, and had not long proceeded when infernal spirits began to enter the house or barn in which it was performing, in the form of black cats. The first cat that entered, after darting a furious look at the operator, said: 'Lachunn Odhar, thou son of Neil, that is bad usage of a cat.' Allan, who superintended as master of the rites, cautioned Lachunn that whatever he should hear or see, he must continue to turn the spit; and this was done accordingly. The cats continued to enter, and the yells of the cat on the spit, joined by the rest, were tremendous. A cat of enormous size at last appeared and told Lachunn Odhar that if he did not desist before his great-eared brother arrived, he never would behold the face of God. Lachunn answered that if all the devils in hell came he would not flinch until his task was concluded. By the end of the fourth day there was a black cat at the root of every rafter on the roof of the barn, and their yells were distinctly heard beyond the Sound of Mull in Morvern." Another account is given by the late Rev. Dr. Clerk of Kilmaille, [344] who states that Allan nan Creach, one of the Lochiels of the fifteenth century, had recourse "to the oracle of the Tigh Ghairm or House of Invocation (sic)." While incorrect in his spelling of the name, which has nothing to do with tigh 'house,' most of the other details agree with the preceding account. The king of the cats is named therein Cluasa Leabhra from his ears of portentous magnitude. The command given to the operant was: 'Hear you this or see you that, Round the spit and turn the cat.' [345] If the presumptuous mortal quailed he would become the prey of the Evil One; if bold enough the cats would answer any question in return for the release of the tortured beast. This Lochiel succeeded in attaining: he asked, it was said, 'What must I do to be saved?' and the answer of the oracle was a command to build seven churches, one for each of his great forays, and thus to expiate his sins. Another account [346] tells how the MacArthurs at Glassary made a taghairm. It is explained that "it seems if you make a Taghairm the Mac Molach (recte, Mag Molach, i.e. Hairy Hand or Paw) will come and tell you anything you ask him." MacArthur offered to fight all that was dead or alive within the sea, and from the evil consequences he was only saved by the virtues of the Need-Fire. But more important animals were sacrificed. Just as a white steer was sacrificed to the sky-god on the Capitol at Rome, [347] we hear of white bulls which the Gaulish druids sacrificed under the holy oak before they cut the mistletoe. [348]

It is recorded by Sir James Simpson, the discoverer of chloroform, that in the latter end of the eighteenth century his own father "was in early life personally engaged in the offering up and burying of a poor live cow as a sacrifice to the spirit of Murrain." [349] This was done within twenty miles of Edinburgh, and by a shrewd farrier who yet laid aside a corner of a field—'the gude-man's croft,'—as an offering to the Evil One. I well recollect how in the Highlands, when any loss occurred among cattle in spring (earchall) the hooves and sometimes the head or parts of it were taken away to the wood and buried secretly in the soil under great trees where nobody could possibly molest them. It was still better to bury them on an adjoining estate, and across a river. This was to put away the earchall and to prevent the loss of more animals. It was a giving of part for the whole. In some of the Isles there is still a memory of a cure for a species of cattle-plague [350] which was especially destructive of heifers. The old people said if the heifer's head were struck off at a single blow with a clean or stainless sword that the plague would cease, and that no further death would occur. [351] This was done in the eighteenth century. One who lived until 1820 remembered seeing his father bring home the decapitated heifer. The man's father explained the reason; he was wont to say likewise that they lost no more cattle by the plague.

"In Wales," says the Rev. John Evans in 1812, "when a violent disease breaks out amongst the horned cattle, the farmers of the district where it rages join to give up a bullock for a victim, which is carried to the top of a precipice from whence it is thrown down." He says this is known as "casting a captive to the devil." [352] In Cornwall, about 1800, a calf was burnt to death, the object of the sacrifice being to arrest the murrain! In Devon a ram was slain. [353] At Gaulish communal sacrifices Diodorus (v. 284) tells that close to the worshippers on certain religious occasions were "hearths laden with fire, and having upon them cauldrons and spits full of the carcases of whole animals." Animals were even bought for sacrifices, according to Arrian. [354]

I would not wish to press what Keating denies, but in the light of other survivals among the Celts the statement of Giraldus Cambrensis [355] can hardly be the offspring of his own imagination, but a survival in old belief, though not in the custom of his day. When the king of the Cineal Conaill used to be inaugurated, says Giraldus, an assembly was made of the people of his country on a high hill in his territory; a white mare being slain, and put to boil in a large pot in the centre of the field; on being boiled he was to drink up her broth like a hound or beagle with his mouth, and to eat the flesh out of his hands without having a knife or any instrument for cutting it. He would have to divide the rest of the flesh among the assembly, and then bathe himself in the broth. If this be a case of tribal totemistic communion-sacrifice part of the ritual is to be compared with that of the tarbh-feiss, or bull-feast, mentioned in The Sick-Bed of Cuchulainn as a means of divination, and with references to the horse as sacred elsewhere. We know the strong aversion we entertain against eating horse-flesh. It seems to be very old among the Celts. When Vercingetorix had sent away all his cavalry by night from Alesia, having barely corn for thirty days, Critognatus later on proposed to support life by the corpses of those who appeared useless for war on account of their age, as alluded to by Caesar for "singular and detestable cruelty." [356] A modern general would have utilised his horses for food. We seem to be in the presence of a taboo from a time when horses were sacred, as they were among the Icelanders, who up to the time of their adoption of Christianity ate horseflesh on certain occasions,—a liberty allowed them even after baptism, but soon discarded.

A Highland example is the sacrifice of bulls at Loch Maree. It is attested by the Records of the Presbytery of Dingwall, [357] from which I give the relevant extracts, omitting the parties' names for brevity's sake:

"At Appilcross, [358] 5th Sept. 1656.

... the presbyterie of Dingwall ... findeing amongst uther abhominable and heathenishe practices that the people in that place (Applecross) were accustomed to sacrifice bulls at a certaine tyme upon the 25 of August, which day is dedicate, as they conceive to S^n Mourie as they call him; and that there were frequent approaches to some ruinous chappels and circulateing of them; and that future events in reference especiallie to lyfe and death, in takeing of Journeyis, was exspect to be manifested by a holl of a round stone quherein they tryed the entering of their heade, which (if they) could doe, to witt be able to put in thair heade, they exspect thair returning to that place, and failing they considered it ominous; and withall their adoring of wells, and uther superstitious monuments and stones, tedious to rehearse Have appoynted as follows—That quhosoever sall be found to commit such abhominationes, especiallie Sacrifices of any kynd, or at any tyme, sall publickly appear and be rebuked ... six several Lord's dayis in six several churches, viz., Lochcarron, Appilcross, Contane, Fottertie, Dingwall, and last in Garloch paroch church. . .

"At Kenlochewe, 9 Septr 1656.

"Inter alia, Ordaines Mr Allex M'Kenzie, minister at Lochcarron, to cause summond Murdo M'conill varchue vic conill vic Allister in Torriton, and Donald Smyth in Appilcross, for sacrificing at Appilcross—to compeire at Dingwall the third Wednesday of October, with the men of Auchnaseallach.

"The brethren taking to their consideratione the abhominationes within the parochin of Garloch in sacrificing of beasts upon the 25 August, as also in pouring of milk upon hills as oblationes quhose names ar not particularly signified as yit—referres to the diligence of the minister to mak search of thease persones and summond them as said is in the former ordinance and act at Appilcross 5 Sept: 1656, and withall that by his private diligence he have searchers and tryers in everie corner of the countrey, especiallie about the Lochmourie, of the most faithful honest men he can find; and that such as ar his elders he particularly poseit, concerning former practices in quhat they knowe of these poore ones quho are called Mourie his derilans [359] and ownes thease titles, quho receaves the sacrifices and offerings upon the accompt of Mourie his poore ones; and that at laist some of thease be summoned to compeire before the pbrie the forsaid day, until the rest be discovered; and such as heve boats about the loch to transport themselves or uthers to the Ile of Mourie quherein ar monuments of Idolatrie. . . . The brethren heiring be report that Miurie hes his monuments and remembrances in severall paroches within the province, but more particularly in the paroches of Lochcarron, Lochalse, Kintaile, Contan, and Fottertie, and Lochbroome It is appoynted that the brethren ... heve a Correspondence, in trying and curbing all such. . . .

"At Dingwall, 6 August 1678.

"Inter alia, That day Mʳ Roderick Mackenzie minister at Gerloch by his letter to the prebrie, declared that he had summoned by his officer to this prebrie day Hector Mackenzie in Mellan in the parish of Gerloch, as also Johne Murdoch and Duncan Mackenzies, sons to the said Hector—as also Kenneth M'Kenzie his grandson, for sacrificing a bull in ane heathenish manner in the iland of St Ruffus commonly called Ellan Moury in Lochew, for the recovering of the health of Cirstane Mackenzie, spouse to the said Hector Mackenzie, who was formerlie sicke and valetudinaire:—Who being all cited, and not compeiring, are to be all summoned again pro 2°."

St. Maolrubha, whose death is recorded for the year 722, and whose historical double is Ruffus, was not the only saint on the way of being deified. Reginald of Durham has a notice of a bull being offered to St. Cuthbert, at his church on the Solway, on the festival kept on the day of the dedication of the church in the year 1164. [360] St. Maolrubha's well was desecrated through a mad dog having been brought to drink of its waters. Animal cures, moreover, were sometimes attempted by offering them the life of another animal. An instance is recorded by Hugh Miller in his Schools and Schoolmasters. He had paid a visit to his aunt's house at Gruids, Lairg, and saw "his cousin, George, administer to an ailing cow a little live trout, simply because the traditions of the district assured him that a trout swallowed alive by the creature was the only specific in the case." Again, the animal life offered may be simply buried alive as a sacrificial rite, as when a live cock or a live toad is buried in the hope of curing some bodily ailments. The idea here is that of putting the disease away—do ut abeas, 'I give that thou mayst be gone.' With the burial act one may compare the rite of burying a murdered man's boots to prevent his spirit from returning to earth again. [361] A certain disease among cattle, Na Geumraich, or 'cattle lowing,' was held to be curable only by human blood. The Rev. C. Robertson [362] gives an independent account which corroborates the one I now quote by a clergyman lately deceased and long familiar with the district.

"The most horrible of sacrificial remedies was that in vogue at one time for the cure of cattle-madness. It is reported that a farmer in Kinlochewe had his cattle infected with that disease, and was unable to heal them by ordinary means. He was told that if he could get the heart of a man who did not know his parents, and dip it in a tub of water, that he would have his remedy. By sprinkling the water on the cattle the trouble would be washed away. He could not expect to get that, but the idea got hold of him, and kept him on the alert for the charm. A travelling pack merchant or pedlar happened to come to his house one evening, and he was hospitably entertained. In course of conversation the man gave as much of his history as he remembered at the time. Among other things, he said that he knew nothing of his people, that he did not know even the names of his parents. He got up next morning and set out on his journey towards Torridon. When about half-way through the glen he was overtaken by his host of the previous evening who demanded his life. The poor man said that he might have all his goods without a struggle on his part if that was what he was after. But the murderer told him plainly that he wanted no less than his life, that he followed him for his heart to cure his cattle. He took out his heart there and then and prepared the remedy. It is said that the cattle had been cured, but that the disease was transferred to his family. Some of his descendants, who inherited the transferred madness, were spotted up to the middle of last century as families who were under a more terrible ban than that of Gehazi." [363]

In Breadalbane "there is a tradition that, once upon a time, when a pestilence raged among the herds on the south side of Lochtay, a ghastly tragedy was enacted. Actuated by a heathenish desire to propitiate some evil spirit or other, the people seized a poor 'gangrel body,' bound him hand and foot, and placed him in the ford of Ardtalnaig burn ... a little further up the stream than the present bridge. All the cattle in that district were then driven over his body, and the poor creature's life was crushed out." [364]

A manuscript of Cormac's Glossary gives an alternative, though unscientific, derivation for the name Emain: "No em ab ema [αἱμα] id est sanguine quia ema sanguis est. Uin i.e. unus quia sanguis unius hominis [effusus est] in tempore conditionis ejus." In other words, the wrong etymology there given is a suggestion that the word 'Emain, Emain' signifies 'the blood of one,' because the blood of one man was poured forth at the founding of Emain.

The need of immolating a human being to ensure the stability of a building Dr. Stokes notes in his edition of Cormac as a superstition still current in India. Grimm tells us that in 1843, during the building of the new bridge at Halle, it was a popular superstition that one required to bury a child in the foundation, and he cites similar beliefs among the Danes, Greeks, and Servians. We find a parallel belief in Britain, as is recorded by Nennius. When Guorthigern wishes to build Dinas Emris his druids say "Nisi infantem sine patre invenies et occidetur ille, et arx a sanguine suo aspergatur, nunquam aedificatur in aeternum." A child without a father has to be found and slain, and the fortress is to be built in such an one's blood if the building is to stand. The Irish-Gaelic Nennius expressly says that Guorthigern, with his hosts and with his druids, traversed all the south of the island of Britain until they arrived at Guined, and they searched all the mountains of Herer and there found a Dinn (Dùn or fort) over the sea, and a very strong locality fit to build on; and his druids said to him: "Build here thy fortress," said they, "for nothing shall ever prevail against it." Builders were then brought thither, and they collected materials for the fortress, both stone and wood, but all these materials were carried away in one night; and materials were thus gathered thrice and thrice carried away. And he asked of his druids: "Whence is this evil?" said he. And the druids said: "Seek a son whose father is unknown, kill him, and let his blood be sprinkled upon the Dùn, for by this means only it can be built." Messengers were sent by him throughout the island of Britain to seek for a son without a father; and they searched as far as Magh Eillite, in the territory of Glevisic, where they found boys a-hurling; and there happened a dispute between two of the boys, so that one said to the other: "O man without a father, thou hast no good at all." The messengers asked: "Whose son is the lad to whom this is said?" Those on the hurling green said: "We know not," said they; "his mother is here." They asked of his mother whose son the lad was. The mother answered: "I know not that he bath a father, and I know not how he happened to be conceived in my womb at all." So the messengers took the boy with them to Guorthigern, and told him how they found him. On the next day the army was assembled that the boy might be killed. And the boy was brought before the king, and he said to the king: "Wherefore have they brought me to thee?" said he. And the king said: "To slay thee and to butcher thee, and to consecrate this fortress with thy blood [dod marbudsa, ar sé, ocus dod coscrad ocus do cosergud in duin sea dod fhuil]." The boy said: "Who instructed thee in this?" "My Druids," said the king. "Let them be called hither," said the boy. And the druids came. The boy said to them: "Who told you that this fortress could not be built until it was first consecrated with my blood?" And they answered not. [365]

Dr. Todd seems of opinion that the practice of auspicating the foundation of cities, temples, or other solemn structures was not of remote antiquity, and throws some doubt upon parallel instances from a ninth century compilator, Johannes Malala, who records that at the foundation of Antioch, Selecus Nicator erected a pedestal and statue of the virgin Aemathe sacrificed as the Fortune of the city, as he likewise is said to have done at the foundation of Laodicea in Syria, where the walls were dug in the track of the blood of a wild boar, and a virgin named Agave is said to have been sacrificed and a brazen statue erected to her as the fortune of the city. But Dr. Todd emphasises the point that the narrative in Nennius has this distinction, that repeated failures had shown the necessity of some piacular rite wherein it more nearly agrees with the legend of St. Odran (Oran) of Iona. It is quite true that the story of St. Odran's self-sacrifice is unnoticed in Adamnan's Life of Columcille, a story which Bishop Reeves calls "curious and not very creditable." Historic fact, however, has an interest entirely apart from quality of action, the belief has to be accounted for quite apart from what actually happened to St. Odran. It is not possible that any such thing happened in Columcille's following, but the legend points to the popular folk-belief in what was expected to occur.

But the Gaelic 'Life of Columcille' in the Book of Lismore, dating from a late age when legend was more active with Columcille's memory than even the embellishments of Adamnan's age could tolerate, we read how the saint reached Iona on the night of Pentecost. Two bishops who dwelt in the land came to expel him from it. But God revealed to Colomb Cille that they were not bishops in truth.

Wherefore they left the island when he told them of their own conclusion and their account. Said Colomb Cille to his household: [366] "It is well for us that our roots should go under the ground here." And he said: "It is permitted to you, that some one of you should go under the earth here or under the mould of the island to consecrate it." Odrán rose up readily and this he said: "If I should be taken," saith he, "I am ready for that." "O Odrán!" saith Colomb Cille, "thou shalt have the reward thereof. No prayer shall be granted to anyone at my grave, unless it is first asked of thee." Then Odrán went to heaven. Colomb founded a church by him afterwards.

This narrative cannot be historical, inasmuch as Odrán is not included in the oldest list of Columcille's companions, and the Annals of the Four Masters record his death in 548 i.e. fifteen years before Columcille came to Hy. Yet the narrative undoubtedly is a piece of folk-belief. It is hard for men to realise that the gods as spoken of in legends really never had actual outward existence, great as is the part they played in the history of man and of mind. The Divine Life was ever perfect and One. And a narrative like this, while not historically true to fact, is historically true as a record of belief, and points to a possible time when there was an actual basis of fact. I do not know when certain legends arose which detail the story of a beggar woman, who while passing the way at the time was buried alive under the foundation-stone of a Highland manse I know well, along with a live cock. It was believed, and yet the building did not exist at the date specified, although the legend may have been transferred from another building more than a mile away, which latter could have come by this association from a pre-Christian sacred place. In like spirit it is still related that Odrán had offered himself in sacrifice, for the walls of Columcille's first edifice in Iona fell down as soon as built owing to evil agencies. Oran was duly interred alive, and spoke as follows to Colomb Cille who on the third day went to the grave to see how his friend fared, when he was told by St. Oran

Chan eil am bàs 'na iongantas
No Ifrinn mar a dh'aithrisear

i.e.

Death is no wonder
Nor is Hell as it is said.

Shocked by such a speech Colomb Cille called out: ùir, ùir sùil Odhrain! mun labhair e tuille còmhraidh i.e. Earth, Earth, on Oran's eye! lest he talk more. St. Oran was credited with laxer views than Columcille, if we follow the version of his answer which Sheriff Nicolson got from Tiree:

Chan eil an t-Eug 'na annas
  s chan eil Ifrinn mar a dùbhrar;
Cha teid math am mùthadh
  's cha bhi olc gun dìoladh.

i.e.

Death is nothing strange,
  Nor Hell as has been said;
Good will not perish,

Nor evil be unpunished.

These theologians of Tiree may never have heard of Aristophanes, but their irony reminds one of the passage in The Frogs where, pointing out the difference between the old style of officials and the new, he says that nowadays State offices are filled with the pharmakos or human scape-goat, from which we infer the existence of such similar practices among the Greeks:

Any chance man that we come across
Not fit in old days for a pharmakos
   These we use
   And these we choose
The veriest scum, the mere refuse.

To expel a pharmakos or human scape-goat was among the Greeks a symbolic act of purification. If a calamity, a Greek historian tells us, overtook a city, whether it were famine or pestilence, or any other mischief, they led forth, as though to a sacrifice, the most unsightly of them all as a purification and a remedy to the suffering city. They set the sacrifice in the appointed place, and gave him cheese with their hands and a barley cake and figs, and seven times they smote him with leeks and wild figs and other wild plants. Finally they burnt him with fire with the wood of wild trees, and scattered the ashes to the sea and to the winds, for a purification. [367]

Later on I shall speak of the Sin-Eater under Funeral-Rites. Here suffice it to say I am reminded of the Gaelic phrase: cuir am mach am Bàs, referring to the expulsion of death in a symbolic act, as is often the case in primitive ritual. Death is symbolised as an old woman or cailleach, who undergoes the process of expulsion by representation. The survival of the ceremony, although the Gaelic phrase is not given, is described in Stewart's Highland Superstitions and Amusements: [368] "Some wiseacre by some lucky chance discovered that at this festive season (Xmas), when the asperity of its character is probably much softened, even relentless death himself can be compromised with on very advantageous terms. By the sacrifice of an old woman, or any other body whom he wished in a better world, and whom, by the following process, he chose to send to it, death was debarred from any farther claim to himself, or his friends, until the return of the next anniversary. He went to the wood this night, fetched home the stump of some withered tree, which he regularly constituted the representative of some person of the description ... mentioned, and whose doom was inevitably fixed by the process, without resort or appeal. Such a simple mode of obtaining security from a foe whom everybody fears, could not be supposed to fall into desuetude; and the custom is therefore retained, whatever faith may exist as to its utility, in some parts of the country even to this day."

Death as expelled through symbol in the Highlands may be paralleled by the old Greek rite of the 'expulsion of hunger,' which Plutarch speaks of as an ancestral sacrifice. This riddance or expulsion did not amount to a purification ceremony, but was magical. A household slave was beaten with rods of agnus castus—a plant of cathartic quality—and driven outside, with the words, "Out with hunger, in with health and wealth." The nearest thing to this in the Highlands is when, on the occasion of death visiting a house, one who condoles is given the answer at times: Is math nach e'n t-acras thainig, ''tis well it is not Hunger that has visited us.'

Where human life is required for the prevention of an evil we come upon the principle of vicarious sacrifice. Among literary references I note that St. Finnian of Clonard "died on behalf of the people of the Gaels that they might not all die of the Buidhe Chonaill." [369] In the tale of the Expulsion of the Déisi the druid of one of the opposing armies sacrifices himself to secure victory to his own side. [370] Eimíne Bán and forty-nine of his monks vicariously sacrificed themselves by voluntary death in order to save Bran úa Faeláin, King of Leinster, and forty-nine Leinster chiefs from the pestilence which was then desolating Leinster. [371]

Of the idea that one must die to secure the recovery of another a striking instance is given in Leslie Forbes's Early Races of Scotland. When Hector Monro, XVIIth Baron of Fowlis, was ill in 1588, a witch whose amulet-water had proved in vain informed him that he could not recover unless in the words of the indictment, "the principal man of his bluid should die for him." Another authentic instance, that of Hugh Mackay of Halmadary, I have quoted elsewhere. [372] Insane imagination and religious frenzy had transformed a black cock into a satanic spirit. The decision to offer Hugh Mackay's son as a sacrificial victim was prevented by the humanity of a girl who had reason enough left to protect the child: when the roof was taken off the house at the instance of outsiders the spell of madness was broken. Afterwards the Good-Man of Halmadary and his associates showed sincere repentance and shame, as well they might! But the principle on which they went was parallel to the belief which Caesar attributes to the Gauls that unless the life of a man be offered for the life of a man the mind of the immortal gods cannot be propitiated. In Gadhelic verse the Dinnshenchas of Mag Slecht tells of the great idol Cromm Cruaich: "to him they used to offer the firstlings of every issue and the chief scions of every clan." Around him were four times three stone idols (trí hídail chloch fo chethair).

"It made every tribe be without peace.
Twas a sad evil!
Brave Gaels used to worship it.
From it they would not without tribute ask
To be satisfied as to their portion of the hard world.
He was their god

. . . .
To him without glory
They would kill their piteous wretched offspring
With much wailing and peril
To pour their blood around Cromm Cruaich.
Milk and corn
They would ask from him speedily
In return for one-third of their healthy (or whole) issue:
Great was the horror and the scare of him
To him
Noble Gaels would prostrate themselves;
From the worship of him with many manslaughters
The plain is called Mag Slecht." [373]

Tradition still faintly whispers of sacrifices at the altar stone of Callernish Temple in Lewis: and there are folk-surmises to say the least as regards some other 'Druid' circles on the mainland. Analogy would point to similar rites as those in honour of Cromm. The poem quoted states that to the coming of Patrick "there was worshipping of stones." [374] Such incidents as have been referred to seem to show that sacrifice is a complex act of offering which embraces commensality and purification with their train of joyous thoughts and acts; giving with a joyous expectation of being given unto; propitiation with the fearsome hope of averting ills; culminating in the case of humanity in the thought of substitution, or life for life. Doubtless there was much variation over the Celtic areas, while for Gaul Caesar's account [375] holds. "The nation of the Gauls is extremely devoted to superstitious rites; and on that account they who are troubled with unusually severe diseases, and they who are engaged in battles and dangers, either sacrifice men as victims, or vow that they will sacrifice them, and employ the Druids as the performers of those sacrifices, because they think that unless the life of a man be offered for the life of a man the mind of the immortal gods cannot be rendered propitious, and they have sacrifices of that kind ordained for national purposes. Others have figures of vast size; the limbs of which, formed of osiers, they fill with living men, which being set on fire the men perish enveloped in the flames. They consider that the oblation of such as have been taken in theft or in robbery, or any other offence, is more acceptable to the immortal gods; but when a supply of that class is wanting, they have recourse to the oblation of even the innocent."

In a previous chapter Caesar tells that to be interdicted from the sacrifices was among the Gauls a most heavy punishment: "Those who have been thus interdicted are esteemed in the number of the impious and the criminal: all shun them and avoid their society and conversation, lest they receive some evil from their contact; nor is justice administered to them when seeking it, nor is any dignity bestowed on them." [376] Sacrifice was thus a most vital bond. Procopius, [377] in referring to the inhabitants of Thule, relates that they regarded their first prisoner of war as the best: the victim was hanged from a tree, cast among thorns, or otherwise horribly done to death. Plutarch [378] particularly emphasises that with the Gauls human sacrifices was the most perfect form of sacrifice. This is confirmed by a rite among the Gauls of Massilia (Marseilles) of which we learn from Servius's Commentary on Vergil. [379] As often as there was a pestilence one of the poor offered himself to be hospitably entertained at the public expense and on the choicest of foods for a full year. Thereafter, having been decorated with boughs and raiment such as were used at sacrifices, he was led through the whole city amid execrations that he might take upon himself the sins (mala) of the whole community, and was thus thrown down from a height as a propitiatory sacrifice.

All these observances in Celtic lands hang more or less together in the matter of fundamental ideas. The gods must not be treated with neglect; the right social observances constitute religion, which is a stated carefulness of rites that is the opposite to neglect. The individual must not come empty-handed for the primitive god is often a magnified human chief in his ways; [380] he must know how to appease the angry deity; he may even feel he has to slay the god's human representative, while his vigour has not suffered decay. Whether it be through the communal-sacrificial meal, or through identification of himself with the nature of the animal offered, or by imitation of such identity as in the case of the man clad in cow-skin, [381] or by human sacrifice, it is only thus that he attains to magic contact with what is taken for divine. The divine touch puts all fear to rest. The essence of sacrifice is contact in the sense that ceremonial contact with sacred objects brings strength. A word may bring one into such contact; to partake of particles of the sacred object begets contact; to place a stone on the cairn where the funeral procession rests brings one into ceremonial contact with the spirit of the deceased, who of old was thought to live on in the body and rest where it rested. Or one may even get into contact with the spirit of the living, as when one makes a vow after missing any article of value that should it be recovered one will give a gift or its equivalent to the saint of the place. This is the West Sutherland rite of putting a shilling (or whatever it be) on a good man. With the element of contact which brings strength there goes the possibility of compulsion or magical control, and hence arises a code of things to be avoided as well as done.

The things proper to be done are positive enactments full of wonder-working power; most of the religious ritual is of this sort, for there is a binding of the object of one's faith, which in Old Irish is iress, 'on-standing,' surviving in modern amharus, i.e. an + iress, 'non-faith or doubt,' and this attitude throughout a series of ceremonial acts is summed up in the attitude of a supreme act of trust, crābhadh; Old Irish crabud, 'faith,' Cymric crefydd, Sanscrit vi-çrambh, 'trust.' The magic or wonder-working element at the basis of even the most rudimentary cult abides throughout and survives in the highest religion on its ceremonial side where the transition is made to awe. How else can we account for the Gaelic ōrtha, from the Latin orationem, 'prayer,' being now the current word for 'spell': e.g. in speaking of a witch one says: chuir i an ōrth' ann, i.e. 'she put a magic spell on him.' There is also the native Gadhelic ubaidh, ubag, 'a charm,' Old Irish upta, 'fascination,' Manx obbee, 'sorcery,' all ultimately from a root ba, 'to speak.' Yet prayer in its essence precedes magic. The rudiments of a voice of conscience speak or whisper in the manadh or 'warning,' and of old it was felt that natural signs follow to corroborate a just verdict. Thus we read in Keating, [382] for example: "When Fachtna delivered an unjust judgement, if it was in the autumn he delivered it, the fruit fell to the ground that night in the country in which he was. But when he delivered a just judgement, the fruit remained in full on the trees; or if in the spring he delivered an unjust judgement, the cattle forsook their young in that country. Morann, son of Maon, gave no judgement without having the Morann collar round his neck, and when he gave an unjust judgement the collar grew tight round his neck, and when he gave a just judgement the collar stretched out over his shoulders. . . . And so it was with several Pagan authors, they were subject to geasa (prohibitions, tabus), preventing them from partiality in history or judgement."

Surrounded by so many dangers, it was unavoidable that even in rudimentary religion there should arise a code of what was 'crossed' or forbidden (air a chrosadh), or tabu, not to be lightly approached,—hence a series of negative precepts or prohibitions.

It is forbidden (tha e air a chrosadh) for a young lad or a young woman to sweep out the room in which a corpse has been. This should be done by a woman who is past child-bearing. The idea is that the influence of Death is about and may endanger the potency of the developing life; one is reminded of the practice in the Congo region, where they abstain for a whole year from sweeping out the house where a man has died, lest the dust should offend the ghost; [383] as also of the Albanian custom of refraining on the day of the funeral from sweeping the place where the corpse lay. [384] In the Highlands it is forbidden for a male child to sweep the floor and the hearthstone in a room where a death has just been; [385] the sweepings seem as if in such intimate consecration to the powers of death that there is a danger of injuring the development of virility. Take not the ashes from off the hearth, the old folks used to say; nothing else is so 'blasting' as to wipe the hearth clean. I would prefer the fire to be alive thereon than not. Others would cast a shower of ashes before them ere entering. That's what the old folks would say: I don't know if they were right, but there were witches since the beginning of the world, and there will be unto the end, so long as the world is a world, [386] according to my authority.

Here is a series of things Taboo which the Rev. A. Macdonald tabulated for the Isle of Eriskay and its neighbourhood: It is not right to throw a comb to a person; do not throw a comb but at thine enemy; [387] it is not right to bury a person on a Friday, nor to kill a sheep on a Friday, nor to cut hair nor pare nails on Friday or Sunday. It is not right to plough on Good Friday, though it is allowable to plant potatoes with a wooden dibble (pleadhag) and to rake the ground with the three-toothed wooden hammer called a rake. It is not right to change residence going from north to south except on Monday, and when going from south to north one should go on Saturday. [388] It is not right to sew clothes on Sunday: no man who has had his clothes stitched on the Lord's Day will walk straight. [389] If a woman tells you that the new moon is visible, it is not right to go and look at it; when making the frìth, if a woman be seen she is the omen of some untoward event.

It is not right to count the number of teeth in a comb. It means that you are numbering the days of your life.

It is not right to be touching the chain (slabhruidh) over the fire. It is said to be cursed. The devil is called Am fear th'air an t-slabhruidh, 'the man on the chain.' I remember once when there was a talk of a public official leaving the island of Uist that I remarked that he might be replaced by a worse. The reply was: cha'n urrainn gun tig mur a tig an t-slabhruidh a nall buileach = 'such a one could not come unless the chain break entirely.'

There was a man who noticed that his cows ceased suddenly giving milk. He had a strong suspicion that a woman in the neighbourhood was at the bottom of the mischief. He went into her house one day in her absence. He found nobody in but a little innocent child,—the daughter of the woman in question. He asked her if her mother gave her any milk to drink. The child said Yes. Where does your mother get the milk? was the next query. Bhiodh i ga bhleoghainn as an t-slabhruidh = 'she would be drawing it from the chain,' said the child. Siuthad, a ghradhag, dian thusa mar a bhitheas i 'dianamh = 'Come, darling, do you as she is in the habit of doing.' The child did go and the milk came from the chain. The man tore down the chain and took it with him, and the lost toradh, 'milk produce,' returned to him (Anne M'Intyre). There was a plant, the torannan or toradan, that was used as being held able to prevent the milk being spirited away.

To recover the toradh filched away. One plan is to go to the house of the party suspected of taking it, and to pull off the roof of his house as much thatch and divot as he can with his two hands, and to proceed home with this. Then a pot is put on the fire and this thatch is thrown gradually on the fire beneath the pot. In the pot is put the little milk that has been left, and the thatch is kept burning under it until it dries up. This brings the toradh back. [390] A male is preferable for the ceremony of the thatch-snatching.

To a person who makes a very brief call and is in a hurry to get away they say: An ann a dhiarraidh teine thàinig thu, i.e. 'is it to seek fire you have come? '

It is not right to mend or stitch clothes while the clothes are on the person. It interferes with the rights of the dead, to whom alone belongs the privilege of having their death linens sewed upon the body (Mary Ann Campbell, 1895).

It is not right (ceart) for a man to cut his own hair or even part of it. Whatever it means the meaning has reference 'to raising the scissors above one's own breath' (togail an t-siosar os cionn analach). Perhaps it refers to cutting the breath of life which is the thread of life (do. do.).

It is not right to return to the meal-chest the leavings of meal that may be on the table when baking (cha'n eil e ceart an fhalaid a thilleadh dha'n chistidh).

It is not right to be humming a song while baking (cha'n eil e ceart a bhi ri gnōdhan orain an am a bhi fuine).

It is not right to leave the band on the spinning-wheel when you are setting it past for the night. The sign of the cross should be made over it.

It is not right to card or spin or work in wool on Saturday night. It is said that a woman who was twisting threads with a spinning jenny on Saturday night had her forefinger and middle finger joined together ever after, these being the fingers that would be used.

It is not right to spin if there be a corpse in the same township.

It is not right to take fire out of a house where there is a child who has not got teeth yet. It is said that the child will never get teeth if the fire be taken away.

It is not right for a woman to comb her hair at night. Every hair that she loses will get entangled about the feet of a relative who is sailing in a ship (cha'n eil gas a dh'fhalbhas asaibh nach bidh dol mu 'chasan duine bhuineas duibh ann san t-saghach [391]).

It is not right to lose the buarach or the spancel tie that goes about the cows' feet at milking time. It is considered by the older people as something holy and venerable. The best are made of horse hair. Some, after milking the cattle, take the ties in their hands while walking after the cattle and have a fixed spot for hanging them up on their return from driving the cattle out. The reason was that a person finding the tie (buarach) might get the toradh, or produce, of your cattle.

It is not right at milking time if a person passes who is suspected of having the evil eye to answer him even though he addresses you. Your silence, or the animosity signified thereby, has an influence in checking any harm that might come from him.

THE EARTHLY JOURNEY (PART 3)

IT was not right to make a cake of the kind known as Bonnach Boise(adh), i.e. a small cake shaped and made on the palm of the hand, without making a hole in the middle of it. The reason assigned is that thus the fairies would not be able to take it away if it were so marked (John Smith, Jun., S. Boisdale). Possibly the origin of the ceremony is due to the time when certain placenta were used as emblems in phallic worship (Father Allan).

It was a source of danger to the soul of a warrior if he fell in battle fasting. Such was the case with one of the Macleans of Lochbuy, in Mull, known as Eoghann a chinn bhig, 'Eoghan of the Little Head,' whose grave is in Iona. His spirit found no rest and his apparition (taibhse) has been fabled for 300 years to have been seen: he rides his mettlesome horse as he did when he fell in battle, in consequence of his having fought on the fatal day without having broken his fast (thuit e na thrasg). [392]

The multitude of restrictions are so numerous that it would serve no purpose to further amplify the above; suffice it to refer to the curious restrictions on the old Irish kings, derived probably from the earlier ages of the priest-kings. The sun might not rise at Tara on the King of Ireland in his bed, with which compare Ossian's advice to his mother; [393] he was not to alight on a Wednesday at Magh Breagh, nor traverse Magh Cuilinn after sunset: on Monday after May-day (Bealltuine) he must not go in a ship; the Tuesday after Samhuin he was not to leave the track of his army upon Ath Maighne. The King of Leinster was forbidden to do certain acts on Mondays and Wednesdays. The King of Ulster might not listen to the fluttering of the birds at Linn Sailech after sunset [because he had some bird-ancestor?]; might not celebrate a certain bull-feast nor drink of the water of Bo-Neimhidh between two darknesses. The King of Connaught might not sit on the grave mound of the wife of Maine in harvest time, nor go on a grey steed in a speckled garment to Dal Chais, nor conclude a treaty concerning his palace at Cruachan after having made peace at All-H allows. [394]

Even before the Christian mission had familiarised the Gadhelic tribes with the Latin peccatum, which has become peacadh, 'sin,' the language testifies to burdens which must be inferred to have pressed heavily if we may judge from the native Gadhelic word fine, 'sin': ar fine glossed .i. ar pectha in Sanctáin's Hymn, as to which Stokes thinks cognation with Latin vieo, vitium, Anglo-Saxon wídl seems probable. [395] Irish cean, cion, means 'transgression, fault, sin.' Another word, immorbus, is frequent in the sense of 'trespass, sin, scandalum.' [396] The magician's spell (òrtha, ubaidh, obaidh, etc.), the wizard's word (facal), the incantation-charm (eòlas) of native medicine-men, the sacrifices (ìiobairtean) of Druids were alike impotent and vain, but were not and could not be abandoned until it was brought home to the more thoughtful minds that magical ceremonies and incantations did not really effect the results they were designed to produce. The spirit of the hymn ascribed to St. Patrick in the energy with which it abandons the nature-worship, and the spirit of the scathing words of Gildas as to a blind people that worshipped rivers and stocks and stones could not become readily diffused among the folk. Nor is it still; the eòlas or charm is resorted to, and in this parish in which I write there lived quite recently a man who was credited with the ability of stopping a flow or issue of blood by a spell; and another not long deceased had a like power ascribed to him in Assynt; while there are still living more than one in Ross-shire who will transmit this secret as carefully as the Druid wizards of old, passing it by word of mouth, with necessary restrictions, from father to daughter, and so forth through a continual alternation from man to woman, from woman to man. Eòlas Casga Fola, [397] 'the charm for staunching blood,' was known in the Isle of Man; Moore gives a charm to staunch the horse's blood: "Three Maries went to Rome, the spirits of the church stiles and the spirits of the houghs or sea-cliffs (ny Keimee as ny Cughtee), Peter and Paul, a Mary of them said, stand; another Mary of them said, walk; the other Mary of them said, may this blood stop (or heal) as the blood stopped which came out of the wounds of Christ: me to say it and the Son of Mary to fulfil it." Another Manx charm to stop blood I give in Moore's translation: "Three godly men came from Rome—Christ, Peter, and Paul. Christ was on the cross, his blood flowing, and Mary on her knees close by. One took the enchanted one in his right hand, and Christ drew a cross over him. Three young women came over the water, one of them said, 'up'; another one said, 'stay'; and the third one said, 'I will stop the blood of man or woman.' Me to say it, and Christ to do it, in the name of the Father, and the Son, and the Holy Ghost." [398]

The resort to similar charms is by no means quite a thing of the past. I gave in my Leabhar nan Gleann a short charm for toothache which I know to have been believed in in my own time. The exorciser—a very decent shepherd—invariably resorted to a wood and made a notch in a tree, which is a reminiscence of the cult of tree spirits and of the belief in the tree-soul. And I well recollect a certain Barbara Ghriogail (sic) who was possessed of a small crystal pebble which possessed some magnetic property, as it was often of use in removing things from the eyes of cattle and of persons. She practised a charm—Eòlas a' Chronachaidh—which I already gave. These are charms for averting evil, and come under the head of ἀποτροπη, or 'averting'; the Latins personified the spirits that controlled this process into Dii averruncii, the gods that avert evil.' In the averting ritual water had to be lifted in a wooden ladle at a stream over which the living and the dead passed; it was not suffered to touch the ground, and when taken up it was done in the name of the Sacred Trinity; silver coins were put into the ladle and also a copper coin; the whole was blessed with the sign of the cross, and according to a ritual of divination it was thought that a wise-person could tell whether it was a male's or a female's eye that had been the bewitching agent. Thereafter the patient was sprinkled with some of the lustral water, and what remained over was dashed against a huge boulder-stone not likely ever to be moved. Evil was thus transferred for ever to the stone, and the 'evil eye' was lifted from off the sufferer. On the other hand, the opposite process could take place, and a transference of virtue be effected: rites connected with the biting of the tearnadh, or 'afterbirth' (see Ch. I.), may be cited in illustration; a simple case is that of getting the razor with which a person well-to-do has committed suicide, which is the magic means of transferring the luck of the dead to the happy possessor through 'contact '; perhaps one may adduce the possession of a caul—or thin membrane covering a child's head at birth—which in the Isle of Man and elsewhere was supposed to be a preventive against shipwreck and drowning. Similarly in West Ross-shire water drunk from the skull of a suicide—and a suicide ranks as a criminal—was held to be a cure for epilepsy; in East Inverness-shire it was held to bring good luck and to be a cure for toothache.

A proper witness for West Ross is the late Rev. Kenneth Macdonald of Applecross, [399] who states: "Another cure for epilepsy is a drink from the skull of a suicide. One may be found in Torridon on the west of Ross-shire still. Two years ago a man from Shieldaig declared that he used the skull himself for that purpose, and that he knew where it was kept. They (i.e. the suicides) had to be buried in some hole in a hill out of the sight of the sea. If his grave could be seen from the sea it was supposed to be enough to drive all fish from the coast. So strong was this belief that cases are on record in which the remains of suicides which had been buried by their friends in their own burying-ground were exhumed by the neighbours and removed to a spot hidden out of the sight of the sea. And yet by some perversity of human nature the withered skull of a suicide is supposed to be a blessing to mankind. It would appear then that the Druid still lives and competes with the evangelist in some localities. The Druid of the first century made no secret of his belief that human sacrifices were acceptable to the gods. Criminals as a rule were used for this purpose. And if a man was cannibal enough to eat a bit of the victim's flesh, he by that act rose in the good-will of heaven. He was supposed to have absorbed into his system so much of the substance of what was consecrated to God. He was in fact part of the atonement and therefore had a special claim to the blessings secured. Human sacrifices are now forbidden by the law of Britain and the druidical Highland worshipper cannot got nearer participation in the gruesome sacrificial feast than to lick the skull of one of a class who would have been sacrificed to Apollo had he lived 2000 years ago."

Mr. Macdonald was for many years Free Church minister in Applecross and his testimony is indisputable. And there is the further witness of an authentic writer which I may quote: "It was a popular belief among the old people that a suicide buried within sight of the sea drove away the herrings for seven years. Any person who came by his or her death in this way was invariably buried behind the church. I well remember as a child hearing a discussion about the burial of a woman who 'put herself aside,' as it is expressed in Gaelic. Her people, who were by way of being superior to such beliefs, were anxious that she should be buried in the family grave; but this was not at all relished by the community, and after a good deal of wrangling she was interred in a remote corner of the churchyard, well out of sight of the sea.

"More than a generation ago, a certain Englishman, who happened to be staying in our neighbourhood, committed suicide, and in spite of all protests he was buried by his relatives in full sight of the Loch. So indignant were the natives at this violation of their traditions that one night shortly afterwards, a party of them disinterred him at midnight, carried the remains away to another churchyard in an inland parish ten miles away, and there re-buried him. It must have been a very grim sort of performance; though grimmer still is another rite which to this day is, I am told, practised sub rosa in connection with this self-same person. It is, I believe, a fact, that the skull of this long-dead Englishman is lying perdu somewhere about the churchyard, its whereabouts being known only to one or two privileged individuals, and is used by epileptics to drink out of; a common belief being that if these unfortunates drink out of the skull of a suicide, the complaint will be cured. Only last summer, a woman whose son is afflicted in this way, said to me: 'Oh! we have done everything for him and tried every known cure; we had him prayed for in church and we even sent down for so and so's skull (mentioning the Englishman) to see if it would do any good.'" [400]

A correspondence on this subject, styled "A Torridon Myth," took place in the Scotsman in 1901, I think, and though the minister of the parish denied both the superstition and the existence of the skull, a correspondent finally declared that he himself had drunk water from the skull as a cure for epilepsy. The two points to be noted are (1) that the suicide is a criminal, (2) that the criminal is a sacrificed victim. Acting on this belief witches in former ages endeavoured to get portions of the body of such as were hung on the gallows in order to make potent charms from them; and in 1591 in Scotland a case was proved against these witches of having opened graves at the devil's orders and taken the fingers and toes of the dead "to make ane powder of them, to do evil withal." In the Middle Ages the Templars were said to have made use of human skulls in their secret rites at midnight; and the early Celts, if we believe Livy, used the head of an enemy, i.e. in their idea, of a criminal for secret purposes, while the Boii are said to have used the head as the appropriate vessel out of which to make drink offerings. A copan-cinn, i.e. the 'pan' of the skull, I have in my own time heard spoken of with subdued awe. A man touched with the hand of one who had been hanged was, in Cornish belief, held to be cured; pickled and dried such was a 'hand of glory' potent in discovering treasure. For further cases compare Southey's Thalaba and the Ingoldsby Legends. The skulls of slain enemies were coveted trophies of valour, doubtless because the luck and prowess of the dead were thus secured. The criminal, too, was slain sacrificially to take the place of 'devoted' persons; and it is likely that it was from personating the latter class that in most human sacrifices the victims were criminals. These, as they had not completed their cycle of life—and life was held to be a constant or complete quantity—had such virtues left which constituted a 'luck ' to be transmitted. But before the criminal life was accepted there was the earlier stage of certain ones devoted' to the god; I think of the ritual of certain Gaulish priestesses on an island at the mouth of the Loire. No man durst visit this isle of women; it had a roofed temple, which the women annually unroofed, but it had to be re-roofed before sunset. Each woman brought on her shoulders a burden of the roofing materials, and if any one suffered her burden to fall to the ground she was torn to pieces instantly by her companions and her mangled remains carried round the temple. See the account in Rhys's Hibbert Lectures, following Strabo. Another account in Pomponius Mela adds the trait that these perpetual virgins could rouse the sea and wind by their incantations, turn themselves into whatever animal form they chose, cure diseases, and were 'devoted' to the services of voyagers only who have set out on no other errand than to consult them (Mela, iii. 6). There was a witch in Assynt, near Drumbeg, known as Mór Bhán, who had a similar gift of raising wind for becalmed sailors, and her memory is still fresh among the people. [401] In the isle of Gigha, too, there was a similar 'witch.' The tabu against any of the roofing material touching the ground reminds me of the holy water got from the Willock family in Strathnāin, which lost its virtue if the bottle containing it were allowed to touch the ground before it reached the house where it was sprinkled in the ritual of 'averting,' of cronachadh or ἀποτροπή in the widest sense, and the water received its virtue through the wizard being possessed of the bridle of the water-horse (srían an eich uisge), ultimately the bridle of Manannan, who had the gift of making himself invisible, as we read at the end of Serglige Conculainn.

A violation of tabu suffices to cause criminality. But I have pointed out that possession of the razor of a suicide helps to transmit the luck he would have had if he completed his span of life; and there is the reciprocal or complement to this belief when for the good of a community the individual possessed of greatest life-power is not suffered to complete his life-span or end it in weakness. To prevent this his life is taken from him, and such a ritual act was liable in the reports of half-informed travellers to assume the appearance of cannibalism. A current explanation, treated at length in Mannhardt and in J. G. Frazer's interesting works, is that the divinity or spirit of vegetation, all-important to the community, was incarnate in chief and priest and 'rain-king,' and if such persons were allowed to die of weakness and age the divine power would be lost to the community, which accordingly marks such persons as 'devoted,' so that at stated periods they are put to death and their power transmitted untarnished to a successor. A man (or even animal, with some peoples) could thus be slain as a god;

while, on the other hand, a suicide criminal, or criminal as such, could readily personate one 'devoted,' and to partake of any part of his members was to participate in the divine life. A suicide's skull, as in close touch with an uncompleted luck of life, would be thought of as imparting divine virtue and be capable of magic transmission by contact; and by imbibing the brain-particles with the water the epileptic's minimum of life was put in the way of becoming a maximum or normal.

Apart from this category, as having no ritual association, I put such references as I note from Keating, who says that in the reign of Loingseach there was a famine for three years in Ireland, "so that the people devoured one another there at this time " [402] (go m-bídís na daoine ag ithe a chéile innte an trath soin). Not alike is the reference to Eithne Uathach, daughter of Congain, wife of Criomhthann, son of Eanne Cinnsealach, King of Leinster, fostered and "fed by the Deise on the flesh of infants (is ar fheoil naoidhean do biathadh leis na Déisibh i) that she might grow up the more quickly; for a certain druid had foretold that they would get territory from the man whose wife she would be." [403] Here there may be a reflex of the need of keeping the divine life in the tribal representative at its fullest and highest. It is not ordinary cannibalism, but a ritual act reflected on as possible for dark thought and for darker practice on the lines of a dark and revolting belief.

(c) Faith-healing. Psychic suggestion associated with stones and wells is very prominent in folk-belief. Thus, when Burns's Highland Mary (Mary Campbell) fell ill, her friends at Greenock supposed, it is said, that she had come under the malign power of the evil-eye. To avert this, seven smooth stones were procured from the junction of two streams. These were placed in milk, which, after being boiled, was administered, but without success. There are many still living who have heard mention at some time or other of a pebble or crystal (grìogag) and of witch-stones (clachan buitseachd), to which various virtues were ascribed in the Highlands.

Sacred stones linked with the cure of human ills are at least as old as the days of Colum-Cille, so far as written record among the Celts enables us to infer. In the country of the Picts, says Adamnan, the saint took a white stone from the river and blessed it for the working of certain cures, saying: "Behold this white pebble by which God will effect the cure of many diseases among this heathen nation." The Druid Broichan, foster-father of King Brude, was thereafter stricken with sickness as punishment for having refused to free a female slave at Colum-Cille's request. Having repented, he sent a message expressing his readiness to do so, whereupon Colum-Cille sent two of his company with the pebble, which he blessed, saying: "If Broichan shall first promise to set the maiden free, then at once immerse this little stone in water and let him drink from it, and he shall be instantly cured; but if he break his vow and refuse to liberate her, he shall die that instant." The captive was freed, and we read: "The pebble was then immersed in water, and in a wonderful manner, contrary to the laws of nature, the stone floated on the water like a nut or an apple, nor, as if it had been blessed by the holy man, could it be submerged. Broichan drank from the stone as it floated on the water, and, instantly returning from the verge of death, recovered his perfect health and soundness of body. This remarkable pebble, which was afterwards preserved among the treasures of the king, through the mercy of God effected the cure of sundry diseases among the people, while it in the same manner floated while dipped in water. And what is very wonderful, when this stone was sought for by those sick persons whose term of life had arrived, it could not be found; thus, on the very day on which King Brude died, though it was sought for, it could not be found in the place where it had been previously laid."

Such sacred stones or charms were once extensively used: faith in them is not yet quite extinct. [404]

The Loch mo Nāir stone is egg-shaped, and "it measures two inches in the long diameter and rather over one and a half inch in the shorter, weighs exactly four ounces, and has a specific gravity of 2.666, or almost that of Aberdeen granite. The stone exhibits a beautifully mottled cream and liver coloured surface, with delicate touches and streaks of pink here and there on the cream colour." [405] Gems and crystals early impressed the imaginative faculty, and the water-rounded pebble of white quartz is associated with early burials so often, one has remarked, as to point "to an underlying significancy so highly esteemed as to have rendered it not unfrequently to all appearance the only relic thought worthy of preservation among the ashes of the dead." [406]

The tradition as told by Dr. Gregor is: "Once upon a time, in Strathnaver, there lived a woman who was both poor and old. She was able to do many wonderful things by the power of a white stone which she possessed, and which had come to her by inheritance. One of the Gordons of Strathnaver, having a thing to do, wished to have both her white stone and the power of it. When he saw that she would not lend it, or give it up, he determined to seize her and to drown her in a loch. The man and the woman struggled there for a long time, till he took up a heavy stone with which to kill her. She plunged into the lake, throwing her magic stone before her, and crying, 'May it do good to all created things save a Gordon of Strathnaver!' He stoned her to death in the water, she crying, 'Manaar! Manaar!' (Shame! Shame!). And the loch is called the Loch of Shame to this day."

The remainder of the account adds that the first Monday in May and August (old style) were the most popular days for frequenting the loch. The patient was kept bound and half starved for about a day previous, and immediately after sunset, on the appointed day, he was taken into the middle of the loch and there dipped. His wet clothes were then exchanged for dry ones, and his friends took him home in the full expectation of a cure. "Belief in the loch's powers was acknowledged till recently, and is probably still secretly cherished in the district." [407]

I know this to be the case: a few years ago this method of cure was tried. Here is an account by an eye-witness:

"At a loch in the district of Strathnaver, county of Sutherland, dipping in the loch for the purpose of effecting extraordinary cures is stated to be a matter of periodical occurrence, and the 14th August appears to have been selected as immediately after the beginning of August in the old style. The hour was between midnight and one o'clock, and the scene, as described by our correspondent, was absurd . . . beyond belief, though not without a touch of weird interest, imparted by the darkness of the night and the superstitious faith of the people. The impotent, the halt, the lunatic, and the tender infant were all waiting about midnight for an immersion in Lochmonaar. The night was calm, the stars countless, and meteors were occasionally shooting about in all quarters of the heavens above. A streaky white belt could be observed in the remotest part of the firmament. Yet with all this the night was dark, so dark that one could not recognise friend or foe but by close contact and speech. About fifty persons, all told, were present near one spot, and I believe other parts of the loch side were similarly occupied, but I cannot vouch for this—only I heard voices which would lead me so to infer. About twelve stripped and walked into the loch, performing their ablutions three times. Those who were not able to act for themselves were assisted, some of them being led willingly and others by force, for there were cases of each kind. One young woman, strictly guarded, was an object of great pity. She raved in a distressing manner, repeating religious phrases, some of which were very earnest and pathetic. She prayed her guardians not to immerse her, saying that it was not a communion occasion, and asking if they could call this righteousness or faithfulness, or if they could compare the loch and its virtues to the right arm of Christ. These utterances were enough to move any person hearing them. Poor girl! what possible good could in immersion do to her? I would have more faith in a shower-bath applied pretty freely and often to the head. No male, so far as I could see, denuded himself for a plunge. Whether this was owing to hesitation regarding the virtues of the water, or whether any of the men were ailing, I could not ascertain. These gatherings took place twice a year, and are known far and near to such as put belief in the spell. But the climax of the absurdity was in paying the loch in sterling coin. Forsooth, the cure cannot be effected without money cast into the waters! I may add that the practice of dipping in the loch is said to have been carried on from time immemorial, and it is alleged that many cures have been effected by it." [408]

In the Statistical Account for the Parish of Farr, written in August, 1834, the Rev. David M'Kenzie, minister of the parish, notes that connected with its antiquities he "may mention a few particulars regarding a loch in Strathnaver, about six miles from the church, to which superstition has ascribed wonderful healing virtues. The times at which this loch came to be in repute with the sick cannot now be ascertained. It must, however, have been at a period of the history of this country when superstition had a firm hold of the minds of all classes of the community. The tradition as to the origin of its healing virtues is briefly as follows:

"A woman, either from Ross-shire or Inverness-shire, came to the heights of Strathnaver, pretending to cure diseases by means of water into which she had previously thrown some pebbles, which she carried about with her. In her progress down the strath, towards the coast, a man in whose house she lodged wished to possess himself of the pebbles; but, discovering his design, she escaped, and he pursued. Finding at the loch referred to that she could not escape her pursuer any longer, she threw the pebbles into the loch, exclaiming in Gaelic, Mo nar, that is, 'shame,' or 'my shame.' From this exclamation the loch received the name which it still retains, Loch-monar, and the pebbles are supposed to have imparted to it its healing efficacy. There are only four days in the year on which its supposed cures can be effected. These are the first Monday (old style) of February, May,

August, and November. During February and November no one visits it; but in May and August numbers from Sutherland, Caithness, Ross-shire, and even from Inverness-shire and Orkney, come to this far-famed loch. The ceremonies through which the patients have to go are the following: They must all be at the loch side about twelve o'clock at night. As early on Monday as one or two o'clock in the morning the patient is to plunge, or to be plunged, three times into the loch; is to drink of its waters; to throw a piece of coin into it as a kind of tribute; and must be away from its banks so as to be fairly out of sight of its waters before the sun rises, else no cure is supposed to be effected. Whatever credit may be given to such ridiculous ceremonies as tending in any respect to the restoration of health, while ignorance and superstition reigned universally in this country, it certainly must appear extraordinary to intelligent persons that any class of the community should now have recourse to, and faith in, such practices; but so it is, that many come from the shires already mentioned, and say they are benefited by these practices. It is, however, to be observed that those who generally frequent this loch, and who have found their health improved, on returning home, are persons afflicted with nervous complaints and disordered imaginations, to whose health a journey of forty or sixty miles, a plunge into the loch, and the healthful air of our hills and glens may contribute all the improvement with which they are generally so much pleased."

One of the three charm-stones purported to have been thrown into Loch mo Nāir was said to have come into the possession of the Lord Reay, who gave it to an ancestor of Mr. Eric Ross, Golspie, who owned it in 1900, and whose notes thereanent are as follow: [409]

The Witch's Stone.—". . . This stone, which had been in possession of the Reay family for generations, was highly esteemed by the country people, who came from all parts of Sutherland, when their cattle fell ill, for a small bottle of water, in which the stone had first been immersed. This water was faithfully administered to the ailing animals. Lord Reay was so bothered by these visitors that he gave the stone to my father, who in his turn was often called upon for the magical water. My father bequeathed the stone to my elder brother, who dying about three years ago, the ancient stone became my property. I remember well in my young days the people coming for the water, and their anxious faces as they watched the stone being put into the bowl of water. It is to be regretted that no particulars of the early history of the stone are known, except the fact that it was once the property of a notorious witch. History is silent also regarding the recovery of the stone from Loch Mon-aar, [410] how it came into the possession of the Reay family, and the fate of its fellow-stones. The stone was never used, except for the purpose already mentioned. If the stone dried quickly after being taken out of the water, the sick animal would get well rapidly; but if slowly, it would be a lingering recovery: so the poor people believed. What the stone was used for in ancient times it is impossible to know. The loch, however, into which the witch-woman threw the precious stones was ever afterwards regarded as a place of healing; and hundreds of people have been known to journey from far to the loch for the sake of plunging into its dark waters to heal some real or imaginary ills. The plunge had to be taken at midnight and the bather out of sight of the loch before the sun rose and shone upon its waters, or else the charm would fail to work."

By reason of the honorific prefix Mo-, one looks, in the first place, for the saint's name; as the name of St. Munn, Munda, Gadhelic Munnu, comes from Mo-Fhindu, so Mo-N-Aar may come from Mo-Fhinn-Bharr, Findbarr or St. Barr, venerated in Sutherland, and whose name occurs in Kilmorack, i.e. Cill Mo-Bharr-óg, 'the church of my little Barr' (with the diminutive of endearment), and also' in Barra. The Rev. A. Gunn has already made this feasible suggestion as to the loch name, but I cannot associate therewith the parish name Farr, with its short ă and thin r (i.e. Fa˙r), which again seems of like origin with the place-name Far in Inverness-shire, and both apparently Pictish.

But in his legend the St. Bairre of Cork has annexed some of the attributes of a marine deity; he rides on St. David's horse across the Irish Sea, and, as Mr. Plummer [411] points out, his full name Findbharr 'white-crest' points in the same direction.

My suspicion is that the saint's name led to association with the ancient goddess Nāir, sometimes termed a bain-leannán, or female sprite. The Adventures of Crimthann Nia Nāir is among the list of the primary tales in the Book of Leinster, and this shows that in the 11th century it was current among the people. She is the goddess of the Wonderland, in the same category as Fand, who leaves Manannan her spouse, an immortal god, from her love for Cuchulain, like Níam, the bride of Oisin, and like the lady who wooed Connla Ruadh, son of Conn of The Hundred Battles,—Conn Cetchathach,—to the Sídh. Crimthann Nia Náir, Crimhthann, husband or hero of Náir, figures as a high king in Ireland at the dawn of the Christian era, was a son of Lugaid Sriabderg, Lugaid of the red-stripes or circlets. This Lugaid was the son of three brothers, Bress, Nar and Lothur; their sister Clothru was his mother.

Lugaid was united to Clothru, who thus in pre-Christian legend was both his wife and mother, The legend of Crimthann Nia Nāir (i.e. C. hero of Nāir) is summarised in the tract known as Flathiusa h-Erenn. [412] The goddess Nāir brought him to an over-sea land, where he abode for what seemed a month and a half. A longing seized him to return, and he brought back a chariot entirely wrought of gold; a chess-board of gold ornamented with three hundred precious stones; a sword with serpents chased in gold; a shield with silver reliefs; a spear that caused mortal wounds; a sling of unfailing cast, two dogs bound by a silver leash valued at three hundred bondmaids,—things, in short, which point to riches acquired by a journey to the happy Other-World over sea. Through a fall from his horse he found his death, 'six weeks after his return to Ireland,'—the usual fate of the hero who returns among mortals from a visit to the land of the Immortals, the Ever-Young.

The diminutive form of the name Nār, Nāir, is Nārag, a name I recollect applied to a woman who was 'touched' with frenzy, and I infer that this other-world being Nāir was a being like Fann, who wrought the sickness of Cuchulainn, and of whom it is specially said that she made men mad. In this aspect of her being she was a goddess of death, whom sick men would seek to propitiate as they longed for a new life and happiness. Death and Night are closely associated in primitive myth. The rites at Loch mo Nāir, which invariably took place at night, were to propitiate Death, the spirit of disease, of evil, of night with terrors dire. This would not exclude a trace of initiative magic; as the sun dies in the ocean at night and returns renewed, so by imitating his. bathing and death in the waters a similar renewal of life might be looked for; nay, if by imitative magic the bather returned ere the sun arose he procured virtue anew. The diving into the lake I take to be a remnant of an Other-World journey across sea, such as meets us in the Book of Leinster tale about Loegaire Liban, where the scene is laid at Enloch or the Lake of Birds. There the unknown warrior from Mag Mell, the Happy Land, the joyous home of the dead, seeks mortal aid, and having declared the glories of that land, he went back into the lake. Thereafter Loegaire dived down into the lake, and fifty warriors followed him. Later on he returns to bid his father Crimthann Cass farewell. He would not be touched: "Come not nigh us," he cried; "we are but come to bid you farewell," and he sang of the marvels of his new abode to his father:

What a marvel it is, O Crimthann Cass!
I was master of the blue sword.
One night of the night of the gods!
I would not exchange for all thy kingdom. [413]

The going at night into the lake then was some form of obeisance to the Other-World past. The bathing in Loch mo Nāir, in the waters sacred to the goddess, was like undertaking a visit to the Land of the Dead, the gods' land.

The dead could cure, it may have been thought. O'Davoren's Glossary gives a word Nár as meaning noble (uasal), good (maith), holy, pure, which Stokes equates with Greek νήφω, 'to be sober, pure.' But the goddess Nāir in character reminds of the Greek Νηρεύς, 'a water-nymph, Nereid.'

Other well-cures of special significance were resorted to. At Strath-fillan in Pennant's [414] time it is observed that the saint "is pleased to take under his protection the disordered in mind; and works wonderful cures, say his votaries, even to this day. The unhappy lunatics are brought here by their friends, who first perform the ceremony of the Deasil, thrice round a neighbouring cairn; afterwards offer on it their rags, or a little bunch of heath tied with worsted; then thrice immerge the patient in a holy pool of the river, a second Bethesda; and, to conclude, leave him fast bound the whole night in the neighbouring chapel. If in the morning he is found loose, the saint is supposed to be propitious; for if he continues in bonds, his cure remains doubtful; but it often happens that death proves the angel that releases the afflicted, before the morrow, from all the troubles of this life." Near hand there formerly lived an old woman of the name Dewar, who was custodian of St. Fillan's fairche or mallet, [415] which was used to stir the sacred waters, if not to impart them virtues.

The Laird of Macfarlane tells of a chapel in Appin called Craikwherreellan, as he spells it, where "there are springs of fresh water, and the opinion of the wholesomeness of the water draweth many people thither upon St. Patrick's Day yearlie in hopes of health from disease by drinking thereof; the town or village of Ardnacloich is hard by, renowned for a well also, where, they allege, if a person diseased go, if he be to die he shall find a dead worm therein or a quick one if health be to follow."

St. Mary's Well at Culloden was visited on the first Sunday of May; about a dozen years ago or so it was calculated that about two thousand persons made the pilgrimage. Its waters were held to have the power of granting under certain conditions the wish of the devotee. Old men are known to have held that in their early days its waters had distinct healing powers. It was believed that at mid-night on the first of May its waters turned into wine for a short time. A visitor some years ago wrote regarding the ritual:

"At any rate two thousand people visited it last Sunday, and the observer might extract, as his temperament led him, either ridicule or much food for thought in noting with how much apparent earnestness—one could almost say seriousness—the appointed rites were performed by the majority of the visitors. The procedure to be gone through is this: A draught of the water is taken, the drinker at the same time registering a wish or desire for success in some form or another throughout the coming year. To facilitate the wish a coin of small value is usually dropped into the water. Yet the rite is not altogether completed. The worshipper who intends to be thorough ties a piece of cloth—nearly always taken to the well for that particular purpose—to an adjoining tree as a symbol of the belief that thereby his cares and troubles for a year at least are left behind him. How small a price to pay for so great a boon!

SOME OF THE DEVOTEES

Here come a group of happy boys, all of whom drink solemnly of the water, no doubt wishes corresponding with their ages and experiences being the while registered. But, alas! the ceremony is left in some degree uncompleted, for on examination it is found that no member of the group possesses a solitary copper. This part of the rule is thereupon brushed aside. But the tying of pieces of cloth on the tree is strictly observed, for, besides costing nothing, it gives each boy an opportunity of indulging in a little tree-climbing, the desire for which is doubtless inherited from his prehistoric ancestors; and soon variously-coloured pieces of cloth are floating gaily on the breeze. Here is another and much more interesting arrival—a young man and a pretty girl. The girl drops a coin into the well, glancing shyly at her companion's face the while. . . ."

The same rites as at Loch mo Nāir were observed at the same time of the year at St. John's Loch, Dunnet, and at St. Trostan's Loch, Papa Westray. Pagan cultus and Christian superstition we're here blended.

The well at Loch Maree, called after St. Mael Rubha of Abercrossan, has been often written about.

Most interesting of all is Pennant's description (1772) of 'the favoured isle of the saint': "In the midst is a circular dike of stones, with a regular narrow entrance; the inner part has been used for ages as a burial place, and is still in use. I suspect the dike to have been originally Druidical and that the ancient superstition of Paganism had been taken up by the saint as the readiest method of making a conquest over the minds of the inhabitants. A stump of a tree is shown as an altar, probably the memorial of one of stone; but the curiosity of the place is the well of the saint; of power unspeakable in cases of lunacy. The patient is brought into the sacred island, is made to kneel before the altar, where his attendants leave an offering in money, he is then brought to the well, and sips some of the holy water, a second offering is made; that done, he is thrice dipped in the lake; and the same operation is repeated every day for some weeks; and it often happens, by natural causes, the patient receives relief, of which the saint receives the credit. I must add that the visitants draw from the state of the well an omen of the disposition of St. Maree; if his well is full, they suppose he will be propitious; if not, they proceed in their operations with fears and doubts; but let the event be what it will, he is held in high esteem; the common oath of the country is by his name; if a traveller passes by any of his resting places, they never neglect to leave an offering; but the saint is so moderate as not to put him to any expense, a stone, a stick, a bit of rag contents him."

Sacred wells are met with in all countries where a Celtic speech has been spoken. I need not linger over the Holy Wells of Cornwall, [416] but pass at once to a great shrine of present-day repute in Wales. It is a special account contributed to The Baptist of November 23, 1905, by Mr. W. Harris of Oxford; I may be allowed to quote it in full, as it is I believe quite reliable, and of special interest in this connection:

"It was our privilege a few days ago to pay a visit to Holywell, North Wales, a place famous among Roman Catholics for its spring of water known as St. Winefride's Well, which is supposed to possess miraculous healing power, and I thought perhaps an account of what we saw would interest Baptist readers. 'Traditions' inform us that somewhere about the twelfth century a wicked youth made infamous proposals to the maid Winefride, which she rejected. She was thereupon slain by him, and the head severed from the body. St. Beuno, on his way home from the church, discovered the remains, placed the head to the body, and prayed, upon which the maiden rose up. Immediately there sprang a stream of water from the spot where the head lay, and from that day to this has not ceased to flow.

"Having arrived at the outer gate (about a half-hour's good walk from the railway station), upon payment of an entrance fee of twopence we were admitted to the outer courtyard, and were directed to a doorway in the crypt of an ancient church. Upon entering, we found ourselves in a cold, wet, vault-like place, in size perhaps eighteen feet square, in the centre of which is the well, protected by a strong stone balustrade, octagonal in design, from the points of which spring eight finely-lined columns supporting an equally interesting fan-shaped roof. The water is allowed to accumulate in the well about three feet deep, and is clear as crystal and icy cold. It just wells' up from the centre of the mud and stone covered bottom, and is thus forced to the circumference of the well. Alongside the well is a baptistery of the usual dimensions, with steps at each end. A richly moulded flying stone arch separates the well from the baptistery. The only outlet for the water is through the latter, and then under the floor out into a large swimming-bath in the courtyard, to which we shall have occasion again to refer; the water passes down to another swimming-bath. This is under cover, and is called 'the Westminster' bath, and to this bath admission can be gained at all reasonable hours upon payment of the entrance fee only. The water then passes away to the rear of the premises, and, by a sluice arrangement, part is conducted to drive a mill of some kind, while the other part is diverted into St. Winefride's Brewery!

"But to return to the well and its interesting surroundings. Upon first gaining entrance to the crypt, we could scarcely believe we were in the British Isles. During the previous month we had scarcely heard a word of our mother tongue, having toured to Pwllheli, Carnarvon and the Snowdonian range, where Welsh is spoken; now we were surrounded by a number of Italians of both sexes in their gay characteristic attire; while there was also a goodly number of our own fellow-countrymen and women speaking with a north-country dialect.

"The walls of the place were well covered with texts of Scripture appropriately selected; these were interspersed with crutches, etc., while in the four corners and on the floor were piles of crutches and walking sticks, cork boots, bandages, belts, metallic and otherwise, bearing unmistakable signs of years of wear, dirt and dust. Against the wall was fitted up an altar, upon which rested a large statue of St. Winefride in a richly carved and draped canopy. We arrived at the wall just at noon, and upon asking the meaning of the number of people present, we ascertained that they were pilgrims from various parts of the world, who had come to a service which would be held at 12.30. We estimate that there were four or five hundred people present. Every available inch of standing room was occupied, and a large number of pilgrims were promenading round the bath in the outer courtyard.

"Seeing a Catholic priest among them, I went and joined myself unto him. He, in reply to my request, very readily lent me an ear for a few moments' conversation. Said I, 'By happy experience I know that faith in our Lord Jesus Christ'—here my friend the priest reverently raised his silk hat and as reverently bowed his head—will tend to the saving of the soul, but when I look round upon these crutches and other implements my faith is—' 'Strengthened?' queried the priest. 'Nay, sir, rather it is staggered.' 'Then,' said a lady, who was standing near, 'surely, if you were told that an old man, a cripple all his life, had bathed here, was healed, and had gone away, having no further use for his crutches, you would believe it.' 'I should believe it,' I replied, 'if I had known the old man as a cripple, and had known him afterwards as a sound man.' 'Well,' broke in the young priest, 'I must say, seeing is believing. But,' he added, 'surely all these crutches and sticks should satisfy any reasonable man of the healing virtue in the waters of this well, but I admit, if you like, that not all who bathe are healed, but only those who have faith in the water.'

"As it was on the stroke of 12.30, by mutual consent we crowded into the crypt for the service, which opened with a hymn accompanied by a harmonium. The tune, judging by the way it was immediately taken up, was well known to all except perhaps our two selves; indeed, I do not think I should be far wrong if I said we were the only persons present who were not Catholics, as the sequence proves. Then followed a remarkable litany, a copy of which is before me as I write, and from which I cull a few petitions. After each petition the response was instantly taken up, and spoken rapidly.

"Priest: O blessed St. Winefride,—(response) pray for us; O glorious Virgin and Martyr,—pray for us; O faithful Spouse of Christ,—pray for us; O sweet comforter of the afflicted,—pray for us; O bright example of Chastity,—pray for us; O hope and relief of distressed pilgrims,—pray for us; That all non-Catholics be converted to the Holy Catholic faith,—pray for us.

"Then followed another hymn and an eloquent address from Psalm cxxi. first verse. The first part of the sermon was very enjoyable, but as the preacher proceeded, he somehow took our eyes off the help coming to us in our need, and sought to fix our gaze ' upon St. Winefride.'

"As I 'retrospect' a little, I can now understand why the preacher's attention was fixed upon our face. He evidently saw gathered thereon 'a cloud about the size of a man's hand.' Another hymn and prayer brought the service to an end. The caretaker then in a loud voice requested 'all ladies to retire, as the men are about to bathe.' The congregation one and all, excepting ourselves, filed past the priest as he stood at the altar, he presenting a 'relic' to be kissed, many persons evidently requesting to be 'touched' on the shoulder, chest or back. The relic appeared to be a silver medallion fixed into a wooden disc with handle, somewhat in shape and size of a quarter-pound butter print.

"When all, excepting ourselves, had passed out, the priest took his departure. My companion then left me, and as I happen to belong to the sterner sex, and desired to be 'in the know,' I, quite unnecessarily, supported one of the pillars already referred to, while, as the priest had retired, the caretaker commenced walking rapidly up and down the room counting his beads and praying at a great speed after this fashion: 'Our Father, which art in Heaven,' etc.

"I now noticed that some half a dozen men, mostly of fine physique, had gathered around the baptistery. Among them was a man with a shrunken leg, a blind man, and an Italian boy of about five years with emaciated legs. He was dipped to the waist by an Italian adult. Each man was evidently carefully instructed how to act while in the 'bathroom.' Each in turn descended the steps unaided, submerged himself by stooping, raised himself to an upright position, then three times kissed the flying arch I have already referred to, which came just about level with the mouth; he then left the water, came and knelt on a certain stone in front of the shrine of

St. Winefride, and again descended into the ice-cold water. This each man did three times in rapid succession, without a visible shudder or murmur. The only sound breaking the stillness was that caused by the caretaker at his 'prayers' and beads. This man was pointed out to me as one who had been stone blind, had bathed in St. Winefride's Well and had received his sight. The bathers then proceeded to the next step—viz., to plunge into the swimming bath in the open courtyard, round which they must wade or swim three times, and it was an act of great merit and efficacy to dive and kiss a certain stone in the floor of the well. All the bathers by some means appeared to be familiar with the spot, and all seemed desirous of giving the stone the kiss. But, alas! while they doubtless could easily drown in the well, yet 'for love or money' they could not dive to the bottom. Then followed 'skylarking' unrestrained, in which one man tried by force to put the other's face into contact with the stone.

"I find I have omitted to mention that at the close of the sermon a procession of Italian peasants arrived, bearing lighted candles, banners, etc., headed by a priest bearing a wreath of hand-made silk flowers, under a glass dome, the work of the pilgrim band just arrived and others unable to leave Italy. This he faithfully promised should ultimately be placed upon St. Winefride's shrine in their beautiful chapel, though for the present it would remain upon the 'altar' at the well. During the service I trust we behaved ourselves with becoming decorum, though during a brief spell of silence I whispered in my companion's ear the words of Naaman, 'When I bow myself in the house of Rimmon, the Lord pardon Thy servant in this thing.'

"In the congregation was a beautiful girl of some thirteen summers, stretched upon a spinal carriage, and certainly, if the human face indicates the condition of the heart spiritually, that girl 'was not far from the Kingdom.' We were told that she had been brought to Holywell the day previous to see if the water would heal her of spinal disease; that she had been 'dipped' once, and it was hoped that 'after one or more dips she would be better.' Our earnest prayer was that this might be so. Before retiring, the priest came to her carriage and presented the relic to her lips. She at the same time raised a suspended wrist-charm to be touched. This she again most affectionately kissed.

"Thus came to an end this never-to-be-forgotten service. Alas, alas! through lack of faith, or other cause, the blind man did not receive his sight, the lame man was not able to leave his cork boot behind, the skin on the legs of the child did not 'become like the flesh of a little child,' so neither was faith found in him. Then remembered I the words of the priest, uttered before the service, 'Not all who bathe are healed, but only those who have faith in the water.'"

At Killin, Perthshire, two springs, Creideag Bheg and Creideag Mhór, had curative qualities. [417] Children were dipped in the Lady of Lawers' Well at Beltane, and sprinkled when the sun was visible. [418] Immersion in the Dòchart was resorted to for insanity. [419]

Of a parallel nature, if on another plane, are the rites associated with St. Patrick's Purgatory, Lough Derg. A saint specially connected with the spot is St. Dabheoc, [420] who is credited with having had a vision there ere he died. It is this saint who gives his name to the sacred well in Gigha, Argyll, known as Tobar Da Bheathag or Tobar ath Bheathag, but correctly written Tobar Dha Bheoc, with the accent on the bhe (Bhe-oc). The Gigha well since the time of the Druids has been credited with special virtues: [421] if a stone is taken out of it a great gale of east wind is aroused, which was taken advantage of when the islanders were given to smuggling, so that excisemen were kept from the island. Not many years ago a man from the south end went to the well (which is at the north end) purposing to take a stone out of it, and have his revenge on the captain of a vessel then anchored on the Kintyre side of the Sound. He returned, however, without fulfilling his purpose, having remembered just in time that a nephew of his was in another vessel in the vicinity. Da Bheoc is an early sixth century saint commemorated in Gorman's Martyrology under January 1. Loch Derg was of old Loch Geirc or Geirg, and was noted for its cave, visited by Knight Owen in the Middle Ages for the purpose of washing off his guilt. Legend has it that St. Patrick, while preaching to the pagans, miraculously opened up the place of punishment, with its four fields guarded by fire, ice, serpents, where souls are in torment; its narrow bridge, its wall bright as glass, its golden gate, its Garden of Eden, where are the happy souls who had expiated their sins, and were waiting to be received into the Celestial Paradise. Ere entering, the penitent had to pass a probation of fifteen days in prayer and fasting; on the sixteenth, having received the sacrament, he was led in solemn procession to the gate, which, after the penitent had entered, was locked, and not opened till the following day. In 1497, on the representation of a disappointed Dutch monk, who saw no visions, the cave was destroyed by authority of the Pope as not being the Purgatory which St. Patrick obtained from God, but the pilgrimages have never ceased, and are in vogue from 1st June to 15th August, despite a second destruction in 1632, and an interdict in 1704. Through the work of Henry of Saltrey, a Benedictine of the middle of the twelfth century, the legend spread all over Europe, and was later dramatised by Calderon. It is most likely that long before St. Patrick's day this island was associated with burial or with death and visions of the entry into the other world, partly to be inferred from island names like H-irt, i.e. Death, the Gadhelic name for St. Kilda; and from Ròcabi and the Green Island of Highland legend, the Caer Is of Brittany, and other sources, such as the English versions descriptive of the water and of the bridge of St. Patrick's Purgatory itself:

   ... they come to a great wattere
Broode and blakke as any pyke [pitch],
Sowles were theryn mony and thykke;
And also develes on eche a syde
As thykke as flowres yn someres tyde.
The water stonke fowle therto
And dede the soles mykylle woo [much woo].
   .   .   .   .   .   .
Over the water a brygge there was,
Forsothe kenere then ony glasse;
Hyt was narowe and hit was hyge
Onethe that other ende he syge.

This last is the Brig o' Dread, and like the Bridge Cinvat of the Avesta and the Bridge Sirāt of Islam. The Middle Ages lived in contemplation of the other world, and had many visions of a Divine Comedy long before Dante gave them eternal literary consummation. In the Vision-literature, of which much is due to the Celt, the Vision itself, by the aid of Faith, helped to cleanse the soul. Terror to a certain extent purified. There was a further basis in practices somewhat similar to the rites of incubation which still take place in Tenos, in Greece; and of old the temple-sleep [422] in the cult of Asklepios at Epidaurus, where suppliants approached the god by sacrifices and rites likely to win his favour, and lay down to sleep awaiting the divine visitation. All such rites had healing and revelation for their end.

(d) Folk-Medicine. Only things significant in virtue of their magic or by reason of their being credited in belief with healing power remain to be considered. Cures wrought by substances of ascertained physical properties must be set aside here for lack of space, forerunners though they be in some instances of later science. [423] Whatever is outside of the usual produces a certain counter-shock on the soul or soul-body: this psychological fact is not forgotten in folk-medicine. If connected with what is held to be holy, the mental-contact itself suffices, although this is strengthened by visible means. In 1849 the people of Carrick were in the habit of carrying away from the churchyard portions of the clay of a priest's grave and using it as a cure for several diseases, and they also boiled the clay from the grave of Father O'Connor with milk, and drank it. [424]

Things connected with or named after a priest's belongings, such as a biretta (currachd sagairt) or a processional canopy (puball beannach), are used in love-charms, whereby a girl can magically attach a lover. A sacred girdle is sometimes still worn by pious women who feel they are soon to add to the number of the faithful. This is to 'sain' the expected child as well as the mother from all harm, and to attach all good spiritual powers on her side. Parallel is the magic or wizard belt of St. Fillan (sianchrios Fhaolain [425]), whereby MacUalraig of Lianachan, Lochaber, tied the Glaistig or water-nymph in front of him on his horse, and swore that he would not let her go until he showed her before men. In return for her release she promised to enrich him with cattle and with house; on fulfilling each stipulation he let the siren (an t-suire) go free, and when parting with her he put the red-hot coulter into her crooked fist, and then she laid on him the curse of the Fairy-Host and of the Goblins, her wishes being that his race might "grow as the rushes, wither like the ferns, turn grey in childhood, die at the zenith of strength." Her imprecation fell short of wishing that a son might not take his father's place.

If sacred human things had such 'saining' power, how much more semi-sacred creatures which brought one in contact with the substance of the god! Epilepsy was held to be curable as follows: "A live snake was caught and placed in a bottle, which was then filled with pure water and corked. After standing for a short time, the infusion was given to the patient, who was kept ignorant of the nature of the drug." [426] To check whooping-cough it was recommended to hold a live frog over the sufferer's mouth. What is unusual has magic virtue: King's evil or scrofula could be cured if water were poured into a basin and applied by the seventh son in a family of nine—a daughter being the eldest and a daughter being the youngest, with seven sons between. Also by the seventh son of a seventh son, although the person concerned is unconscious of the secret of his healing gift.

Water drunk from a live-horn (adharc bheò), or from a spoon or cup made out of horn taken from off a live animal, had virtue in curing whooping-cough. Another remedy was mare's milk from an aspen spoon. Fasting-spittle used at early dawn, as also swine's blood, was used to cure warts, the right hand being placed on the earth under the left foot (or the reverse, as the case might need) in name of the Trinity at the time of waning of the moon. Children born feet first were held to cure epilepsy, and certain charms were used to transfer the fits from day to night. Against epilepsy a black cock without a white feather was taken and buried where the patient had the first fit. A special modification was "the taking of the parings of the nails of the fingers and toes, binding them up with hemp, with a sixpence in a piece of paper, on which was written the name of the Father, the Son and the Holy Ghost. The parcel was then taken, tied under the wing of a black cock, and buried in a hole dug at the spot where the first fit occurred, by the oldest God-fearing man of the district, who must watch and pray all night by the fire, which must not be let out. Another very universal remedy was drinking water out of the skull of a suicide at dawn." [427] Serpent-bite was cured by a decoction of water wherein a serpent's head had been boiled. In Tiree "water taken from the crest of nine waves, and in which nine stones had been boiled, was an infallible cure for jaundice. The shirt of the patient, after being dipped in this magic infusion, is put on wet." [428]

On the west side of the same island there is a rock with a hole in it, through which children are passed when suffering from whooping-cough or other complaints. [429] "On the point of Oa, Islay, there is a small arch formed in a huge boulder, which had been resorted to by invalids for ages. Any person who passed through it was supposed to have left his malady behind him, whatever it was. The transit was a cure for all diseases. Within the last twenty years a poor man carried his sickly wife on his back for miles to give her the benefit of the charm.

One fact to be observed was that the disease of the last person healed would stick to the next passing through it unless he got a substitute to pass before him. Probably a valuable animal of the clean kind was the original substitute required, but latterly any living creature was considered sufficient. An old worn-out dog was supposed to be as good as a first-class ram." [430] The water-vole (labhalan), referred to in Rob Donn, is mentioned also by Pennant: [431] "The country-people have a notion that it is noxious to cattle: they preserve the skin, and as a cure for their sick beasts give them the water in which it has been dipt. I believe it to be the same animal which in Sutherland is called the Water-Mole." The mole itself is held to be an omen of death if it is perceived as making its runs in the direction of the foundation of a dwelling. The cure may be a sort of counter-magic, just as an ointment from snakes' tongue was once used as an antidote to snake-bite, and in England the herb 'adder's tongue' (ophioglossum vulgatum); in the south they nailed to the byre-door and to field-gates adder-stones, saucer-shaped pieces of hard blue marl, rounded and perforated in the centre by the action of water, which was probably the origin of the ovum anguinum of the Gauls, the serpent's egg so phantastically described by Pliny.

Goats especially were held to be proof against adders, and the minister of Kirkmichael, Banff, in 1794, quotes [432] a Gadhelic saying which implies that the goat eats the serpent or adder: cleas na goibhr' ag itheadh na nathrach, i.e. 'like the goat eating the adder or serpent.' Red woollen thread which has been 'sained' (snàithlein) has various virtues: in the shape of a cross it may be tied to cows' tails or put underneath the milk-pans or over the byre-door to counteract the evil eye; bound on the hand, if one has sprained a vein, it is held to be a blessed remedy, and termed sgo-chadhfèithe, i.e. a magical 'incision of the vein.' In some districts the magic thread is thrice passed over a horn spoon; the ends of the thread are placed together, and the spoon is thrice passed round the crook, and the sufferer's disease is rightly named or diagnosed whenever the thread stays on. If one sprains one's foot a good remedy is to take the crook full of soot, and make the sign of the cross over the aching part; the chimney-crook is ascribed great virtue. Equally so is the magical operation of turning the heart in lead (cridhe-luadhainn) on behalf of a person suffering from heart disease. The patient may be resident far away in another glen, but doubtless has some knowledge that a good friend is 'turning his heart.' The lead is molten and poured through an iron key taken from the outer door into a bucket full of cold water. The state of the heart is diagnosed from the formations made by the liquid lead falling into the water. Another code requires the patient to be present, and to kneel near the fire: a sieve is placed on the head, and in the sieve is put a bowl full of water; into this bowl molten lead is poured through iron (the finger-hole of scissors suffices). One of the dropping pieces of lead is thought to take the rough shape of a heart, and the lead has to be melted over and over until a smooth or 'whole heart' is produced with no hole in it, whereupon the patient may rest assured that his heart is whole. [433] In the ritual of cow-healing and of turning the evil eye off children, lustral water, literally silverwater (būrn airgid), water which has been blessed in the Triune Name and has had silver coins cast into it, is given to cow or child as the case may be; a portion must be drunk by the ailing, a portion sprinkled over them, and the remainder poured over a large stone that cannot be moved. This stone is a sort of altar.

The evil cannot go further; it is thought to have passed into the stone. If cracks appear, the saying is applicable: envy will split the stone (sgoiltidh farmad a' chlach): this is the properly magical part of the rite; the religious part is the careful observance of the earlier portion of the ritual, and the trusting spirit in which one goes about lifting the water, blessing it and giving it to the sufferer. Similarly, when rags are placed at wells or on trees and bushes near hand, the real idea is not that of transferring the disease to the tree or bush, but of taking the spirit of the place, either of the well or of the tree, to witness, in evidence of having done one's own part: the deity may then be trusted to do his. What Carleton, in his Traits and Stories of the Irish Peasantry, puts into the mouth of one of his characters is apposite: "To St. Columbkill I offer up this button, a bit o' the waistband o' my own breeches, an' a taste o' my wife's petticoat, in remembrance of us havin' made this holy station; an' may they rise up in glory to prove it for us in the last day!" In a similar spirit, if on a different plane, is the cry of the religious: God is my rock.

Man in his inner life is opposed to negligence of those rites which are realised as pertaining to his economic and social welfare in the highest and widest sphere; he in this spirit is strengthened to endure the further burdens of his pilgrimage.

Evidence of his magic-compelling belief in his spiritual power is seen in the old Irish custom of fasting in order to obtain justice or legal redress, to injure an enemy, to obtain a request as if by magic force; [434] to ward off a plague. [435] The rite has its parallel in the sitting dharna (sic (dharana)—JBH) of the Hindoos. The explanation is that as eating keeps the body in life so fasting is a feigning of death; the dead-body does not eat. The spirit of Eoghan of Lochbuy cannot rest, for the warrior fell fasting. [436] Fasting makes a man more accessible to magic power whereby he may get his wish, just as it renders the body open to magical transformations; fasting elevates one on a par with the dead who eat not. Thus a fasting man may get his 'wish,' which becomes equal to an imprecation, which has magic-compelling power according to the Highland proverb. [437] That request or 'entreaty' passes into 'conjuration or exorcism' is shown by the meaning of geas, Irish geiss, from a word signifying 'I bid, entreat ': the magic word is mighty to place one under a prohibition from doing a certain act, which is tantamount to an obligation to doing another thing. The magic-spell (Irish feth fia: the Highland fāth-fīthe) has power to cause invisibility. The root is *vet, 'to say.' [438] Power centres in the magic word, and this is the justification of embracing a part of folk-medicine along with sacrifice. The word makes sacred.

One word in retrospect. Consciously or unconsciously, religious rites have an implied reference to the supra-sensible; the motives of religion are manifold, and are inclusive (1) of the power of the word, (2) of the unseen objects of fear or faith which on the lower plane may be simply demons, (3) of acts of faith which issue in expiatory offerings. Religion embraces more than magic. There is felt or implied that some Power exists outside and beyond the actual words recited. In charms of the older period names of deities, such as Goibniu and Diancecht, occur. By easy transitions, as in the case of the pre-Christian Brigit, all [439] such deities make way for Christian saints. The lower rites anticipate the higher. The Divine Life is to man as man is to the Divine Life. There is freedom on both sides. Priority remains with the greater. It is the higher that gives, it is the lower that gets. Every giving reveals.

Folk-consciousness thinks in pieces: it gives small answers to great questions; it never reveals a sovereign content of existence, with its fullness of labour and sorrow, as well as love and joy. Truth is the whole. Celtic, like other folk-consciousness, betrays a longing after messages and signs of the will and favour of God. Its holy or naomh, Old Irish nōib, has its nearest cognate in the Old Persian naiba, 'beautiful.' Holiness in its spiritual depths and inwardness is a product of Christian associations. Non-Christian folk-consciousness is 'yet without strength'; [440] it does not know God as Holy. In Christianity alone is God seen as giving up Himself without giving up His Love.

INDEX

A' Bhean Mhath, 109.

adha, ae, 14.

Affric, 149.

after-birth, 15.

aibhseachadh, 17.

ainm, 12, 13, 35.

aìre chlaidh, 3, 32 (an fhaire chlaidh), 39.

aisling, 7.

anam, 29.

animal-fasting, 62.

baist, 132.

Beannachd na Cuairte, 129.

bear, 140.

Beltane, 158.

bile (tree), 114-117.

bird-man, 140.

birth-token, 45.

blithe-meat, 128.

blood, 18, 19, 20, 21, 134, 168.

blood-covenant, 20, 22, 23.

blood-staunching, 182.

Bodach an Dūin, 109.

bonfire, 151.

bonnach bainnse, 152.

boobrie, 83, 90, 95.

Boyne, 92.

bréid, 153.

Brian, 40.

Brian Carabine, 143.

bricht, 11.

Brigit, 103.

Briid's bed, 141.

buarach, 180.

bubaire, 88.

bull-feast, 140, 165.

bull-sacrifice, 165.

burial, symbolic, and divination, 205 n.

bùrn airgid, 16.

Caesar on sacrifice, 175.

Caisean Callaig, 160.

caisean-uchd, 160.

Calluinn a' Bhuilg, 97.

cat, 66, 163.

clach na brataich, 138.

clachan aoraidh, 126.

clachan carraghan, 122.

cloicheir, 43.

cnāmhlach, 39.

Coinneach Odhar, 141.

comh-dhalaiche, 138 n.

copan-cinn, 14

corp-criadh, 10, 11, 32.

corrachd, 9.

couvade, 36.

cow-healing, 205.

cràbhadh, 5, 176.

crane, 96.

Creideag Mhōr, 201.

creideamh, 6.

cridhe-luadhainn, 10.

Crithreamh Gorm, An, 271 n.

crō-codaig, 20.

Crom Cruach, 125, 174.

cronachduinn, 122.

crosadh (forbidding, lit. crossing), 177.

cruentatio, 24.

crystal-gazing, 144.

cuckoo, 54, 55, 137.

currachd sagairt, 203.

dailgneachd, 7.

dā-shealladh, 7.

Deae Sequae, 92.

dearbadan Dē, 49.

Death, expulsion of, 172.

Deasoil, 152.

deō, 28.

Devona, 92.

devoted (in symbolic sacrifice), 159.

Dia, 30.

distaff, power of, 145.

donn, 97.

dreag, 138.

Druid, 135.

Dusii, 44.

earchall, 119, 164.

eāric, 150 n.

eōlas, 182.

epilepsy, 162.

erdáthe, 131.

Esus, 98.

evil-eye, 16.

facal, 12.

faith-healing, 187.

faoighdhe, 150.

farmad, 27, 122.

fasting, 181, 206.

fasting-spittle, 204.

fàth-fìth, 8, 135, 207.

feet-laving, 149.

féille fairc, 133.

fī, 9.

fiosachd, 141.

fire, 129, 178.

fire-circumambulation, 151.

fīs, 7.

fitheach, 56.

frìth, 136.

fuatharlan, 48.

Garland Sunday, 126.

Gaulish sacrifices, 175.

gealbhan (moving light), 137.

gearraidh, 633.

geas, 6, 8, 9, 12, 14, 35, 76, 177, 207.

Geumraich, na, 167.

ghost-bird, 57.

glaim, 135, 138.

gōbhlachan, 87.

gonadh, 9.

goose, 75.

Gruagach, 154.

guidhe, 6.

Guorthigern, 169.

Halmadary and Sacrifice, 173.

H-irt, 202.

horn, live-, 204.

horse, 71, 104.

imleag, 15 n.

immolation, 168.

infant-flesh, 187.

iress, 6, 176.

kirking, 132.

labhalan, 204.

Labhraidh Lorc, 121.

Lady of Lawers, 141.

lead-divination, 10 n.

lead-turning, 205.

leigheas cuairte, 128.

Līa Fāil, 122.

liū, 130.

Loch Maree, 196.

Loch mo Nāir 193.

Lōchy, 92, 122.

lostey-chainley, 132.

Lough Derg or Geirc, 201 n.

Lug, 98.

lustration by fire, 128.

magpie (v. pigheid), 104.

Māg Molach, 34, 44 n, 109, 164.

Mag Slecht, 174.

man in cow-skin, 290.

Manannan's bridle, 186.

manadh, 7, 13 n, 176.

marca, marcach, 92.

mare, 138.

Mark, King, 119.

marriage by capture, 150.

Mathair mhór, 15 n.

menmain, 21.

minn (mionn), 7, 13.

mīre Mīchil, 259.

mole, 205.

Mōr Bhān, 186.

Morc, 72, 74.

mother-affinity, 3, 4.

Nair, 34.

naomh, 31, 207.

Nār, 194.

Nārag, 193.

navel-string, 15.

need-fire, 130.

Ness, 92.

oath by the elements, 13 n.

òb, 6.

obaidh, 8, 176.

omphalos, 128.

òrtha, 6, 9, 176.

Ossian (Oisín), 75, 79.

peallaidh, 109.

pharmakos, 172.

Phynnodderree, 44 n, 110.

pigheid, 55 n.

Pīreig, 113.

plut, 68.

priest-kings, 181.

pruch, 61.

puball beannach, 203.

ram, 164.

réite, 149.

religion, 4, 5, 8, 31, 176, 177, 207.

religion, multiple motives of, 207.

right, things, 179.

riochd, 65, 135.

rowan, 111.

ruad, 118.

Sabarios, 158.

sacrifice, 7, 163.

sacrifice, psychological essence of, 176.

scapulimantia, 141.

second-sight (or sight of the two worlds), 148.

serpent, 33, 102, 103, 104, 105, 205.

serpent-bite, 204.

Shony, 155.

sin (cean, cion; fine; immorbus; peacadh), 182.

sīthich, 154.

skull, water from a, 185.

slān treabhaidh, 157.

soot, 149.

soul, 30.

soul-in-weapons, 47.

srannan, 43.

sreot, 14.

St. Bairre, 192.

St. Colum Cille, 170-171, 187.

St. Fillan's fairche, 194.

St. Fillan's girdle, 194 n, 203.

St. Kentigern, 113.

St. Maolrubha, 167.

St. Mo-Bharr-óg, 192.

St. Mulvay, 155.

St. Nun's Well, 196 n.

St. Odran (Oran), 170.

St. Patrick's Purgatory, 201.

St. Winefride, 196.

stones, 122.

stones, for raising wind, 201.

Struan, 156.

suicide, 184.

suire (siren), 203.

taboo, things, 177.

taghairm, 162.

tairrngearacht, 7.

taisbein, 7.

tannasg, tāsc, 113.

tarbh, 82, 83.

tārmachduinn, 148.

tārmachan Dé, 49.

tāsc, 29.

tathaich, 9, 25.

teàrnadh, 15 n, 183.

teine-Dé, 135.

Temair, 120.

Tobar Dha Bheoc, 201.

tong, 7, 13.

toradh, 17, 178.

tree worship, 122.

tree-witness, 206.

treith chuileanach, 108.

trom-laighe, 12.

trugeranos, 91.

tuar, 7, 137.

vicarious sacrifice, 173.

water, 133-134.

water-horse, 100.

wedding-day, 151.

whooping-cough, 204.

witch-stones, 187.

wolf; 105.

wooden ladle, 183.

word, 11.

wren, 59.

ENDNOTES

[1] Tribal System in Wales, pp. 54-60. (p. 3)

[2] Is e cáirdeas na mathar as dilse. (p. 3)

[3] Cha chan mi brathair ach ris a' mhac a rug mo mhathair. (p. 3)

[4] Frazer, Early History of the Kingship, p. 238. (p. 4)

[5] Ib. p. 244. (p. 4)

[6] Ib. p. 245. For the Picts v. Zimmer in my Leabhar Nan Gleann. (p. 4)

[7] The Rise of the Greek Epic (Heinemann), p. 76. Miss Harrison refers to a clue to matriarchal theology in Pythagoras (Prolegomena, 262) and points to indications of Mother-Right in St. Augustine (ib. 261n) "Matriarchy gave women a magical prestige," says Miss Harrison (ib. 285, cf. 272). (p. 4)

[8] Res ipsa, quae nunc religio Christiana nuncupatur, erat apud antiquos nec defuit ab initio generis humani. . . . (p. 4)

[9] Bergson's Time and Free Will, p. 231. (p. 5)

[10] The L. religio implies carefulness and diligence in things pertaining to rites of devotion; it is the very opposite of negligence. The recent attempt to connect it with religare in the sense of 'binding the god' is erroneous to my thinking. (p. 5)

[11] Gheobh baobh a guidhe ged nach fhaigheadh a h -anam tròcair. (p. 8)

[12] Cŏrrachd. (p. 8)

[13] Carmina vel caelo possunt deducere lunam. (p. 8)

[14] Chuir i an òrth' ann. (p. 8)

[15] Also ubaidh; ubag; ob (rarely)—all from the root ba, 'to speak,' utter. (p. 8)

[16] Thug i facal da (common speech). (p. 8)

[17] v. Carmina Gadelica. Joyce has suggested that here we have the origin of the words which head St. Patrick's hymn Faeth Fiada (with the d aspirated?), long rendered as the guardsman's cry, the deer's cry, but really a 'spell' for rendering invisible. The story of the deer may have arisen from a folk-etymon. When Patrick, with his eight companions, went before King Loigaire, the king saw but eight deer and a fawn making for the wilds. The monarch returned to Tara in the morning twilight, disheartened and ashamed. For Transformation into Animal Form, v. ch. ii. (p. 8)

[18] Anthropological Essays presented to E. B. Tylor, Oxford, p. 293. (p. 9)

[19] For Ness, Lewis, I noted the word with a long ō: tha mi 'ga chur cōrachd ort, i.e. I place on thee a stipulation not to be broken; while for Lorne I got the phrase: chuir e cōrachd air a theangaidh, 'he spoke as if he disguised or hid his speech,' which must be a secondary meaning; in any case it is not mine, which is invariably 'a death-bed entreaty.' (p. 9)

[20] "Apparently of Greek origin is the widely-received custom of pouring out lead; even Ihre mentions it: cf. molybdomantia ex plumbi lique facti diversis motibus (Potter's Arch. i. 339), i.e. lead-divination from the divers motions of liquid lead."—Grimm's Germ. Myth. 1118. (p. 10)

[21] Sébillot, Le Paganisme Contemporain chez les Peuples Celto-Latins, pp. 152-157, re envoûtement. (p. 10)

[22] Moore, Folk Lore of the Isle of Man, p. 90, quoting Train. (p. 10)

[23] Sheila MacDonald in Folk Lore for 1903, 373-374. (p. 11)

[24] Folk Lore of the Isle of Man pp. 96-99. Cf. for Ireland O'Foharta's Siamsa an Gheimhridh, and An Lóchrann (Tralee, Kerry, 1910). (p. 11)

[25] Bezz. Beit. xxiv., Göttingen, 1899, p. 113. Allerhand Zauber etymologisch beleuchtet. (p. 11)

[26] Gill's Myths and Songs of the South Pacific, pp. 86-87. (p. 12)

[27] J. G. Campbell's Superstitions, p. 245. (p. 12)

[28] What trom may be here is uncertain: cf. trom-dhée, 'household gods,' in E. Irish; trom usually is 'heavy, oppressive.' (p. 12)

[29] Primitive Paternity, i. 225 (Folk-Lore Soc. issue). (p. 13)

[30] The power of the word as seen in the curse is evidenced by the Manx phrase Mollaght Mynney, which Moore (Folk-Lore of the Isle of Man, 11n) says, "is the bitterest curse in our language, that leaves neither root nor branch, like the Skeabthoan, the besom of destruction." It seems to originate from the old custom of swearing by the relics of a saint, for the word is different from Manx Monney, 'a sign, an omen, a portent,' G. manadh, 'omen.' Noticeable also is the reference in this Manx oath to sun and moon (ry ghrian as eayst), met with also in present-day Ireland: dar brígh na gréine 's na gealaighe, 'by the virtue or essence of the sun and of the moon' (Lúb na Caillighe, p. 20; ed. S. Laoide, Connradh na Gaedhilge, i mBaile Atha Cliath). (p. 13)

[31] Cf. The Last Days of Charles II., by R. Crawfurd, M.D. (Oxford: Clarendon Press). (p. 14)

[32] Bha iad glē thoigheach mu'n teārnadh: nan rachadh an teārnadh a losgadh ann san rathad chlī cha bhiodh tuille cloinne aig a bhean (sic). Bha eagal mór air na mnathan glūine roimh so mus biodh iad a gabhail beatha fheadhainn eile. Ach nan itheadh a bhean teārnadh bean (sic) eile thigeadh a' chloinn (sic) air ais. B'ābhaist do bhean I. G. nach maireann a thoir air bean air a chiad chloinn trī caoban thoir as a' chochull bha m'an cuairt do'n leanabh. Chan fhuilingeadh am mathair piantan cloinne an deighidh sin. (p. 15)

[33] Kinahan's Notes on Irish Folklore; v. Folklore Record, iv. p. 104. (p. 15)

[34] G. imleag, ilmeag, E. Ir. imbliu, cognate with L. umbilicus, Gr. ὀμφαλός, E. navel, Skr. nābhi, nâbhîla. (p. 15)

[35] Harrison's Prolegomena, 321. As to Earth-Mother, I noted a children's game in Eriskay called Mathair Mhór, 'Big Mother,' where the mother was feigned to be a pig! It is possibly a relic of early ritual. (p. 15)

[36] Hist. of Brazil, i. 238. (p. 15)

[37] Crawley: Tree of Life, p. 226. Mr. Crawley points out that the soul is often placed on a tree for safe keeping. Cf. Hazlitt's Dict. of Faiths and Folklore, sub Heam = after burthen, secundine. The afterbearth of cows was put on a hawthorn bush with faith that they shall have a cow next year (ib.). (p. 15)

[38] Hartland, Prim. Patern. I. 70; ii. 276. (p. 15)

[39] Lady Wilde's Ancient Legends of Ireland, vol. i. p. 37. (p. 16)

[40] E.g. Non istic obliquo oculo mea commoda quisquam limat,—Horace, Epist. I. xiv. 37; Nescio quis teneros oculus mihi fascinat agnos,—Virgil, Bucol. Ecl. iii. 103; conspiciturque sinus,—Juvenal, Sat. vii. 112; Ter cana, ter dictis despue carminibus,—Tibullus, Eleg. I. ii. 56; veniam a deis petimus spuendo in sinum,—Pliny, xxviii. 4, 7. The shepherd in Theocritus (Idy. vi. 39), following the injunctions of a 'wise' woman, spits thrice into his own lap in order to save himself from the consequences of self-admiration. (p. 16)

[41] Cf. G. Borrow, The Zincal, pt. I. c. viii. (p. 16)

[42] P. 126. (p. 16)

[43] Superstitions and Witchcraft. (p. 16)

[44] The Evil Eye in the West Highlands. There is a German work by S. Seligmann, Der böse blick u. Vermandtes: Ein Beitrag zur Geschichte des Abenglaubens aller Zeiten u. Völker, 2 vols. (p. 16)

[45] Labhair Criosd an dorus na cathrach
Trī ghairmeachduinn cho ceart:
tillidh seachd paidrichean Moire cronachduinn sūl'
co dhiubh bhios e air creutair no air bruid:
cia b'e air bith chuir ort-s' an t-sūil
gu'n till i orra-fhéin no air an cloinn
's mar 'eil a chlann ann gu bheil a chuid ann.
's mar 'eil a chlann ann gu bheil a chuid ann.
   [An t-ainm]
Thu-sa bhiodh 'nad iom-shlāint
Ann an ainm an Athar, a Mhic, 's a Spioraid Naoimh. (p. 16)

[46] I.e. cuidh-lainn, 'cattle-folds': may God bless these cattle-folds! This I am asking in the name of God, nor am I asking but for mine own. (p. 17)

[47] Lactantius ait: Alii animam ignem esse dixerunt, alii spiritum, alii sanguinem. Ignem dicunt, quia vivificat corpus, spiritum quia spirat per membra, sanguinem, quia cum sanguine migrat. Wasserschleben, Die Irische Canonensammlung, 2nd ed. 1885, p. 233. (p. 18)

[48] The original of the last stanza I quote from memory:

Chuir iad a cheann air ploc daraich
 agus dhōirt iad fhuil mu lār
Nan robh agam-s' an sin copan

dh'ōlainn dith mo shāth.

A version of the original is accessible in Rev. Maclean Sinclair's Gaelic Bards. (p. 19)

[49] Western Isles, p. 109 of ed. of 1716. (p. 20)

[50] Rev. Celtique, 13, p. 75. (p. 20)

[51] Ib. 13, 75. (p. 20)

[52] The original words are:

Dh' ōlainn deoch ge b'oil le cāch e
Cha b'ann dh'fhīon dearg na Spāinne,
Dh' fhuil do chuim 's to 'n deidh bāthadh. (p. 21)

[53] Otia Mersiana, iii. 48. (p. 21)

[54] Rev. Celt. ii. 197. (p. 21)

[55] Keating's Hist. of Ireland (Irish Texts Soc.), i. 323.; cf. what Keating says of the Druids, ib. 349. (p. 21)

[56] Wilde, Irish Popular Superstitions, pp. 92-93. (p. 21)

[57] Eleanor Hull, The Cuchullin Saga, p. 82. (p. 23)

[58] S. Hartland, Primitive Paternity, vol. i. p. 261 (Folk-Lore Society). (p. 23)

[59] The Blood Covenant, p. 219, quoting Buxtorf's Synagoga Judaica, c. ii. (p. 24)

[60] For other references, cf. Strack, Blutaberglaube, 1892, p. 125; Christensen, Baareprøven, Copenhagen, 1900, investigates 'bier-proof'; cf. Wood-Martin, Elder Faiths, i. 323. Herodotus (iii. 18) speaks of the drinking of blood as the highest sanction of a treaty, and alludes to it as an Arabian custom. Mohammed had to forbid it as one of the heavy sins (Kremer, Studien zur verg. Kultur Geschichte, p. 35). Stanley, the African traveller, speaks of exchanging blood through marks on each other's arms, after which there was a treaty of peace, as firm as any made in Europe, he thought. (p. 24)

[61] Quoted from Celtic Monthly in Inverness Northern Chronicle, 16th August, 1905. (p. 26)

[62] Rev. Walter Gregor's Folk Lore of North-East of Scotland, 1881, p. 208. (p. 26)

[63] Wardlaw MS. pp. 516-521 of Scottish Texts Society, edited by William Mackay, p. 517. (p. 26)

[64] The minister quotes Genesis 9:6 Numbers 35:3 to show that only blood can atone for blood. John M'Keanire at the end of two years was discovered; he confesses; he was compelled to the deed by John Mackeanvore,—both were hung near the parish church of Wardlaw, the present Kirkhill, Clunes, Inverness. (p. 28)

[65] Folk-Lore of the Isle of Man, p. 145. (p. 28)

[66] Lettsom's translation, p. 183. (p. 28)

[67] Benson's Remarkable Trials, p. 94n. (p. 28)

[68] Scotsman, March 8, 1907. (p. 28)

[69] Sola ex omnibus superfutura, Pliny's Nat. Hist. lib. II, c. 53. (p. 28)

[70] Chan eil a h-anail romham. (p. 28)

[71] Mar cheo no mar thoit gheal. (p. 28)

[72] Ralston, Songs of the Russian People, p. 116; for soul thought of as breath, wind, vapour, cf. Skr. atmán cognate with O.H.G. âtum, breath, soul; Irish athach, breath. Modern Greeks speak of the soul at death escaping through the mouth, 'with the soul between one's teeth,' while ψυχή at times denotes 'stomach '--Abbott's Greek Folk-Lore, 193n. (p. 28)

[73] Cognate with G. deò, breath, are Lithuanian dwesuì dwêsti, to breathe; dwãse, breath, spirit; dùsas, vapour. Schrader connects Latin Fêralia, from a proto-Italic *dhvêsâlia, a festival in honour of the dead, also probably L. fêriae for *dhvêsiae, feralis, belonging to the dead or underworld, and festus. Certain is the connection with Lithuanian daũsos, in plural meaning 'the air'; Lettic, dwascha, breathe, breath; Greek, θεός, god, from θϝεσός (Brugmann). From a long form of the root, *dhu̯ēs, comes the Middle High German ge-twās, ghost; Lettic dvêsele, soul, life, breath (with which Walde would connect the Latin bestia). From *dhŭ, another form of the root, come Lithuanian dustù, dusau, 'aufkeuchen'; dùsas, sigh; dūsiù, to gasp; Lettic dusu, dust, 'aufkeuchen.' (p. 28)

[74] Here tannasg, apparition, is either shortened or confused with Ir. tásc, report, etc. (p. 29)

[75] Spiorad, 'spirit,' is a loan from L. spiritus. (p. 29)

[76] Bezz. Beiträge, 19, 276; cf. ib. 21, 212, where Mikkola equates Gothic saiwala with O. Bulg. sila, force, energy, power; Prussian seilin, exertion, effort, zeal, from *seilā, sei̯(u̯)l,—the primary root in Servian do-sin-uti se, 'potiri' from *sei̯i̯u-n-. (p. 30)

[77] Phil. of Religion, p. 396. (p. 31)

[78] v. Schrader's article on Aryan Religion in Hastings, Ency. of Religion and Ethics. (p. 31)

[79] 'Tuatha adortais síde'—Old Irish Hymn ascribed to Fiacc. (p. 31)

[80] Trevelyan, Folk-Lore and Folk-Stories of Wales, p. 165; cf. the veneration for snakes in Lithuania. (p. 33)

[81] Cf. Dr. Carmichael's Carmina Gadelica. (p. 33)

[82] The Gael, vol. v. 330 = Dh'òrduich e a thiodhlaiceadh am bian an fhéidh sin. (p. 33)

[83] The stress is on Nāir, not on the preceding Mo, which is a suffix of endearment. The accent is quite different from that in Loch Monar in Ross-shire, which has the stress on the first syllable. (p. 34)

[84] Folk-Lore, Sept. 1893, pp. 357, 359, 'The Women's War-of-Words in the Feast of Bricriu' alludes to the couvade. The Irish tale Cess Noinden Ulad, 'the Nine Days' Debility (?) of the Ulidians,' may reflect this practice among the Cruithne or Irish Picts, possibly conjoined with the old custom of racing for a bride. Cf. Frazer's Kingship, 261. (p. 36)

[85] Totemism and Exogamy, iv. 252. (p. 37)

[86] Crawley's Tree of Life, p. 211; v. Spencer and Gillen's Native Tribes of Central Australia. (p. 38)

[87] Researches, 2nd ed. p. 301. (p. 38)

[88] The Highland phrase is: chuir i na piantan air an duine = 'she put the pains on the husband.' This transference is understood as being due to the wife or else to the wise-woman who first attended her. (p. 39)

[89] v. Scott's Poetical Works. Edin. MDCCCLI. Robert Cadell, St. Andrew Square. Not all editions give this note in full. (p. 39)

[90] A. Clerk, Memoir of Colonel John Cameron, Fassifearn, 2nd ed. 1858. Appendix, Note A. (p. 39)

[91] Macfarlane's Geographical Collection, vol. ii. p. 520 (Scot. Texts Soc.), 3907, ed. by Sir Arthur Mitchell. (p. 40)

[92] Miss F. Tolmie's 'Highland Folk Songs'; it is given also in The Gael. The significant lines are: Gun robh neart Chonchulainn leat | Agus neart na Féinne | Neart Oisein bhig agus Osgair threuna | Neart an daimh duinn as àirde leumas] Neart na fairge thruime threubhaich | Gun robh neart na cruinne leat| Agus neart na gréine | Gun robh Brian dhuit mar tha mise dhuit | Gu bheil mise mar dhearbh phiuthar dhuit | S mur h-eil ni 's mó tha 'cheart uibhir |. (p. 41)

[93] Luighim sìos le Dia is luigheadh Dia lium
Cha luigh mi sìos le Briain 's cha luigh Briain lium.
       (Carmichael's Carmina Gadelica.) (p. 41)

[94] Religious Songs of Connacht, vol. 2, p. 409. (p. 41)

[95] Carm. Gad. ii. 232. (p. 41)

[96] Bu to gaisgeach na misnich
Dol air astar na fiosachd
Is tu nach siubhladh air criplich
Ghabh thu steud Briain Mhìcheil,
E gun chabstar 'na shliopan,
Thu 'ga mharcachd air iteig
Leum thu thairis air fiosrachadh Naduir.
       (Quoted in Carm. Gad. i. p. 200.) (p. 41)

[97] v. D'Arbois de Jubainville's Irish Mythological Cycle, Best's trans. p. 82. (p. 42)

[98] v. Kuno Meyer in Eriu, iv. 69. (p. 42)

[99] Srannan, hoarseness, murmuring in sleep, snorting of cattle, rattling in the throat; srannan a bhàis = death rattle. (p. 42)

[100] Original in Campbell's Leabhar Na Féinne, p. 200; a variant where Brian is used instead of an Sealbh in Waifs and Strays of Celtic Tradition, iv. 79. (p. 42)

[101] Lit. thine half-hand. (p. 43)

[102] Quosdam daemones quos Dusios Galli nuncupant, hanc assidue immunditiam et tentare et efficere plures talesque asseverant.—Augustine, De Civ. Dei, xxiii.; cf. Breton Duz; E. Deuce? The Manx hairy satyr, Phynnodderree,—'its hair or fur is its covering,' says Craigeen (Dicty. 130),—is parallel: story pictures him as an Elfin Knight who fell in love with a Manx maiden (Moore, p. 53). He is the 'Dun Haired One,' and parallel to the Mag Molach (Hairy Paw or Hand) of the Highlands, where it is a synonym for the Devil. (p. 44)

[103] Rev. Celt. V. 275. (p. 45)

[104] Hartland, Primitive Paternity, i. 8, quoting Sébillot's Contes Pop. i. 124 (Story No. 18). (p. 45)

[105] See The Celtic Dragon Myth, p. 37, where Campbell of Islay's retelling is given (Edinburgh, J. Grant). (p. 46)

[106] J. A. MacCulloch, The Childhood of Fiction, 134-5. (p. 47)

[107] Legends of Strathisla, Inverness-shire, and Strathbogie, Elgin, 1862, p. 10. (p. 47)

[108] Ib. p. 105. (p. 47)

[109] § 2 of 'Serglige Chonchulaind' in Windisch's Irische Texte; cf. "I swear by my shield and by my spear" (Ériu, iv. 99). (p. 47)

[110] "Air laimh t' athar 's do sheanar is air do dhā laimh fhéin ga saoradh sin"-v. Barra version of 'Deirdire and the Sons of Usnech.' (p. 47)

[111] Usener's Götternamen, 1896, p. 280. (p. 47)

[112] Mionn; E. Ir. mind, oath, diadem, the swearing relics of a saint, cognate with O. Welsh minn, sertum. (p. 48)

[113] Spenser's View of the State of Ireland, 82, 99. (p. 48)

[114] Pennant's Tour, i. 96. (p. 48)

[115] Lady Wilde's Anc. Legends, i. 66-67. (p. 49)

[116] Sébillot, p. 342.

With the priest's thought compare the Indeterminates or questions barred by Buddha: whether the Soul is the same as the body or different from it: v. Rhys Davids, Dialogues of the Buddha, vol. i. 186 fol. (p. 49)

[117] Chuir Iain Bān aodach dubh air na seilleanan nuair chaochail a bhrathair = John Bayne placed black clothing on the bees when his brother died. Cf. telling the bees of the death of the owner (a custom widely spread in England). (p. 50)

[118] Rev. W. Forsyth, Dornoch, Folk-Lore Journal, vi. 171. (p. 51)

[119] Condensed from Le Braz's La Legende de la Mort en Basse Bretagne. (p. 54)

[120] Sébillot, 339. (p. 55)

[121] Pigheid bās 's a dhā banais. Seemingly old British; cf. the belief in the Cotswolds that to have a magpie cross one's path in the morning means that a death will follow. (p. 55)

[122] Fios fithich. (p. 55)

[123] v. 'The Tobermory Treasure Ship in Fact and Legend,' by Rev. D. McGillivray, in Northern Chronicle, January or February 16, 1910. (p. 56)

[124] St. Kilda and its Birds, by J. Wiglesworth, M.D., F.R.C.P., Liverpool, 1903, p. 37; cf. A. B. Cook, in Folk-Lore for 1904, p. 387 n. (p. 57)

[125] The literary evidence for which is seen in the myths of Caeneus (Ovid's Metam. 12, 514 ff.) and Ctesylla (Ant. Lib. i.); the monumental evidence in works like G. Weicker's Der Seelenvogel and J. E. Harrison's Prolegomena to the Study of Greek Religion (p. 197 In Egypt the king's soul is referred to as a hawk under the twelfth and nineteenth dynasties (Flinders Petrie, Religion and Conscience in Ancient Egypt, p. 30). (p. 57)

[126] Orgain Brudne Da Dergae, ed. Stokes, § 7, 13. (p. 57)

[127] Girald. Cambr., Itinerarium Cambriae, l. i. c. 2. (p. 58)

[128] Napier's Folk-Lore of the West of Scotland, p. 111. (p. 58)

[129] Indogerm. Forschungen, 1910, 2nd pt. p. 143. (p. 59)

[130] A. W. Moore, The Folk-Lore of the Isle of Man, pp. 133, 144, where the various accounts are quoted, also the music of 'Hunt the Wren.' (p. 60)

[131] Keating's History of Ireland, vol. iii. p. 91 (Irish Texts Society ed.). (p. 60)

[132] Duanaire Fhinn., pt. i. p. 119. (p. 60)

[133] Bertholet, The Transmigration of Souls, 64. (p. 61)

[134] Reinach's Orpheus (French ed.), p. 168. (p. 62)

[135] Rev. Celtique, 12, p. 441. (p. 62)

[136] Elton's Origins of English History, 287. (p. 62)

[137] De Bello Gallico, V. 12. (p. 62)

[138] Conqu. Hibern. i. 31. (p. 62)

[139] Dion. Cass. lxii. 3. (p. 62)

[140] Cf. Figuier, Prim. Man (Tylor), 268. (p. 62)

[141] Pennant's Tour Through Montgomeryshire and Sikes's British Goblins, 162. (p. 62)

[142] O'Curry's Man. and Cus. ii. 141. (p. 63)

[143] The Folk-Lore of the Isle of Man, by A. W. Moore, p. 147. (p. 63)

[144] Trevelyan, p. 77. (p. 63)

[145] Sébillot, 196. (p. 63)

[146] Folklore as an Historical Science, 287-288. (p. 65)

[147] v. my trans. in Irish Texts Society ed. (p. 66)

[148] Ta'a—Tiree dialect. (p. 69)

[149] Sort of slang for 'paw, hand.' (p. 70)

[150] Atha Cliath, Connradh na Gaedhilge, 1910. (p. 70)

[151] Craveth Read, Natural and Social Morals, p. 85. (p. 72)

[152] Superstitions of the Scottish Highlands, p. 269. (p. 72)

[153] For his Midas-like story see Y Cymmrodor, 6, 181-3; cf. for Breton, Rev. Celt. ii. 507-8, re le Roi de Portzmarch. (p. 74)

[154] Gum bu sheatha (spelling doubtful) duit fein = 'happy, lucky, may you be.' [Probably sheagha; cf. Irish seaghais, 'pleasure, joy, delight'—G. H.] Shèamha would be possible, only the e has no nasality. (p. 74)

[155] Ma bhrathas tu, etc. = 'If you locate, discover.' (p. 74)

[156] O'Curry's Manners and Customs, I. ccclxx. (p. 75)

[157] Gordon-Cumming's Hebrides, 369; transformation into the shape of a wild goose was known in some parts of Wales (Trevelyan, 214); cf. Trans. Gad. Soc. Inv. 25, 132 for witch in hen-form. (p. 75)

[158] Glasgow Herald, Aug. 20, 1910, by the late Alex. Macpherson, Kingussie. (p. 78)

[159] The doe is some fair lady bound by enchantment, but able, for a short time only, to appear to her lover in her natural figure. The enchanter in this instance permits her offspring to assume the human form. Bran was the daughter of Fionn by a lady who came to him as an enchanted hound, but the enchanter threw his spells over her as well as over her mother. Oisin was half-brother to Bran, who, instinctively, found out the relationship when the hounds seized Oisin. (p. 78)

[160] Pp. 221-224 of Poems of Oisin, Bard of Erin. From the Irish by John Hawkins Simpson. London, 1857. The section cited comes under the heading of 'Mayo Mythology.' (p. 79)

[161] Campbell of Islay MSS., Advocates' Library, vol. xxii. p. 8. (p. 79)

[162] v. MacBain's 'Study of Highland Personal Names,' The Celtic Review, 1905, p. 71; and Trans. Gael. Soc. Inverness, vol. xx. 304-305. (p. 80)

[163] O'Grady's Silva Gad. p. 102 of the Eng. vol. (p. 81)

[164] Ib. 225; also Irische Texte, 4 ser. I heft, p. 140. (p. 81)

[165] Frazer's Golden Bough, 1st ed. vol. ii. 363. (p. 81)

[166] Camden's Britannia, by Gough, ii. 81. (p. 81)

[167] References in Gomme's Governance of London, p. 112. (p. 81)

[168] Karl Pearson's Chances of Death, ii. 19; in vol. ii. 64 n. he adds: "There are a considerable number of local saints,—fossils of district goddesses,—who have the roe or stag as their attribute." On the Cult of the Stag, cf. Journal of Hellenic Studies, 14, 134. (p. 82)

[169] P. 185 of Sermons of a Buddhist Abbot, by Soyer Shaku (Chicago Open Court Publishing Co.). (p. 82)

[170] Windisch's ed., l. 6162; and Hull, p. 225. (p. 82)

[171] Faraday, Translation of Tāin, ix. (p. 82)

[172] Nutt's Bran, ii. 58. (p. 82)

[173] The word rhymes with oighre, but might be spelt boidhbhre, as if from bo + od + ber, with meaning of cow-giver, cow-bestowing. Different is boirche, 'a large hind,' O'Brien's Irish Dictionary, 1832; others give it as 'buffalo,' and MacBain suggests alliance with L. ferus, E. bear. Dineen in his Irish Dictionary under ortha gives tarbh ortha, 'an enchanted bull.' A writer in an extinct Highland periodical writes tarbh fhaire (The Gael, vol. v. 50). In West Highland Tales Campbell writes tarbh eithre. These are all corrupt forms. Final -bh in tarbh would tend to change initial b into bh in a rare word like boibhre. (p. 83)

[174] In those days ploughs were almost always made of wood. (p. 85)

[175] Tarbh a nathar-neimhe (sic) .i. cuileag mhór no gobhlachan mór riabhach donn; fad do lùdaig ann's e glé dhona air son bhith toirt full a na h-eich. (p. 87)

[176] Tha'n t-each uisge coltach ri duine; 'na bhodach coltach ri creutair is riobanan no luideagan air; chan fhaic a h-uile neach e agus is e comharradh romh bhàthadh a th'ann. (p. 87)

[177] Rev. Cel. 12, 347. (p. 87)

[178] Book of The Twelve Prophets, vol. ii. 65. (p. 90)

[179] The name is the same as in the goddess name Ness, mother of Conchobar; proto-Celtic *nesta, √ned, wet, water; German, netzen, to wet; nass, wet; Sanskrit, nadi, river; cf. the river Neda in Greece, Nestos in Thrace. MacBain in Trans. Gael. Soc., Inverness, 25, p. 62. (p. 92)

[180] Esquisse de la Religion des Gaulois, par H. Gaidoz, Paris, 1879, p. 12. Even Cicero reasons: "ergo et flumines et fontes sunt dii" (De Nat. Deorum, iii. 20). (p. 92)

[181] Cf. Mackenzie in Proceed. of Society of Scottish Antiquaries, 1895-96, pp. 69-76, on 'Traces of River Worship in Scottish Folk-Lore.' (p. 93)

[182] This signifies the presence of divinity or of inspiration in the votary. In the early cult of sacred trees and pillars, birds of various kinds play an important part: the spirit descends on the tree or stone in the form of a bird. In Greece the dove is connected with a sepulchral cult. "It is, in fact, a favourite shape in which the spirit of the departed haunts his last resting-place, and in accordance with this idea we see the heathen Lombards ornamenting their grave-posts with the effigy of a dove." It is the dove that bears the nectar to Zeus (Ody. xii. 62, 63); v. Harrison's The Dove Cult of Primitive Greece, p. 7. (p. 94)

[183] 'Celtic Inscriptions of France and Italy,' from Proceedings of the British Academy: reviewed by me in The Scottish Historical Review, July, 1908. (p. 95)

[184] v. Sitzungsberichte of Berlin Academy, 16th April, 1896. (p. 95)

[185] Cumont, The Mysteries of Mithra, Eng. trans., Chicago, 1903, pp. 135-6. (p. 96)

[186] Archiv für Celtische Phil. ii. B. p. 310. (p. 97)

[187] R.C. 27, 329n. (p. 97)

[188] A. B. Cook in Classical Review, xvii. (1903), pp. 410, 412. (p. 97)

[189] Prolegomena to Greek Religion, p. 537. (p. 97)

[190] Frazer, On the Kingship, 174-5. (p. 97)

[191] v. Gilbert Murray, The Rise of the Greek Epic, p. 127n; and cf. The Pilgrimage to Loch Derg. (p. 98)

[192] Táin bó Cúalnge, ed. Windisch, pp. 190-1, ll. 1532-1536. (p. 98)

[193] Ib. p. 82, etc.; also p. 68; Hull's Cuch. Saga, p. 128, sec. 8. (p. 98)

[194] Transl. by Stokes, Rev. Celt. 12. (p. 98)

[195] Book of Leinster, p. 9, col. 1, ll. 5-7. (p. 98)

[196] De Bello Gallico, vi. 17. (p. 98)

[197] v. a chapter in my Memoirs of a Highland Gentleman, E. MacIver of Scourie. (p. 103)

[198] Cf. Irish phrase: ní bhéidh fios an rúin ag an fhár-doras, implying that a secret is well kept when even the lintel stone of the doorway is. unaware of it. (p. 104)

[199] Ralston, Songs of the Russian People, p. 370. (p. 104)

[200] Reinach, Cultes. (p. 104)

[201] Cf. Harrison, p. 325.
For Hebraic belief, v. Exod. 7:9-12; Numb. 21:9; 2 Ki. 18:4, etc. (p. 105)

[202] Macdonald's 'East Central African Customs' in Journ. Anth. Inst. 22, p. 114. (p. 105)

[203] Todd's Irish Version of Nennius, p. 204. (p. 105)

[204] Cóir Anmann, ed. Stokes, p. 399. For further references to the man-wolf compare Eriu, iv. p. 11. (p. 106)

[205] S. Reinach's Orpheus, 5th French ed., Paris (Alcide Picard), 1909, p. 172. (p. 106)

[206] v. references in Gomme, ib. p. 277. He also gives Geraldus Cambrensis re St. Natalis. (p. 107)

[207] Cf. Crimthann, 'wolf,' a name of Columba. (p. 107)

[208] Moore, Folk-Lore of the Isle of Man, p. 62, where the account in Waldron is quoted. If dog names be non-Celtic, even then a parallel is got on non-Aryan ground in the Sacred Dog of China, the Pekeingese. The aunt of the reigning Chinese Emperor in 1860-61 committed suicide on being unable to keep her canine pets out of reach of the foreigner. (p. 107)

[209] Shaw's Province of Moray, ed. 1775, pp. 306-307. (p. 109)

[210] Ralston's Songs of Russian People, p. 120. (p. 109)

[211] Moore, Folklore of the Isle of Man, pp. 54, 57. (p. 110)

[212] Letter from Rev. Dr. K. A. Mackenzie, minister of Kingussie, dated 5th July, 1900. His father was minister of Lochcarron after Mr. Lachlan Mackenzie's death. (p. 111)

[213] Trevelyan, 103. (p. 111)

[214] See the writer's rendering of the Lay in the Celtic Dragon Myth, pp. 20-22 (Edinburgh: J. Grant). For another tale wherein the quicken tree figures, see Joyce's Old Gaelic Romances. (p. 112)

[215] Uhland's Volkslieder, 241. (p. 112)

[216] Deirdire and the Lay of the Children of Uisne, ed. A. Carmichael, p.111. (p. 112)

[217] Aeneid, iii. 27-34. (p. 113)

[218] Metamorph. viii. 741. (p. 113)

[219] Idyll, Xviii. 48. (p. 113)

[220] For a curious custom of telling the trees of certain things in Cornwall, see Couch, History of Polperro, p. 168. (p. 113)

[221] A celebrated one was Tāsg Sheumais Mhóir. The shepherd and the farmer and the miller heard it. All agreed it was Tāsg Sheumais Mhóir. And they were right (they thought). (p. 113)

[222] Cha chreid mi gur h-e beathach ceart th'ann; aig an drochaid thug e sgal chruaidh thug fuaim air na creagan aig Meile-fitheach. Cha'n urrainn tāsg dhol seachad air uisg gun sgrìamhail. Theid an tāsg a réir pearsa an duine: sgread chruaidh bhiorach: bheireadh e air a h-uile gaoistean fuilt umad seasamh air a cheann = I do not believe that it was a right (i.e. natural) creature: at the bridge it gave a harsh yell that resounded among the rocks of Meile-fitheach. A ghost cannot go across water without screeching. The ghost bears a proportion to the human personality; a hard piercing yell (in this instance, of Big James's ghost); it would make every hair on thee stand on end. (p. 114)

[223] Proceed. Soc. Antiq. Scotland, vol. xii., year 1876-1877, by Mr. William Galloway, architect. (p. 115)

[224] Joyce's Irish Names of Places. (p. 115)

[225] Proceed. Soc. Antiq. Scot. viii. 104 (p. 116)

[226] Cf. poem on three celebrated trees of Ireland in Celtische Zeitschrift, v. 21. (p. 116)

[227] Campbell of Islay, MS. Collection, Advocates' Library, vol. x., last tale. (p. 117)

[228] Leabhar na g-Ceart, 151n, and v. Battle of Magh Leana and Tochmarc Momera, ed. O'Curry, p. 67n. (p. 117)

[229] O'Curry's Magh Leana, 95n, after MS. H. 2, 16 (Roy. Ir. Acad.). (p. 117)

[230] Issin Chroeb-ruaid, imorro, no bitis narríg, edhon ba ruad do na rigaib. See O'Curry's trans., Manners and Customs, ii. p. 332, from Bk. of Leinster = H. 2, 16, fol. 69 b.b. (p. 118)

[231] Voyage of Bran, ed. Meyer, pp. 4 and 6. (p. 118)

[232] S.C. § 33 and Leahy's translation. (p. 118)

[233] Cf. E. Hull, 'The Silver Bough', in Folk-Lore. (p. 119)

[234] Curr, The Australian Race, ii. 199; and Palmer in Journ. Anthr. Inst. xiii. 292. (p. 119)

[235] Brinton's Religion of Primitive Peoples, p. 150. (p. 120)

[236] Cormac's Glossary, ed. Stokes, p. 155. (p. 120)

[237] Keating's History of Ireland, ed. Irish Texts Society, vol. ii. 173-175. (p. 121)

[238] Skeat and Blagden's Pagan Races of Malay Peninsula, i. 13. (p. 121)

[239] Such concepts fit in with the matriarchal stage of society. Mr. Gomme remarks: "The soul-bird belief and the tree-naming custom are different phases of one conception of social life, a conception definitely excluding recognition of blood-kinship, and derived from the conscious adoption of an experience which has not reached the stage of blood-kinship, but which includes a close association with natural objects" (Folk-Lore as an Historical Science, p. 248). Thus among the Arunta tribe in Australia the child is thought to be the reincarnation of one of the spirits which haunted the spot or totem-centre where the mother first felt herself quickened. There is sympathetic association with the object or external soul. Totemism is really no product of any conceptual theory, as Dr. Frazer argues for; it falls under the wider category of Manism. (p. 122)

[240] H. Gaidoz, Esquisse de la Religion des Gaulois, p. 12. (p. 122)

[241] Bk. ii. 53 (ed. Dinneen). (p. 122)

[242] Ib. i. 101. (p. 122)

[243] Ib. 209; cf. O'Grady's Silva Gadelica, ii. 264; Meyer and Nutt's Bran, i. 187, and the tale of 'Baile an Scāil' in the same work. (p. 122)

[244] Rev. K. Macdonald of Applecross, Social and Religious Life in the Highlands, p. 34 (Edinburgh, 1902). Mr. Lang (Hist. of Scotland, ii. 560) speaks of a seat with a stone in it as still existing in Glasgow, and of a black capping-stone at St. Andrews, and asks: Is this a relic of fetichism?' (p. 123)

[245] Cultes, iii. 365-433. (p. 124)

[246] Contra Gentes, vii. 49. (p. 125)

[247] For association of a white stone with a new name, cf. Rev. 2:17. (p. 125)

[248] Lúb na Caillighe (ed. Lloyd), Connradh na Gaedhilge, 1910, p. 34. (p. 125)

[249] Proverbs, p. 167. (p. 126)

[250] Proc. Soc. Antiq. Scot. for 1900. (p. 126)

[251] Moore, Folklore, etc. 157. (p. 128)

[252] Ibid. 156. (p. 128)

[253] Rogers, Social Life in Scotland, i. 135. (p. 128)

[254] Frazer, On Certain Burial Customs, p. 84. (p. 128)

[255] Year 1889-90. (p. 128)

[256] A. Carmichael, Carmina Gadelica. (p. 130)

[257] Joyce's Soc. Hist. i. 335; Silva Gadelica, trans. by O'Grady, pp. 15, 16, 41. (p. 130)

[258] Cf. J. G. Campbell's Witchcraft, p. 247; Train's Hist. and Stat. Acct. of Isle of Man (Douglas, 1845), ii. 116; Solinus, xxii. 10. (p. 130)

[259] Frazer, G. Bough, iii. 347-9; On the Kingship, p. 281. (p. 130)

[260] Grimm, Deutsche Mythologie4, i. 506. (p. 130)

[261] Stokes and Strachan, Thesaurus Palaeo-Hib. ii. 45. (p. 131)

[262] Anthropological Essays, presented to E. B. Tylor, Oxford 1907, p. 82. With the daimon-protector compare idea in the Faire-Chlaidh, 'the kirk-yard watch,' q.v. (p. 131)

[263] Frazer, On Certain Burial Customs, p. 85n. (p. 131)

[264] K. Maurer, 'Ueber die Wasserweihe des Germanishen Heidenthumes,' Bavarian Acad. of Sciences for 1880. (p. 132)

[265] Cf. the whisky and cheese carried in processions to church by a marriage party and offered to those met on the way; this was etiquette in 1875 to my knowledge, and later. (p. 133)

[266] Hatch, Influences of Greek Ideas and Usages upon the Christian Church, p. 299 (where he quotes Mabillon). (p. 133)

[267] Letter from Rev. D. Macfarlane, the present minister. (p. 133)

[268] Quoted in Warren's Liturgy and Ritual of the Celtic Church, p. 67. (p. 133)

[269] Duchesne's Origins, quoting Synodus Patricii, ii. 19; Victor Vitensis, Hist. Persec. Vandal. ii. 47. (p. 134)

[270] Té chaol a' chòt uaine a' nigheadh a phàisde ann am miosar bhainne. (p. 134)

[271] Chan urrainn domh; tha mi air mo mhiapadh. (p. 134)

[272] Witchcraft and Second-Sight, p. 173. (p. 134)

[273] An Lóchrann, Tralee, 1910, Bk. iii. No. 7. (p. 134)

[274] Trans. Gael. Soc. Inv. 26, 284. (p. 135)

[275] v. Appendix to my Norse Influence on Celtic Scotland. (p. 135)

[276] This derivation by Thurneysen may be upheld, but the name may have been extended also to the 'wise men' of the pre-Celtic peoples who brought over their own rites when the incorporation of the various races took place. (p. 135)

[277] Carmina Gadelica, ii. p. 22, where a specimen of this incantation is given. (p. 135)

[278] Social History of Ireland, i. 386. (p. 135)

[279] Reprint for the Clan Mackay Society, 1892, p. 88. (p. 135)

[280] The Rev. Duncan MacGillivray succeeded in 1817. (p. 135)

[281] There is a rite of blessing oneself when making the frìth if a woman be seen,— she being the omen of some untoward event or other. (p. 136)

[282] Gum bu slàn sin oirn-ne is air ar daoine!
Mas to chuala cha to chaoineas. (p. 137)

[283] See under Bird-Soul. (p. 137)

[284] Le d' iarraidh, dosgadh ort!
Gur e do sheice fhéin a chiad sheic a théid air an sparr. (p. 137)

[285] Forbes, Gaelic Names of Beasts, Birds, Fishes, Insects and Reptiles, p. 263. (p. 137)

[286] Gaelic Soc. Inv. Trans. 26, 126 and 42. (p. 137)

[287] Gall. Soc. Inv. Trans. 265. (p. 138)

[288] Ib. 292-3. (p. 138)

[289] Ib. 25, 127. (p. 138)

[290] Ib. 25, 130. (p. 138)

[291] Chan ann ga mhaoidheadh ort atá mi. (p. 138)

[292] Cha deach' R------ M------ riamh o'n tigh leis an làir aige, gun a chas dheas chur timchioll a ceann an ainm an Athar is crois Chriosda chur p. 227 air; 's cha robh buitseach no droch spiorad sam bith a b'urrainn thighinn 'na chòir. (p. 138)

[293] Comh-dhalaiche; German, An-gang; L. primitiae. (p. 138)

[294] A Brief Account of the Clan Donnachie, with Notes on its History and Traditions. (p. 138)

[295] For the original see Windisch's Irische Texte, i. 213. (p. 140)

[296] Orgain Brudne Da Dergae, a text of about the end of the eighth century. (p. 140)

[297] Duine còir a leughadh slinneagan a' mhathghamhna. (p. 140)

[298] Teut. Myth. ed. Stallybrass, 1113. (p. 141)

[299] Western Isles, 119. (p. 141)

[300] Superstitions of the Scottish Highlands, p. 258. (p. 141)

[301] Targaireacht Bhriain Ruaidh Ui Chearbháin. Dublin: Gill & Son, 1906. (p. 143)

[302] His name is referred to on pages 9, 13, 19, 45, 55, 80 of the 1878 edition; at the foot of page 3, a whole passage is omitted. (p. 144)

[303] Prophecies of the Brahan Seer, pp. 4-5; cf. 1878 ed. (p. 145)

[304] Prophecies, pp. 78-79. (p. 146)

[305] Prophecies, p. 6. (p. 147)

[306] Ib. p. 7. (p. 147)

[307] Highland Second-Sight, ed. by N. Macrae, with Introductory Study by Rev. Wm. Morrison. Dingwall: George Souter. (p. 148)

[308] The shedding of the blood of a cock is inferred by Clay Trumbull (The Blood Covenant, p. 199) for Lowland Scotland from the Uowing of Jok and Jynny; he quotes the lines:

Jok tuk Jynny be the hand
And cryd ane feist and slew ane cok.

If a trace of the Blood Covenant can be inferred here, I can only say that I do not recollect any blood rite associated with Highland betrothals. (p. 149)

[309] v. Stowe Missal in Warren's ed. p. 217. (p. 149)

[310] J. C. Lawson, Modern Greek Folk Lore and Ancient Greek Religion, 592, 594. (p. 150)

[311] Mas maith leat do cháineadh, pós;
Mas maith leat do mholadh, faigh bás. (p. 150)

[312] O. Irish foigde, from fo and guidhe, 'beg,' 'entreat.' (p. 150)

[313] Eàiric (according to my pronunciation); cf. O. Ir. airec (2) in Windisch's Wb. Root in O. Ir. tairciud 'oblation.' (p. 150)

[314] Transactions, Gaelic Soc. Inverness, 26, 298. (p. 151)

[315] Irish Popular Superstitions, p. 49. (p. 151)

[316] Lady Wilde, Ancient Legends of Ireland, vol. i. p. 219. (p. 151)

[317] Burt's Letters, vol. ii. p. 106. (p. 151)

[318] Was this connected with the custom in South Scotland of the bride presenting a marriage shirt to the bridegroom? (p. 151)

[319] An old opinion. Gesner says that the witches made use of toads as a charm, 'Ut vim coeundi, ni fallor, in viris tollerent,' Gesner, de quad. ovi, p. 72. (p. 152)

[320] Pennant's Tour, i. 187. 'Cutting the creel' is a rite known to the fishermen of the Berwickshire coast. (E. B. Simpson's Folk Lore in Lowland Scotland, p. 209.) A knife is given to the newly made wife who relieves her husband of the load, emblematic of the assistance that a help-mate renders. (p. 152)

[321] Celtic Magazine, x. 542. (p. 152)

[322] Ancient Legends of Ireland, i. 219, where one elaborate account of an old Kerry wedding is quoted and of interest otherwise. (p. 153)

[323] Mìle beannachd dhuit-s' fo d' bhréid. (p. 153)

[324] Uibhir aig Dia de a chuid. (p. 154)

[325] Sìthein. (p. 154)

[326] A Description of the Western Isles of Scotland, ed. 1716, p. 28. (p. 155)

[327] Description of the Western Isles, 2nd ed. 1716, p. 89. (p. 156)

[328] Ib. p. 100. (p. 156)

[329] Sheila MacDonald in Folk-Lore, 1903, pp. 381-382, 'Old-World Survivals in Ross-shire'; cf. vol. xiii. p. 44. (p. 156)

[330] Beannachd romham. (p. 157)

[331] Cf. the ritual of the Terminalia (Ovid's Fasti, 2, 643; 2, 655; also 4, 743-746). (p. 157)

[332] Srùbhan Mìcheil, also written Strùan. (p. 157)

[333] Ed. Dinneen, bk. ii. pp. 41-43. (p. 157)

[334] Carm. Gadelica, i. 204. (p. 158)

[335] Golden Bough, i. 319-320. (p. 158)

[336] Sinclair's Statistical Account, xi. 620. The word Beltane, however, has no connection with the Phoenician Baal, but involves the idea of whiteness or brightness from the fires then lit in honour of the sun-god; cf. Lithuanian baltas, 'white,' and the root in Baltic. v. MacBain's Dictionary. (p. 158)

[337] Sinclair's Statistical Account, xv. 517 n. (p. 159)

[338] Carm. Gadel. ii. 239. (p. 160)

[339] As to the man clad in cow-skin, see Ramsay's Scotland and Scotsmen in the Eighteenth Century, ed. 1888, vol. ii. 438; cf. Elton's Origins of English History, 1890, p. 411. The individual essays to assimilate himself with the substance of the victim offered. (p. 161)

[340] Folk-Lore for 1903, pp. 370-1. For cock-sacrifice in France, v. Sébillot, Le Paganisme Contemprain, p. 202. In the Highland p. 267 asseveration, Ged shlugadh an talamh mi = 'though the earth should swallow me' there is testimony to the sacredness of the earth. A vestige of a similar belief exists in the Breton imprecation rendered: 'Que la terre s'ouvre pour m'engloutir' (ib. 308). The Celtic oath was by the elements, and by the essence of the sun and moon as in Irish, tar brígh gréine is gealaighe. (p. 162)

[341] Cf. Folk-Lore, xi. p. 446 (text and note 2). (p. 162)

[342] O. Ir. to-gairm 'invocatio'; Ir. toghairm 'summoning, request, prayer, petition.' (p. 162)

[343] Other accounts in J. G. Campbell's Superstitions, 304, where he designates it as 'giving his supper to the devil'; Norrie's Loyal Lochaber, p. 247; Armstrong's Gaelic Dictionary; Martin, Western Isles, speaks of another method of Taghairm by wrapping a person in a cow-hide, all but his head. His "invisible friends" would answer his queries. (p. 162)

[344] Memoir of Colonel John Cameron of Fassifearn, 2nd ed. 1858. (p. 163)

[345] Ciod air bith a chì no chual' thu cuir mu'n cuairt an cat. (p. 163)

[346] J. F. Campbell, MSS. (Adv. Lib.), vol. xiii. p. 368. (p. 164)

[347] Arnobius, Adv. Nations, ii. 68; Livy, xxii. to. 7; Ovid, Ex Ponta, iv. 4. 31; Servius on Virgil, Georg. ii. 146; Horace, Carm. Seculare, 49. (p. 164)

[348] Pliny, Nat. Hist. xvi. 250. (p. 164)

[349] E. Simpson, Folk Lore in Lowland Scotland, p. 27; for burning a living calf to preserve the rest, see Dalyell, Darker Superstitions of Scotland, p. 184; cattle were buried alive and others driven over the spot to arrest mortality (ib. 185-186). (p. 164)

[350] An Crithreamh Gorm. (p. 164)

[351] Thuirt seann daoine nam biodh an ceann air a chur far fear dhiubh le aon bhuille claidheamh glan gun stadadh a phlàigh agus nach bàsaicheadh a h-aon tuilleadh dhiubh (from a MÓD Competition Paper of 1907, entitled An Crithreamh Gorm.) The writer adds: Tha fhios againn gun dean luchd-ionnsachaidh an là 'n diu gàire fanoid ris a so, ach tha e nis nas fasa gu mór gaire dheanamh ris na tha e mhíneachadh ciod a bhiall da; co dhiubh cha ghabh e àicheadh nach robh an nì ann oir bha e air innseadh am measg nan coimhearsnach ann san eilean uile, eadhon gus a nis agus bha mac Iain Mhic Thearlaich a bha beò gus a bhliadhna 1820 'ga innseadh do m'athair-sa agus gum fac e an t-agh 'ga thabhairt dhachaigh aig athair air slaod agus an ceann dheth agus gun do ghabh e féin ioghnadh mór do'n chùis ciod a b'aobhar dha gus an d'innis athair dha mar a thachair e. Bha e ag radh mar an ceudna nach d'fhalbh aon do'n chrodh aca tuilleadh. (p. 164)

[352] For references v. Forbes-Leslie, Early Races of Scotland, p. 85. (p. 164)

[353] Hastings, Encyclop. of Religion and Ethics, iii. 297. (p. 164)

[354] Cyneg. xxxiv. 1. (p. 165)

[355] Top. Hibernica, dist. iii. c. 25. For refutation see Keating's History, Irish Texts Soc. ed. vol. i. p. 23. (p. 165)

[356] De Bello Gall. vii. 77, vii. 71. (p. 165)

[357] These are published by the Scottish Texts Society and edited by William Mackay. I quote from the Appendix to Mr. Dixon's book on Gairloch, as being at hand. (p. 165)

[358] Abercrossan is the old historical form and means the estuary of the River Crossan. The change from r to l is dialectal. (p. 165)

[359] Afflicted ones or lunatics; founded on Gaelic deireoil 'afflicted,' used in Kirke's Bible (William Mackay). (p. 166)

[360] The Libellus on St. Cuthbert's virtues, Surtees Society, p. 185. (p. 167)

[361] Recorded in a lecture by Mr. Alex. Munro, F.S.A., some years ago for Sutherland. (p. 167)

[362] Trans. Gael. Soc. Inverness, vol. xxvi. (p. 167)

[363] Rev. K. Macdonald of Applecross, Social and Religious Life in the Highlands, p. 31 (Edinburgh, 1902). (p. 168)

[364] Trans. Gael. Soc. Inverness, vol. xxv. p. 129. (p. 168)

[365] Todd's ed. of Nennius, p. 95. (p. 169)

[366] Is maith dhun ar fremha do dul fon talmain sunn ocus doraidh: As cead duib nech eicin uaibh do dul fon talmain sunn, no fo huir na hinnsi-sea, dia coisecrad. Adracht suas Odrán erlathad ocus is ed adubairt: 'Diamgabthasa' ol se. As erlam leam sin, a Odhrain ar Colomb Cille. Rat-fia a logh. Ni tibirter idge do neoch icom lighise minab fortsa iarfaigter ar tos.' Luid iarom Odran do chum nime. Fothaigis Colum eclais aice iarsin (Stokes' Lives of Saints from Bk. of Lismore, p. 30). (p. 170)

[367] Tzetzes, quoted in J. Harrison's Prol. to Study of Greek Religion, p. 98. (p. 172)

[368] Ed. 1851, p. 166. (p. 172)

[369] Lives of Saints from the Book of Lismore, ed. Stokes, p. 82. (p. 173)

[370] Cf. Anecdota from Irish MSS. vol. i. p. 23, where we read: Loiscther an dlai-sea, or si, 7 tabarthar bó mael derg duind 7 ní frith an bó. Maith, or an drai dona Deissib. Ragadsa a richt na bó do ma guin ar sairi dom chlaind co brath.
The point is that when the red hornless cow was not forthcoming a Druid of the Déisi says: "Good! I will go in the shape (i.e. instead) of the cow to suffer (lit. to my wounding) in behalf of the liberty of my clan for ever." (p. 173)

[371] Eriu, iv. 39. (p. 173)

[372] Norse Influence on Celtic Scotland, p. 70, where one should read N. Hjálmar + G. airigh. (p. 173)

[373] Trans. by Kuno Meyer, Voyage of Bran, ii. 304. (p. 174)

[374] Adra for clacha = adhradh air clachaibh; cf. current Highland phrase well known to me: ga innseadh dha na clachan, "telling it to the stones." That arrested the evil spoken of from coming on the person to whom it was mentioned. (p. 174)

[375] De Bello Gallico, vi. 16; trans. in Bohn's Library. (p. 174)

[376] Caesar, De Bello Gallico, vi. 13. (p. 175)

[377] De Bello Gothico, ii. 13. (p. 175)

[378] De Superstit. 13, p. 171 B. (p. 175)

[379] Aen. iii. 57, Auri Sacra fames. (p. 175)

[380] The late Mrs. Mackellar (née Cameron) used to quote the phrase of an old clanswoman who, as she was dying, heard of the return of Locheil, whom she described as: our own great god of the Camerons! Cf. 'the god Mourie,' really St. Maolrubha. (p. 175)

[381] Ramsay, Scotland and Scotsmen in Eighteenth Century, ii. 438. (p. 176)

[382] Irish Texts Society ed. vol. iii. p. 35; cf. Bruiden maic Dareo in New Ireland Review, Oct. 1906, p. 101, § 29. (p. 176)

[383] Bastian, Mensch, ii. p. 323. (p. 177)

[384] Hahn, Albanesische Studien, i. p. 152. (p. 177)

[385] Tha e air a chrosadh do leanabh gille an tigh a sguabadh an deigh a bhàis. (p. 177)

[386] Na toir an luath dhe'n chagailt. Cha'n eil rud eile as gointe an 'chagailt a ghlanadh. Bu doch' leam-s' an teine bhi beò ann na'n teine bhi as. Chuireadh feadhainn eile fras luathainn ann mus tigeadh iad a steach. Sin theireadh an t-seann mhuinntir. Chan eil fhios agam-s (prond: chan 'l'ös a'm's) bheil e ceart. Bha buitsichean ann bho (prond: fo) thoisich (sic) an t-saoghail, 's bidh gu 'dheireadh fhad's bhios an saoghal 'na shaoghal. (p. 177)

[387] Na tilg a chìr ach orra (= air do) nàmhaid. Cf. the comb-symbol on old monuments. (p. 177)

[388] Imrig Sathurna mu thuath, imrig Luain mu dheas, 's ged nach biodh agam ach an t-uan 's ann Di-luain a dh'fhalbhainn leis. (p. 178)

[389] Cha dian duine ceum comhnard is greim an Dòmhnaich 'na, aodach. (p. 178)

[390] Other means used were (a) putting milk into an egg-shell: if carried to the house of an evil-doer the milk would curdle; (b) milking three drops from the ewes of the suspected evil-doer; then the useless milk would get all right; (c) boiling the cattle's urine. Trans. Gael. Soc. Inverness, Vol. 26, pp. 50 and 49. (p. 178)

[391] Localism for soitheach. (p. 179)

[392] N. Macleod in Teachdaire Gaelach, Aug. 1830, p. 93. (p. 181)

[393] See previous chapter sub Deer Parentage of Ossian. (p. 181)

[394] Cf. The Books of Rights, ed. J. O'Donovan. (p. 181)

[395] Thes. Pal-Hib. ii. 351; K.Z. 41, 385. (p. 182)

[396] Windisch's Wörterbuch for references. (p. 182)

[397] Cf. the charms of healing put into the wounds of Cuchulainn. Faraday's trans. of the Tāin, p. 84-5. (p. 182)

[398] Moore, Folk Lore of the Isle of Man, 98. (p. 182)

[399] Social and Religious Life in the Highlands, pp. 29, 30 (Edin. 1902). (p. 183)

[400] Folk-Lore for 1903, p. 370. (p. 185)

[401] Her grave is still pointed out, covered with flagstones in a lonely spot where she is said to have been done to death by a number of young men. She entreated that her slayers should all die a violent death, which tradition says was the case. (p. 186)

[402] Irish Texts Soc. ed. vol. iii. p. 143. (p. 187)

[403] Ib. vol. ii. p. 317. (p. 187)

[404] For an account of charm-stones for curing cattle, see Proceed. Soc. Scot. Antiq. for 1889-90, pp. 483-488. (p. 188)

[405] A. Hutcheson, Proceed. Soc. Antiq. Scot. for May 14, 1900, p. 486. (p. 188)

[406] See Mitchell as to the association of white pebbles with burials, ib. vol. xviii. pp. 286-291. (p. 188)

[407] Quoted in Mackinlay's Folklore of Scottish Lochs and Springs, pp. 249-250. (p. 189)

[408] From the Inverness Courier, quoted in the Celtic Magazine for 1877-78. (p. 190)

[409] Proceedings of Soc. of Antiquaries, Scotland, 14th May, 1900. (p. 191)

[410] Mr. Ross's spelling indicates the true pronunciation, viz. ā long, and bearing the chief stress. (p. 192)

[411] Vitae Sanctorum Hiberniae, vol. i. p. xxxi. St. Barr begged St. David for the loan of his horse that he might make his journey the quicker. Quo concesso, ac benedictione optenta, equum ascendit, et sic super eum mare confidenter [intrauit], et usque ad Hiberniam peruenit. Equum vero prefatum in seruicio fratrum secum retinuit. Set in memoria miraculi discipuli eius fecerunt equum eneum, qui usque hodie apud Corkagiam manet. Ib. 69 n. (p. 192)

[412] Book of Leinster, p. 23, col. 2, lines 2-8; Book of Lecan, fol. 295, v. col. 2. Cf. Keating's History, ed. 1811, pp. 408-9. (p. 193)

[413] D'Arbois de Jubainville's Irish Mythological Cycle, trans. by Best, p. 204. (p. 194)

[414] Tour, pt. ii. 15. (p. 194)

[415] Originally, the mallet for bruising barley, but in later ages used for stirring the pool. St. Fillan's relics further embrace his bell, which was put over the patients in the morning; his Quigerach; his belt or girdle. Cf. Brigit's girdle (Relig. Songs of Connaught, ii. 27). (p. 194)

[416] The Cornish Well of St. Keyne has a unique fame. Its water is gifted with the marvellous property that whoever first drinks of it after marriage will be ruler in the household. The poet Southey was so struck with this well when on his visit to Cornwall, that he afterwards celebrated its virtues in the poem beginning:

A well there is in the west country,
And a clearer one never was seen.
There is not a wife in the west country,
But has heard of the Well of St. Keyne.

The conduct of some of these wells is truly unique. Take for instance the spirited behaviour attributed to the basin which catches the water as it issues from the spring at St. Nun's Well, Pelynt, near Looe. Here is the legend: A farmer once wishing to use this basin as a trough in a pig-sty attempted to move it by means of a team of oxen. At first it resisted every effort made to dislodge it. At length, however, he succeeded in dragging it from its place. But just as it was nearing the top of the hill it burst the chains that were holding it, and started to roll rapidly down again. Finally, when abreast of the well, it made a sharp turn and rolled straight in at the entrance, retaking its old position, where it remains to this day. The oxen then fell dead, and the farmer was struck both lame and speechless. (p. 196)

[417] Trans. Gael. Soc. Inverness, 26, 48. (p. 201)

[418] Ib. 25, 131. (p. 201)

[419] Ib. 26, 145. (p. 201)

[420] Shane Leslie's Lough Derg in Ulster (Maunsel & Co., 1909); T. Wright's St. Patrick's Purgatory, 1844; P. de Félice, L'Autre Monde: Le Purgatoire de Saint Patrice, Paris, 1906. (p. 201)

[421] 'Buaidhean sònruichte'; cf. Gordon Cumming's In the Hebrides and Martin's Western Isles as to the round bluish stone always moist on the altar of Fladda's Chapel in the island of Fladdahuan: windbound fishermen walked sunways round

the chapel and then poured water on the stone, whereupon a powerful breeze was sure to spring up. In Lewis and Man wind might be sold to mariners: it was enclosed in three knots; undoing the first brought a moderate wind, the second half a gale, the third a hurricane. (p. 201)

[422] Cf. Mary Hamilton, Incubation, or The Cure of Disease in Pagan Temples and Christian Churches (Henderson & Son, St. Andrews, 1906). (p. 202)

[423] v. Dr. Masson on 'Popular Domestic Medicine' in Trans. Gael. Soc. Inverness, vol. xiv.; Dr. Clerk's 'Notes on Ancient Gaelic Medicine' in Trans. of Gaelic Soc. of Glasgow, vol. i.; The Caledonian Medical p. 335 Journal, July 1897, January 1898, April and July 1902, October 1904, January-April 1910, has papers by Dr. Gillies, Dr. Mackay, Dr. Maclagan, and by Professor Mackinnon on Gaelic Medical MSS., which in substance follow known Latin works of the Middle Ages, and are on a par with the 'science' of their day. In Pennant's Tour there are interesting remarks on The Diseases of the Highlands. (p. 203)

[424] Gomme's Folk-Lore as an Historical Science, p. 199, quoting Wilde's Beauties of the Boyne, 45; Croker's Researches in the South of Ireland, 170; Rev. Celt. V. 358. (p. 203)

[425] Domhnull Mac-Mhuirich, An Duanaire, Dun-éidinn, 1868, pp. 123-126. A fairly literal rendering is given in J. G. Campbell's Superstitions of the Scottish Highlands (MacLehose), p. 169. (p. 203)

[426] Rev. Kenneth Macdonald, Social and Religious Life in the Highlands, p. 29. (p. 203)

[427] Dr. Aitken in Trans. Gael. Soc. Inverness, 14, 309. (p. 204)

[428] Folk-Lore Journal, i. 167. (p. 204)

[429] Folk-Lore Journal, vol. i. p. 167. (p. 204)

[430] Rev. K. Macdonald, op. cit. p. 35. (p. 204)

[431] Tour, i. 175. Possibly an fhadhbh-alan; alan being a Pictish word, root as in Alnwick, the river-name Alaunos of Ptolemy. (p. 204)

[432] Old Statistical Account of Scotland. (p. 205)

[433] For lead-turning magic, see also Folk-Lore, Sept. 1893, p. 361. Divination by symbolic burial was resorted to: parents were wont to dig two adjacent graves

beside a lake in the parish of Reay in Caithness, and there to lay their distempered children in the interval to ascertain the probability of their recovery from whooping-cough (Brand's Description of Orkney, p. 154). (p. 205)

[434] v. Joyce, Social History of Ancient Ireland, i. 205, for evidence from the Brehon Laws. (p. 206)

[435] E. Hull, The Ancient Hymn-Charms of Ireland in Folk-Lore, xxi. 423. (p. 206)

[436] v. p. 181. (p. 206)

[437] p. 8 (p. 206)

[438] Cymric gwedyd, 'say'; also dywedyd; old perfect dywawt: gwawd, 'carmen, eulogy, poem'; gwawdiaeth, 'sarcasm.' From the ablaut *vat comes the Gadhelic fath; ferba-fath, 'words of magic' (Rev. Celt. xx. 246). (p. 207)

[439] Lady Wilde has a spell wherein the three daughters of Fliethas are invoked against the serpent. (p. 207)

[440] Romans, ch. v. 6 (p. 207)